How to Make the Most of Your Workday

By
Jonathan and Susan Clark

CAREER PRESS
180 Fifth Avenue
P.O. Box 34
Hawthorne, NJ 07507
1-800-CAREER-1
201-427-0229 (outside U.S.)
FAX: 201-427-2037

HOW TO MAKE THE MOST OF YOUR WORKDAY

ISBN 1-56414-143-8, $16.95

Cover design by George Harris

Printed in the U.S.A. by Book-mart Press

To order this title by mail, please include price as noted above, $2.50 handling per order, and $1.00 for each book ordered. Send to: Career Press, Inc., 180 Fifth Ave., P.O. Box 34, Hawthorne, NJ 07507

Or call toll-free 1-800-CAREER-1 (Canada: 201-427-0229) to order using VISA or MasterCard, or for further information on books from Career Press.

Library of Congress Cataloging-in-Publication Data

Clark, Jonathan, 1947-
   How to make the most of your workday / by Jonathan and Susan Clark.
      p.   cm.
   Includes index.
   ISBN 1-56414-143-8 : $16.95
      1. Time managament.   I. Clark, Susan, 1950-   II. Title.
HD69.T54C58   1994
   650.1--dc20
                                                            94-26669
                                                            CIP

What the Experts Have to Say...

"Superb...! To the point...no trash to sift through."
> Susan Dussault
> Director of Client Services
> Mahoney & Associates, Inc.

"Well organized and interesting...outstanding format and interaction..."
> Melvin Morrow
> Supervisory Cantographer

National Press Publications, the product and publishing division of National Seminars Group, originally published this book for the training industry. Now this title is available exclusively to the trade from Career Press. Packed with real-world strategies and hands-on techniques, this resource is guaranteed to help you meet the career and personal challenges you face every day.

National Seminars Group, a division of Rockhurst College Continuing Education Center, Inc., has trained more than 2 million people in every imaginable occupation to be more productive and advance their careers. Along the way, they've learned what it takes to be successful, how to build the skills to make it happen and how to translate learning into results.

DEDICATION

JONATHAN AND SUSAN CLARK have spent the past 15 years in the management training and consulting business. Previously, Jonathan worked as a sports writer and editor and Susan was in education and administration.

Combined, they have taught more than 2,200 full-day workshops on subjects ranging from leadership and supervision to team-building and self-awareness to business writing and priority management. Since 1982, Jonathan and Susan have taught more than 175,000 people in over 400 cities in all 50 states, Canada, England, Guam, Japan and Australia how to become better managers of themselves and their lives.

Approximately 50 percent of the activity in their business, the Fisher Clark Services, is presenting public seminars on a contract basis for National Seminars, Inc. In addition, the Clarks develop, present and implement customized training and educational programs to clients primarily in the Pacific Northwest. The Clarks joined the National Speakers Association in 1983, and have been on the faculty of presenters for National Seminars since 1989.

Jonathan and Susan manage the many priorities of their busy lives and careers from their home in Deer Harbor, Washington.

FOREWORD

A Personal Note. . .

Frustrated by an inability to make decisions because of the seeming importance of everything you have to do? Do many days begin with a feeling of being overwhelmed by the projects and activities on your daily list all crying for attention at the same time? As you return home at the end of the working day, is your exhaustion matched only by the frustration of a lack of visible accomplishment?

If you know life could be more fulfilling, satisfying and productive, we do, too. In fact, that's why we wrote this book.

The ideas contained in these pages are not theoretical: They are proven and practical. And, they can work for you.

This book challenges your thinking, provides workable step-by-step patterns to follow, and makes the process of learning fun and entertaining.

Most people are less than half as productive as they can be. Through good management of priorities, you can channel your time effectively, recapture lost energy and enjoy the warm sensation of accomplishment on a daily basis. You'll get more done, feel better about it and have a sense of balance and relaxation at the same time.

Which brings us to the first adage of this book:

This book does not advocate that you become a fanatic about accomplishment and use of time. If you surrender control of life to the daily action list, the calendar and the watch, you will have only replaced one tyrant with another. The definition of management is to control or handle. Managing priorities means you are in control—not the priorities or the methods used.

Through the careful consideration and selection of techniques from this book, you will be able to form alliances with the ideas that can work for you and make a significant difference in your life.

If "what you've already got" is less than what you want, then this book is for you. Turn to the first chapter and get started—now!

CONTENTS

CHAPTER 1

In The Beginning...

- **The importance of self-management**
- **Developing good habits for priority management**
- **Why things don't get done**
- **The 30-day commitment**

In the beginning is self-management. In fact, self-management will be found in the middle and at the end, as well.

If you want to manage and organize the priorities in your life, you must learn to manage yourself. A fundamental philosophy that underlies every idea in this book is:

I GOT MYSELF INTO THIS MESS,

SO IT'S UP TO ME TO GET MYSELF OUT.

This book does not contain quick fixes. Magic words and pixie dust are simply not available. Self-management requires work and lots of it. It took time for you to get into your situation. It takes time to get out.

We are all the sum total of the decisions we make and fail to make in our lives. Some of our present circumstances were consciously created: We volunteered to take on a project at work because we believed it would have a positive impact on our career.

Other circumstances have arrived in innocent-looking packages, disguised as indecision or lack of assertiveness: We put off making a decision so long it finally became impossible to do anything but plow into solving the problems our indecision created. Because we didn't say no, we were re-elected to an office in the civic organization we really didn't want to handle again.

There are undoubtedly certain aspects of your life and job that you can't control. An invalid parent must move in to live with you. Your business partner is suddenly called out of town for a family emergency. A snowstorm paralyzes the city and the flight to call on your key client is cancelled. Part of effectively applying priority management is determining what those areas are, accepting them and learning to live with them.

However, you have control over the majority of the events and situations that occur. The temptation sometimes will be to say: "I really can't do anything about this particular situation, so I'm not going to try." This can be a major mistake: Much of what you believe you can't control falls into that category only because you have developed habits that prevent you from taking control.

Humans are creatures of habit. We develop habits as we go through life, good ones and bad ones, and sometimes no habits at all. Psychologist William James (often called the "father of American psychology") studied human habits and theorized we are the sum total of the habits we have developed. He further noted that since repeated effort results in creating habits, repeated effort can also change or eliminate habits. The only difference is while existing habits may have been subconsciously developed, new ones require conscious, constant repetition.

Many, many ideas in this book are tied to the development of new habits. Until you have become so familiar with a new method of

> *Good learners talk to themselves. It's part of their success in learning. The most useful lines:*
>
> - *I can learn and improve.*
> - *If I stick with it, I'll get it.*
> - *I'm going to turn this mistake into a lesson.*
> - *It doesn't have to be perfect.*
> - *It's okay to ask for help.*

behavior that your response is automatic, you must think, plan and apply the ideas over and over again. This book is "habit forming"!

Fortunately, the process of acquiring new habits doesn't take forever, but it won't happen overnight, either. James noted that it takes from 21 to 30 days of consistent, spaced repetition of an activity to eliminate an old habit or to develop a new one.

This doesn't mean you won't immediately see some impact from applying good priority-management techniques, because you will. But until the new activity is repeatedly forced on you (through your own self-management), it will be just like so many of the ideas people give up on, saying, "I tried that once, and it didn't work."

The Critical Incubation Period Of New Habits

There is a critical incubation period when you apply new ideas. For any form of life, the first few days are the most critical. Baby chicks spend the first days of life in an incubator. Temperature, light, food and water are provided under controlled conditions. Forgetting to turn the light on the second night after the chicks hatch would prove most disastrous.

By neglecting the chicks at this critical period, the time and money already invested have been wasted. Better to have never started!

So it is with habits. They are ever so fragile in the incubation period! If you haven't taken an idea and carefully nursed it through the critical time of its life, you really can't say, "I tried it, but it didn't work." Did it really get the attention it needed to survive, or did the idea merely represent a wish—a wish you never put into the incubator?

With the passage of time, the habits you grow become strong and secure. They take control, and you yield to them willingly. In order to take control, you must first be in control. Og Mandino's *The Greatest Salesman in the World* contains a series of positive affirmations for success, and one goes like this: "I will form good habits, and become their slave."

SELF-MANAGEMENT IS SLAVERY—
TO GOOD HABITS

Do you want to attack every priority with confidence and assurance? Do you yearn for automatic responses that guarantee control and productivity? That kind of freedom comes only from developing good habits and nurturing them until they control your behavior. And, if you think about it, it's probably the poor habits you've developed throughout your life that keep you from getting things done.

Why Things Don't Get Done

Are you frustrated at the end of the day? Is your daily action list nearly as long at the end of the day as it was in the beginning? Do you sometimes feel that you've spent all day spinning your wheels?

Nearly all productivity problems can be traced back to one or more of the items on the following list.

- **No clear goals.** Without a specific sense of purpose, it's impossible to effectively manage and organize your priorities. Where are you going? Why did you show up for work today? What is your department's specific purpose for existence? Do you have an organizational mission statement, and do you know it by heart?

  In Chapter 4 you'll find valuable tools to help you determine a business and personal mission statement and establish clear, focused goals.

  As a farmer plows a field, the path of the plow is always determined by looking at a specific point at the end of the field. The focus on the goal ensures the shortest, straightest furrow. This is just as true in your business and personal life.

"IF YOU DON'T KNOW WHERE YOU'RE GOING, YOU'LL PROBABLY END UP SOMEWHERE ELSE."

- **Lack of priorities.** The best daily action list ever written is useless and ineffective if the relative importance of each item on the list hasn't been established. It's easy to fall into a trap of getting many things completed, but doing the wrong things. Rather than doing the most important items first, people sometimes work on things that are easiest to accomplish, more fun, or closer at hand.

  If you don't know what's really important to you, or to your organization, you can't make decisions that will make effective use of your time. The organizational tools in Chapter 8 are invaluable in determining what's really important and provide a logical sequence to get things done.

- **No daily plan.** Beginning your day without a plan of action is a formula for spending all day doing the wrong things. It invites anyone and everyone to interrupt your activities with their requests and assignments. You will passively allow unwelcome intrusions, because you'll have no way to defend yourself. Chapter 10 describes how effective your defense can be through prior planning and good communication.

- **Attempting to do too much.** For many, there's not a lot wrong with the way in which projects are planned, tackled and completed. It's the sheer number of projects taken on that becomes overwhelming. If you're thinking "that's me!"—you're right. You must learn how to say "NO" and mean it. Chapter 7 tells how.

- **Perfectionism.** Are you unable to complete and release a project until it is done perfectly? Can you still see ways for something to be done better? Even if you can't see anything, does it nag you that there must be something you've overlooked? How much time and energy do you waste pursuing the impossible dream, perfectionism? Perfectionism can be controlled with the ideas and techniques contained in Chapter 6.

- **Personal disorganization.** No matter how well organized your priorities are or how effective your daily plan, you may be losing valuable, irretrievable time searching

Constant improvement, not perfection, should be your goal. Improvement means finding solutions to problems. The result is not only increased productivity but also a feeling of accomplishment and a boost to morale that leads to further improvement.

for things that are lost in the messes on your desk, files, drawers, closets and even in your car. A few minutes a day, plus some time spent in Chapter 6, will make a difference.

- **Snap decisions and indecision.** The decision-making process is only as good as the planning preceding it. Without adequate planning and prioritizing, there's always the risk of rushing into catastrophe or watching opportunity disappear from a failure to respond with any action at all. Chapter 3 deals with planning, and a portion of Chapter 6 will aid you in confident, effective decision-making.

- **Crisis management.** Life is extremely frustrating when we're caught in the constant search for extinguishers to put out the fires that break out day after day. Productivity can be put on hold, indefinitely, as neglected situations suddenly become urgent. You can't prevent fires if you spend all your time putting them out!

  We had a boss once who was a crisis-management expert—that is, an expert in breeding crises. He would throw gasoline all over things and then toss lighted matches into the pile. What he considered "productivity" was nothing more than putting out the fires he started himself! We called this "arson management."

  One of the greatest benefits of the kind of planning discussed in Chapter 3 is the elimination of many crises from daily activities. When a crisis is unavoidable, as it sometimes is, the steps in Chapter 12 describe a sure-fire method to get you through.

- **Ineffective delegation.** Without a doubt, the "I can do it better myself" philosophy has created more career burnout and lost opportunity than any other single factor. Failure to communicate effectively when delegating probably ranks number two. In Chapter 10 you'll discover a highly effective way to get other people committed to your plans through confident delegation.

- **Interruptions.** Your day can be going according to schedule, and then the telephone rings or an unexpected visitor drops in and productivity instantly wanes. Many of these occurrences can be eliminated; those that can't must be controlled. If this is a problem for you, as it is for many people, you'll be delighted to know the title of Chapter 5 is "Controlling Productivity."

- **Meetings.** Meetings are the only place where "minutes are kept and hours are wasted." Unplanned, unnecessary meetings involving the wrong people waste millions of hours and billions of dollars each year. Often, those that are planned and necessary still suffer because of poor preparation or follow-up. Effective meeting planning, as described in Chapter 5, is the key to making these times useful and productive.

- **Procrastination.** The universal tendency to put off until tomorrow what should be done today is a major productivity killer at work and home. All too often people immerse themselves in unimportant activities while the really important work remains undone. Let's discuss this— later! If you're ready to tackle it now, turn to Chapter 6.

Are you a frequent participant in some of these productivity killers? How many undermine your ability to get things done?

How many of those reasons are within your control, at least somewhat? With the possible exception of some meetings (if you don't plan them but are required to attend), you have significant control over every one of these motivation and productivity killers!

The Commitment To Change

Nothing will change until you decide to do something. We'll be spending more time in all of these areas throughout this book, but it's not too early to make some significant decisions and take back some control. Do it right now!

> *Determine the single most important activity to be accomplished each day and focus your energy on accomplishing this task to ensure your success.*

WORKSHEET—PERSONAL PRODUCTIVITY KILLERS

Directions: Of the productivity killers listed, which can you begin taking steps to control today? List them below:

1. *Indecision*

2. *Crises mgnt.*

3. *No clear goals*

If you had to pick just one—to start to work on immediately— which one would it be? Rewrite it in the box below:

No clear goals.

Now, the challenge! We challenge you to begin today, in a conscious and systematic way, to work on eliminating this unproductive habit from your life and replace it with a good one! Are you willing to work (and work hard) for 30 days to rid yourself of this millstone of unproductivity you've been lugging around all these years?

Things are much more likely to happen when put in writing. To demonstrate your commitment to change, take the following pledge:

"Today I resolve to begin a 30-day period of conscious and repeated effort to *set + focus on clear goals.* . I will continue to apply myself until this problem has been completely eliminated from my life. I am truly excited about the difference this will make as I organize and manage the many demands of life."

Signed: _____

Date: *9.9.94.*

As we said, habits are usually very strong and firmly entrenched. To ensure your success in developing this new habit, here are three pieces of advice about the process:

1. **Begin quickly.** The best time to start working on this new habit is today. Don't succumb to the tendency to procrastinate. Sure, it might be more convenient a month from now, but it will never be more important. Your motivation and resolve will not be stronger in a month than it is now. Start now, and set a goal to acquire this new habit in the next 30 days!

2. **Begin strongly.** You've already committed yourself by putting this goal in writing. Don't stop there. Don't keep this goal a secret. Commit yourself to positive change by telling some other people (at least one!) what you've decided to do and by challenging them to keep you to your commitment. We guarantee if you'll commit yourself to the people most affected by the old, bad habit, they will hound you until you break it!

3. **Allow no exceptions.** Remember the incubation period. No matter what might come up in the next 30 days, don't allow yourself to slip back into the old behavior.

    Remember the last time you resolved to exercise yourself into better shape? Perhaps you decided to get up 30 minutes earlier every morning and run before breakfast. It probably went well for the first four or five days, but then one day the alarm went off and you thought: "I'm tired. I worked too hard last night. It's cold and raining this morning. Just for today, an extra 30 minutes' sleep would really be nice."

    For most, there ends the exercise program. Because the next day, we not only have to begin again, we probably have to begin behind the starting line. And this time, we start with the knowledge that we didn't make it the first time!

In the fragile incubation stage of a new habit, it is disastrous to allow any exceptions. Six months from now, when a new habit is strong and well ingrained, an occasional exception may be permissible, because it won't kill the habit. But not now.

> **YOU CAN'T UNSEE WHAT YOU'VE ALREADY SEEN, AND YOU CAN'T UNLEARN WHAT YOU ALREADY KNOW.**

Summary

What kind of goals would you set for yourself if you knew you would not fail? How about looking at that list of productivity killers one more time and at your list of three you would like to overcome? Your success is guaranteed if you commit yourself, and you'll never want to make the changes more than you do now.

Try it and find out for yourself!

Making It Work

CONCERN	REASON	STRATEGY
poor management and organization	bad habits have been allowed to form	develop new habits with 30-day program
unsuccessfully tried an idea before	gave up too soon; new habit not developed	stick with plan until familiar with it, behavior ingrained

Putting It To Work

- If you want to manage and organize your priorities, you must first learn to manage yourself.

- Recognize and accept areas you can't control; note areas you *can* control and act upon them.

- Look for your personal application of every idea in this manual.

- Successful self-management is the result of developing good habits and letting them control you, thereby giving you freedom.

- It takes 30 days of conscious, spaced repetition of an action to develop a new habit or eliminate an old one.

- If things aren't getting done, there are many common productivity killers that may be at fault.

- Recognize your weaknesses and develop a plan to build new habits there.

- When developing a new habit, begin quickly, begin strongly and allow no exceptions until after the habit is well formed.

Check Your Working Knowledge
Of Self-Management

1. How can you best manage and organize the priorities of your life?

2. What is the "incubation period" of a new idea?

3. To develop a new habit, what should you do? How long should it take?

4. What three rules apply to developing new habits?

5. Which of the 12 reasons why things don't get done are you going to work on first?

6. When are you going to start?

Four Fantasies And Three Rules

> **Mistaken beliefs about time**
> - **Learning to work smarter**
> - **The Law of the Slight Edge**
> - **The Pareto Principle (the 80-20 rule)**
> - **Bowling Balls (using In-Between time)**

For many of us, our inability to organize and manage priorities is a result of certain ideas we accept as true and on which we act accordingly. There are certain rules which, when understood and applied, can be used in all sorts of ways to provide advantages needed to succeed and stand out: to achieve when others are failing. This chapter will expose those fantasies about time and discuss the application of rules that are legitimately useful in priority management.

For starters, the fantasies. Most of these fantasies are related to time. This is a book not only on priority management, it's also on time management, because it's impossible to discuss organizing and managing our projects and activities without a nod in the direction of the clock.

> **FANTASY #1:**
>
> **NO ONE EVER HAS ENOUGH TIME. REALITY:**
>
> **WE ALL HAVE AS MUCH TIME AS THERE IS.**

It's true! Each one of us has exactly 24 hours in each day. That translates to 1,440 minutes. That's it. No more, no less.

What that means is, even though you may wish you had more time than you do, it's just not possible. This is one of the few ways in which all people are equal. You must make do with what you have.

In our workshops, we like to hold up a dollar bill and tell our participants about a bank advertisement we once saw in a financial news magazine.

The ad contained only a picture of a dollar bill with this caption:

> **THIS DOESN'T COME WITH INSTRUCTIONS.**

In this way, money and time are both the same. Time doesn't come with instructions, but you have to use it, nevertheless. Something simple like a toaster oven *does* come with instructions. It makes you wonder, doesn't it?

So, just like money, you have to learn how to use your time—all the time there is—in the most effective ways possible.

Some of us can acknowledge the folly of Fantasy #1, but trip up on the next fantasy.

> **FANTASY #2:**
>
> **THERE ARE MANY WAYS TO SAVE TIME.**
>
> **REALITY: YOU CAN'T SAVE TIME—YOU CAN ONLY SPEND IT.**

The concept of time is well represented by the hourglass. The sand passes through constantly, at the same rate. You can't stick your finger in and stop it. In the last minute each one of us has spent 60 seconds of time that can never be retrieved.

The great Finnish runner Paavo Nurmi set and then lowered several times the world record for the mile run in the 1920s. On one such occasion, a college student who had just learned of the accomplishment exclaimed to one of his professors, "Dr. Rogers, Paavo Nurmi has broken the world record for the mile by two seconds. Two whole seconds!"

His professor looked at him for a moment and replied, "And what does Mr. Nurmi intend to do with the time he saved?"

The bad news, then, is that you simply can't save time. But there's good news as well. You can spend your time wisely by investing it in ways that will give you future payoffs in productivity and freedom in decision-making. Which activities can you invest time in now to give you the greatest Return on Invested Time (R.I.T.)? Some of the answers you'll find ahead in this chapter, and when we get to the chapter on Planning, we'll tell you the rest of the story!

FANTASY #3:

THE LONGER YOU WORK, THE MORE YOU GET DONE.

REALITY: THE LAW OF DIMINISHING RETURNS APPLIES HERE.

Most people accept this fact in theory, but often don't acknowledge it in practice. The old advice holds true: "Don't confuse activity with accomplishment." The computer has driven this idea deep into our minds. Did you ever delete the last hour's worth of input with one tired, fatal mistake? (Writing this sentence just reminded us to save the last 300 words we've just written on this subject!)

If you insist on working yourself past reasonable limits, you are not only inviting major imbalance into your life (more on that in Chapters 7 and 13), you also allow the Law of Diminishing Returns, closely followed by the Law of Counterproductivity, to take over.

Personal Experiences

JONATHAN: In one of my first jobs, I established a pattern of taking work home with me nearly every night. Not that I always did much with it, but it made me feel productive and impressed my boss, I thought.

One day he took me aside and said, "When I had your job, I was always able to get it done in eight hours. You're showing me you must not be very effective with your time if you have to take work home."

Guess what I never did again? Guess what I learned?

FANTASY #4:

PRODUCTIVE PEOPLE WORK HARDER THAN OTHERS.

REALITY: WHEN YOU'RE IN CONTROL, YOU ARE RELAXED.

Of course, productive people don't work harder than others. There's a different word that applies here. You know the word... SMARTER!

Think about the people you know. Do the really productive ones seem to get virtually everything done without breaking a sweat? This, no doubt, explains the saying, "If you want something done, ask a busy person."

Of course, these people probably are indeed "breaking a sweat." What looks effortless is usually achieved only after experience and discipline. When you think about it, the least productive people are often those who continually run around in perpetual commotion. Much like the General of whom it was once said, "He jumped on his horse and rode off madly in all directions."

We must note here that income is not a measure of productivity (just look at the new major league baseball contracts!). Can you honestly say a person who earns $100,000 per year works five times more than one who earns $20,000? Probably not. But, if two people in the same field are earning widely differing amounts of money, it probably boils down to that word again . . . SMARTER.

The main reason some people are able to work smarter than others is that productive people have learned, applied and mastered one of the most important laws you can ever learn:

RULE #1: The Law of the Slight Edge

We encourage you to memorize this law: Write it down any place you'll see it frequently. Make this law so much a part of you it becomes an automatic part of your thought process and, therefore, your action. Use it to understand fully the nearly infinitesimal difference between success and failure. Between productivity and frustration. Between happiness and agony. WARNING: It's so simple it's deceptive! The Law of the Slight Edge is:

```
SMALL CHANGES, OVER TIME,

MAKE A BIG DIFFERENCE.
```

That's it. Profound, no? Yes, it is! Perhaps an illustration from horse racing can illustrate the truth of this simple little idea.

In racing's "Triple Crown" series for three-year-olds, there is a $5 million bonus to any horse that can win all three races: The Kentucky Derby, The Preakness and The Belmont Stakes. Should one horse fail to win all three races, there is still a $1 million bonus for the horse with the best overall record in the three races.

During the 1989 series, two horses, Sunday Silence and Easy Goer, were clearly the best of the field. Sunday Silence easily won The Kentucky Derby, Easy Goer was just as dominant in The Belmont. In each race the other horse finished second. The difference, as it turned out, was the middle race—The Preakness.

In this race the two horses staged a thrilling run down the stretch to the finish line, way ahead of the other horses. In a photo finish, Sunday Silence won the race (and subsequently the bonus) by a nose. First place in the race was worth about $700,000, plus the million dollar bonus for a total of $1,700,000. Second place was worth $70,000.

Sunday Silence got about 25 times more money for his efforts than did Easy Goer! Was Sunday Silence 25 times better than Easy Goer? Hardly. Over three races covering five weeks and nearly four miles of running, one horse was about two inches better than the other. There was virtually no difference, but the payoff was 25 times greater!

That's what The Law of the Slight Edge is all about. Little changes, over time. Maybe just a little more training. Maybe a slightly better method of planning. Maybe just one tiny habit overcome. Maybe all of those and more. Each one almost inconsequential, but when added up, the advantage is incredible!

That's really the major promise of this manual. If you can identify these little advantages you can develop, and add to them enough patience and persistence to carry them through, then look out! The payoff will not be arithmetical, but exponential!

Once you start achieving things, the turnaround gets a life of its own—success generates itself.

The Law of the Slight Edge is the reason that, at the end of each chapter of this book, you have a chance to take time to reflect on the ideas discussed. Sort them through and identify the key ideas FOR YOU that you can apply to your situation to make The Law of the Slight Edge work in your favor. Write those ideas down in the space provided at the end of each chapter.

You certainly don't have to work harder. "Smarter" is achieved in a number of small steps, one at a time. We'll mention The Law of the Slight Edge again in this book. We promise!

RULE #2: The 80-20 Rule (Pareto Principle)

Another rule that you can apply to make a difference in how well you organize and manage your priorities is the Pareto Principle, also known as the "80-20 Rule."

Victor Pareto was an Italian economist and sociologist at the turn of the 20th century who studied the ownership of land in Italy. Pareto discovered that more than 80 percent of all the land was actually owned by less than 20 percent of the people. As he studied other things that people owned (including money), he found the same principle held true: 20 percent or less of the people always ended up with 80 percent or more of whatever he measured.

This law is so well accepted by economists that most agree that if all the world's assets could be evenly distributed to every person in the world, it would only be a matter of time (and a short one, at that) until 20 percent of the people had 80 percent of the assets all over again.

We realize this book isn't about economics; however, the application here is that the law has proven to hold just as true concerning issues like time management and productivity on the job.

Do you work in sales? When we worked in real estate sales several years ago, 20 percent of the agents in our office made more than 80 percent of the transactions (it was actually more like 10 percent—if anything, this law is understated).

Are you a manager? We'll bet 20 percent of your people cause 80 percent of the problems you have to deal with and require 80 percent of the total time you spend with all your people. If you manage five people, you just thought of which one we're talking about!

Are you a volunteer worker? Then you probably agree that less than 20 percent of the people do 80 percent or more of all the work that gets done.

Do you work with many people on your job? Does at least 80 percent of the benefit come from only 20 percent of those people? Who are these productive people? Identify them, and decisions about priorities are already made!

> *The human animal was not designed to function at 20 percent. At that pace it develops enough malfunctions to cause a permanent shortage of psychoanalysts and hospital beds.*

Trying to manage priorities (as we all are)? Look at your list of projects and activities. We'll bet 20 percent of those priorities are producing 80 percent of the results coming from your work. And in many cases, the first 20 percent of the time you spend working on a job will produce 80 percent of the payoff you get. What activities will produce the greatest R.I.T. for you? When you can identify them, you can focus your energy for maximum benefit.

The most astonishing revelation about the 80-20 Rule is its opposite side: If 20 percent of activities are producing 80 percent of the results, then the other 80 percent of activities are, in total, only giving 20 percent of the results.

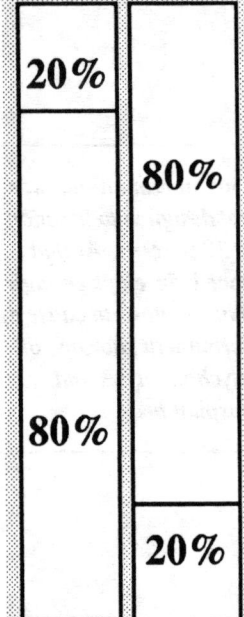

Most people acknowledge the truth of the 80-20 Rule without having a true picture of what it means. Does it mean one person (or one project) will have or produce four times as much? No, it's not nearly that conservative.

Picture five people sitting down at a table to eat a pie cut in five equal pieces. If this pie is apportioned to these people according to the 80-20 Rule, one person will end up with four of the five pieces of pie and the other four will have to share the remaining piece (would you believe one bite each?). The benefit to the one is 16 times greater than to any one of the other four people. Four people get five percent each while the fifth person gets 80 percent!

(Do you hear The Law of the Slight Edge whistling in the background somewhere? Those small advantages add up, and your attention to them will enable you to be that one person in five.)

Engineers know it's possible to draw and redraw a project indefinitely. There's always something else that could be done or another way of doing it, sometimes making it better. Yet, if what has been designed is going to be built, there comes the day when the plans must be taken off the drafting table and put into action.

The point? Perfectionism is frequently the biggest stumbling block to accomplishment when we reach this point. Is the last 10 percent really worth it? In some cases it is, but not usually. Time-management expert Alec Mackenzie writes: "I practiced the art of getting more things done, rather than getting the really important things done well."

Before you slam this book shut and decide Alec, Jonathan and Susan are all heretics, think about it. Getting things done is the name of the game. The more you get done, the greater your productivity. Yet some of us cling to a few "really important" priorities, trying to do them just a little better. You must learn to ask yourself: Is it already good enough? Is it necessary to put any more time and effort into this project?

Lest you think we've gone too far from the 80-20 Rule, we haven't forgotten it. As we determine the best use of our time at any given moment, we must pause and think about the effects of the rule and how it impacts our productivity and, therefore, the decisions we make about what to do and how much time to devote to each task.

Remember: To apply the 80-20 Rule to managing your priorities, remind yourself that 20 percent of the activities on your list are going to produce 80 percent of the results and payoff. Your question must constantly be, "Which activities are the 20-percenters?"

RULE #3: The Bowling Ball Rule ("In-Between" Time)

Obviously, if you do nothing but devote yourself to the really big items on your list, there will be a lot of little things that aren't ever going to get done. Since the fact in itself can lead to big trouble eventually, you can't totally overlook the small stuff. Remember: "For want of a nail, a shoe was lost . . ." etc.? You can't lose your battles if you pay some attention to details. The only question is, "How?" Well, meet The Bowling Ball Rule.

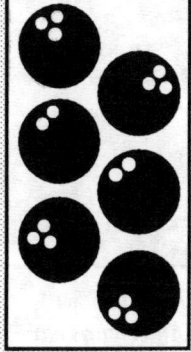

Before us is a box, filled with bowling balls. We all know a few things about bowling balls, such as: They are very big; they are quite heavy; they take up a lot of room. In fact, it would be impossible to put any more bowling balls in this box. There is room for only so many, and that limit has been reached. Such it is with the major priorities of your day. They are big and time-consuming. Try as you might, there is room for only so many and no more.

But here (Ta-Da!) is the "In-Between" Time concept—when The Bowling Ball Rule comes into play. While you can't put any more bowling balls into the box, how many marbles could you still drop in there? How many B-Bs? There's lots of room for something, but it can't be big "somethings."

You can make your days even more productive and satisfying by identifying the little windows of opportunity that pass through your life each day. They don't arrive with much fanfare, so if you're not alert to them, they will sneak right past you. These snippets of minutes we call "In-Between" Time.

Did you ever call someone on the phone and promptly get put on hold? Ever have a 10:00 meeting scheduled with someone who turned out to be five minutes late? Ever finish up a major activity just before lunch? Ever sit in a lobby or waiting room for your appointment?

True, in themselves these five- and ten-minute periods may be insignificant, but taken together they can form a powerful force of accomplishment in our lives and on our jobs. What you must do with your In-Between Time is:

1. **Recognize** it as soon as it occurs.

2. **Utilize** it immediately by taking a premeditated action.

There are many, many ways you can effectively use In-Between Time to your advantage. There's a key point to remember here.

> ## IF YOU DON'T HAVE A PLAN, YOU
> ## WILL WASTE THIS TIME!

That's where the "premeditated" part comes in. The best time to develop a plan of action is... NOW! What are some small activities, without specific deadlines, that could fit into this time? What marbles do you have to throw into your bowling ball box? Here are some suggestions, many of which have been passed along to us by participants in our workshops.

- Return phone calls
- Sign letters that have been typed and are ready to mail
- Keep a reading file at your desk, and read something
- Clean up your desk and return things to their proper places
- Review your Daily Action List and re-prioritize, if necessary

Prepare a small notebook of things that can be done in the one or two minutes it takes someone to answer the phone or for when you are put on hold.

About 25% of Americans eat breakfast in their cars to save time.

- Go through your mail (this doesn't always have to be done right away!)
- Write a quick note or memo
- Relax!

Psychological fatigue is common among executives. Learn to relax, prioritize and delegate.

The last item on this list is one we're always glad to hear somebody suggest. We are concerned, really, that people can become fanatical about time, insisting that every second of every day be accounted for productively. But sometimes what you need most is a couple of minutes to catch your breath, put your feet up, go for a short walk, meditate, even snooze if you're a cat-napper, to recharge and energize yourself again.

The problem is that many people fritter time away and then feel guilty when it's gone. Make a conscious decision to do one of these things (including "relax") and this time will hardly ever be wasted. Have a plan!

Is making the most of even small periods of time worth it? Did we mention that "small things can make a difference"? We did?

Suppose you had three "In-Between" Times per day, averaging five minutes each. That adds up to 15 minutes more productivity per day, more than one hour per week or more than 60 hours per year! Would you feel more in control of your life with an extra week and a half of work time each year, at no cost to your vacation schedule or normal working hours? Would this increase your value to your organization?

There's room for lots of marbles in your box. When you start putting them in, the benefits are going to add up quickly! In truth, The Bowling Ball Rule is really an effective variation and application of The Law of the Slight Edge!

WORKSHEET—USING "IN-BETWEEN" TIME

List here at least three strategies for using "In-Between" Times:

1.

2.

3.

Once you have that plan, you need to develop the awareness to identify the "In-Between" Time opportunities and swing into quick action when they occur! You'll be ready, no doubt about it.

Making It Work

CONCERN	REASON	STRATEGY
not enough time	belief there's more time out there somewhere	use what you have—there isn't any more
how can I save time?	thinking time can be saved	spend it wisely, because you can't save it at all
I need to work longer	if I do, I can get more done	don't confuse activity with accomplishment
I need to work harder	that's how to be productive	work smarter—relax, and keep in control that way
I need to make major changes in my style	I want to improve	apply small changes over time—use the slight edge
too many projects, too many people	all must be treated equally	learn the 80-20 rule: valued few or trivial many?
no time for small demands	can't schedule them in	don't schedule: have ready for "In-Between" times

Putting It To Work

- Destroy and forget your fantasies about time.

- You already have as much time as there is, and there isn't any more.

- You can't save time, you can only spend it. Spend it where it will give you the greatest returns.

- Working too long can actually reduce or erase your productivity.

- If you work smarter, instead of harder, you can be productive and relaxed at the same time.

- Commit to memory The Law of the Slight Edge: Small changes, over time, make a big difference!

- You don't have to be twice as good to do/earn twice as much.

- Apply the 80-20 Rule to your people and projects: Focus on the valued few, not the trivial many (and learn to recognize each!)

- You probably can't put any more large projects into your day, but there are lots of little ones you can do if you use "In-Between" Time.

- Always have small projects ready to work on as soon as you notice that "In-Between" Time is occurring.

- Five extra minutes, three times a day, equals almost two additional weeks of productive time during a year.

Check Your Working Knowledge Of The Fantasies And Rules

1. Which of the fantasies about time did you once believe in?

2. What strategy can you take with your new insight about that fantasy?

3. What is The Law of the Slight Edge? Have you written some Slight-Edge ideas at the end of the chapter yet?

4. In what other ways could you apply the 80-20 Rule to your life to make a difference in productivity or accomplishment?

5. What are the three new strategies you have identified for using "In-Between" Time?

6. If you were to experience "In-Between" Time right now, would you be ready to make it productive?

MY SLIGHT-EDGE IDEAS FROM CHAPTER 2:

Small changes, over time, make a big difference
Don't confuse activity w/ achievement
Work Smarter. Relax + keep in control that way.
80/20 - valued few, trivial many

It's much more fun to work smart, isn't it? More
rewarding, too!

CHAPTER 3

It All Begins With A Plan...

- **The importance of leverage**
- **Benefits of planning**
- **Obstacles to planning**
- **The tyranny of the urgent**
- **The difference between important and urgent**
- **Choose to be proactive**
- **Making planning work for you**
- **Knowing and using prime time**
- **A revolutionary challenge**
- **Every day's 15 most important minutes**
- **Using organizational tools for productivity and control**

... but there's a lot more to it than a simple four-letter word.

Webster tells us a plan is:

1. A method of doing something: A procedure.

2. A detailed program of action: A goal or aim.

3. An orderly arrangement of parts of an overall design or objective.

Our definition of a plan is:

> **DECIDING WHAT YOU HAVE TO DO**
> **TO HAVE A LIVABLE FUTURE**

"But I don't have time to plan," you reply.

> **YOU DON'T HAVE TIME NOT TO PLAN!**

Planning has many wonderful advantages, but the greatest of them all is what it does to the time available to do things. It literally adds to it.

Planning gives you leverage. The financial world uses the word *leverage* as a way of measuring how much can be controlled with personal investment. For example, if you bought a $150,000 house and paid $30,000 down, you are considered to be leveraging $150,000 in assets with your investment. Each dollar you put in is actually controlling five dollars. If you could buy that same house for just a $15,000 down payment, each of your dollars would then control ten. The more of someone else's money you can use and still have control of the asset, the greater your leverage.

It makes sense in finance, and it certainly makes sense in planning. Time spent in planning literally allows you to control more of the remainder of your time—in fact, it actually gives time back.

Time-effectiveness studies conducted by DuPont support this concept: For every one minute spent in planning, the time required to complete an activity is reduced by three to four minutes. Spend ten minutes, reduce completion time by 30 to 40 minutes. Spend an hour, reduce by three to four hours! That's **leverage!**

> **QUESTION: HOW MUCH TIME SHOULD I SPEND PLANNING?**
> **ANSWER: HOW MUCH TIME DO YOU WANT TO HAVE?**

When properly used, 15 minutes of planning can effectively control your time for an entire day. One quarter hour controls eight hours! That's like buying that $150,000 house for less than $5,000 down.

LEVERAGE!

PROJECT A

PLANNING	WORK

PROJECT B

PLANNING	WORK

You probably experience situations like this every day: "If only I had thought to bring this tool, the job would be a cinch!" "Why didn't I remember I had to take Jimmy for a haircut? Now I will have to make two trips!" Time is wasted every day for lack of a plan!

From now on, if someone rushes in and exclaims:

> **"WE HAVE ONLY TEN MINUTES TO..."**

Your best response is:

> **"OK, LET'S TAKE THREE MINUTES TO PLAN."**

Self-Quiz: How's Your Planning I.Q.?

Directions: To learn something about your present orientation to planning, take a moment to go over this quiz, circling the answer that best describes your orientation: (3) agree (2) not sure (1) disagree.

• I take regular time for planning every working day	3 2 1
• I have a personally chosen calendar or organizational system	3 2 1
• Before tackling a project, I carefully plan what it should accomplish	3 2 1
• I usually complete a *Daily Action List*	3 2 1
• I do not have difficulty making decisions	3 2 1
• I daily spend time on projects with long-term benefit	3 2 1
• The gas tank in my car is presently at least half full	3 2 1
• I know exactly when my most productive time of the day is	3 2 1
• I know my most important project for tomorrow	3 2 1
• I have a current Master Project List	3 2 1

In your plans for excellence, use "The Seven Questions." Which? Why? Where? When? Who? What? How? The results depend on your clarity of purpose, vision and objectives.

How Did You Do?

25 or more:	You have a plan, and are working your plan
15 to 24:	Sometimes your day gets the better of you
less than 15:	How are you holding up under your present crisis?

The Benefits of Planning

Planning is truly the key to managing our priorities better. There are many advantages to planning, including the following:

- **Planning makes things happen.** With no plan, chaos reigns. Events are left to chance. There's no priority and no way to measure accomplishment.

  It's fun to get things done, isn't it? The satisfaction of completing any project is rewarding. An artist wouldn't consider attempting a major painting without first doing a sketch on the canvas or a miniature version of the intended work. That's the artist's plan. The actual work is filling in the lines or boxes already there.

  Effective planning ensures completion of your priorities; it increases your chance of achieving success and recognition, no matter what the project. Does that frighten you? Does it seem risky? With an intelligent plan, it shouldn't. In fact, you will never have control over your own life until you understand and attain the results possible through planning!

Thoreau said:

> **"IT'S NOT ENOUGH TO BE BUSY. THE QUESTION IS: WHAT ARE WE BUSY ABOUT?"**

- **Planning promotes job and career advancement.** A simple illustration will suffice here: You are considering two people for promotion. One is a wonderful human being, but never quite has a clear purpose or direction. Effort is being expended, but there seems to be no real sense of what is important.

  The other is continually "planning the work and working the plan." Things really happen around this person. Who would you choose?

- **Planning provides the necessary framework for decision-making.** Did you ever wonder why some people approach a decision with confidence and assurance when so many others start to panic and perspire?

  Once again, the key is a plan. With a plan, you can see how events and activities fit in. With a well-thought plan, even when crisis arises and you have to make quick decisions with limited information, these too can be good decisions.

- **Planning will reduce crises.** The word here is *reduce*, not eliminate. That's because there are two kinds of crises: legitimate ones and false ones. Certain events can't be foreseen, so trying to plan around them is impossible.

  At work, you can't anticipate a personal emergency that calls your key employee away from the job in the middle of the day. But planning effectively, you can anticipate the absence of an employee who has an occasional emergency. Good planning prevents you from counting on 100% availability.

  Lots of crises occur simply because somebody failed to plan; most of these are completely avoidable. You need to realize that some crises will occur that can't be avoided and have some idea what you might do when they arise. (We'll have plenty of useful ideas for those occasions in Chapter 12, entitled: "Crisis and Conflict: Things Just Might Go Wrong.")

Linus (of Peanuts comic strip fame) said:

> **"NO PROBLEM IS SO BIG
> IT CAN'T BE RUN AWAY FROM!"**

- **Planning gives direction to energy.** A rodeo bronco horse has lots of energy, but no direction. Someone attempting to ride this creature has to literally hang on for dear life. However, a trainer can take the horse and teach it to work or be ridden, thereby channeling the energy into positive production. With a plan the "trainer" controls the energy. The average person says, "When in doubt, gallop!"

> *When you face an unpredictable future, nothing takes the place of a good plan.*

31

Obstacles To Planning

Obviously, there are a lot of reasons to become planners. In fact, it seems so obvious, you may be asking, "Why doesn't everybody plan?"

People come up with lots of reasons not to plan. Understanding the truth behind planning obstacles can help you avoid the consequences of poor or inadequate planning.

OBSTACLE #1: Day-to-day operations. Once again, sometimes the feeling can be: "I'm simply too busy to stop to plan." Remember the leverage factor when such thoughts creep into your mind!

Firefighters go to sleep at the fire station, but not before they have laid out their clothes on the floor next to the bed. The day-to-day operation of dressing is already considered, and these professionals have reduced the activity to a quick, predetermined process.

Is there an idea for you in this illustration? How much time do you spend after getting up making "what am I going to wear" decisions? How much time do you spend trying to find (in the dark, with half-opened eyes) the clothes you want? What if the power went off during the night and you unintentionally overslept? Would your plan help minimize the negative effects?

We don't want to deal with the "What" or "How" of day-to-day operations here, but a pretty good question to ask concerning these activities is, "Why?" Why are you doing the things you do? In the firehouse illustration, you're not interested (unless you're a firefighter!) in how the clothes are laid out, or what those clothes are. The question is: Why do firefighters do that? That's not a hard question to answer if it's your house burning at 3 a.m. Your comment then is "I'm glad they did!" instead of "I wish they had..."

Examine your own activities. Why do you do the activities you do every day? Are they all necessary? Do they have to be done daily? Is this merely a habit developed for a reason that is no longer valid? Can any activity be eliminated, or delegated without negative effects?

Do you get important correspondence finished to take to the mail

> *The world is divided into two groups: the few people who make good on their promises (even if they don't promise as much), and the many who don't. Get in the first group and stay there.*

room at 11:00 every morning? Are you doing this because that's
what the person who held the job before you always did, and the
person before that?

Could the reason for doing this be that once the mail carrier arrived
at the office at that time every day? Did you know your company
now has a box at the post office and someone stops by on the way
to work each morning? And, since no carrier stops by during the
day to pick up outgoing mail, someone else takes all the mail at the
end of the day and places it in the box down the street on their way
home from work? It's easy to keep doing something just because
"it's always been done"! But why do you do it? Is it even
necessary any more?

Are you like that sometimes? Are there activities you still perform
daily because the person before you did it? Or because you
watched a person you admired do it as part of his or her routine? Is
there still a valid reason for you to do this yourself? Would there be
more time available by eliminating this behavior entirely?

OBSTACLE #2: Lack of immediate satisfaction. We live in a
society where everyone wants everything now, if not sooner. Why
save money to buy something when a plastic card allows you to
have it now?

Since you can't get time on credit, how will you respond if, on the
first day you plan, things don't go as smoothly as you expected?

Sociologist Robert Merton noted successful people often exhibit a
behavior he termed the "Deferred Gratification Pattern." This
behavior reflects a willingness to put off something now and invest
more work, energy or money to attain something better in the
future. Rather than being disenchanted, logically examine the
situation; the "hidden price tag" is usually the real benefit of
waiting.

> *"The business of life
> is to go forward."*
> — *Samuel Johnson*

Keep this in mind as you look at the early results of the plans you
make. Don't be deceived or discouraged if your efforts don't result
in immediate payoff. Even if it's a good plan, it may take a while.
But it's worth waiting for! (OBSERVATION: Why do many of us
like to make "To Do" lists? For the satisfaction of crossing things
off! There's the immediate payoff, if you need one.)

OBSTACLE #3: What, more paperwork? Some of us have this conditioned response to the word "planning"—we see nothing but paper and more paper. Suddenly there are lists everywhere in our lives—our bathroom, on the refrigerator, in our car, or at the desk.

Don't let this bother you. More thinking creates less paper. Really! Even though it may seem to the contrary, planning actually works to your advantage. With planning, you can make decisions more quickly and effectively, actually reducing the amount of paper you have to handle on the job. (We'll give you some specific ideas about this in Chapter 6.)

OBSTACLE #4: Habits. It's simply a fact that habits are acquired and can be reinforced or changed. If failure to adopt the planning habit is your problem, you're only 30 days away from never worrying about it again. Make the choice today, and make planning a part of your acquired daily habits.

OBSTACLE #5: The fear of failure. You may be thinking, "What will happen if I really make the effort here? What if I sincerely try to change my patterns and spend more time each day planning my activities, and I have nothing to show for it? I'll feel even worse than I do now, because I've tried it and failed."

This simply won't happen! Now, we can't promise just how much more successful you'll be as a result of making planning a part of your life. Maybe it won't make as much a difference as you hoped it would; but it will make a difference! If you try to increase your productivity by 50 percent through planning and only increase results by 10 percent, have you failed? Hardly! You're simply that much better off than you would have been had you not tried and stayed the same.

Amazingly enough, some people are not so much afraid of failing as they are of succeeding. **Fear of success** can also deter actively implementing plans. Once again, it's simply not worth worrying about. You'll grow in so many ways as planning becomes a part of your life. You'll be prepared for the greater responsibility that accompanies success. Plus, you'll know how to plan to accommodate the new challenges!

OBSTACLE #6: Planning is hard work! Work can be fun. If you believe there is only unpleasantness in work, you will shortchange yourself of life's satisfaction. Besides, the most pleasant part of planning is thinking about the benefits you're going to receive as a result of what you're doing!

The key to boosting productivity is to focus on one or two short-term activities that are likely to produce the biggest results.

The Urgent: Our Tyrant

Have you ever been in a situation where a trivial matter suddenly became a major problem that seemed to dominate every aspect of your life? Experiences like these tend to be very convincing testimonials to the absolute necessity of planning. These are the times when we become subjects to **The Tyranny of the Urgent.**

PERSONAL EXPERIENCE

SUSAN: I recall a class I took one semester in college. The first day of class, the professor asked the class members if we wanted to know how our final grade would be determined. We all urged him to keep talking. We were eager to find out just how little we had to do to pass the course.

He told us that 50 percent of our grade would be taken from the average score of the three exams we would take during the semester. The other 50 percent would be determined by the grade we earned for the term paper (which he assigned that day), that was due the last week of class.

This term paper was certainly important—half of the grade depended on it—but it certainly wasn't urgent. At age 19, the end of the semester seemed at least a lifetime away to me.

Well, one of the worst weeks of my entire life was, you guessed it, the last week of class. I stayed up all night three times trying to finish the paper. I fared poorly on exams in other classes that week. I was sick the first week of the next semester. All because of my own neglect, something became urgent. When it was urgent it became my tyrant, and I paid for my neglect in a memorable way.

> **WHEN SOMETHING HAS TO BE DONE,**
> **IT HAS TO BE DONE SOMETIME!**

There's a world of difference between **important** and **urgent.** The first two definitions of important in the dictionary produce these two words: *significant* and *consequential*. Under urgent we find the words *insistent, pressing* and *imperative*.

Nowhere are words like *significant* and *consequential* to be found in the definition of urgent! The things we must pay attention to should be items that are *significant* and that have *consequence*. If your energy is directed to activities right now that are *insistent* or *pressing* or *imperative*, your energy is misdirected!

How do you keep the urgent from becoming your tyrant? Effective planning! Remember, everything that has to be done must eventually be done. The old expression "A stitch in time saves nine" certainly speaks to the Tyranny of the Urgent, doesn't it?

Would a little thinking right now identify some very important information you're going to need for that report due next month? Is there a question you need to ask someone before that person leaves on vacation next week? If the gas gauge in your car is reading half full, would it be easier to stop this afternoon at that service station you pass on the way home from work, instead of waiting "just a little longer"?

WORKSHEET — Planning For The Important

STOP RIGHT NOW. Think about your next working day for a moment, and then list below six things you want to get done tomorrow:

1.

2.

3.

4.

5.

6.

Now, spend a little time analyzing that list, and ask some questions:

- Are some of these items day-to-day operations, which would be on your list virtually every day?

- Are some of these items relatively unimportant—for now—but could become urgent if neglected too long?

- Are some on the urgent list now because of previous neglect?

- Are you putting out fires or taking steps to prevent them?

- Do any of these activities fall into the long-range category? What steps, if taken now, can make life easier and more productive down the road?

Let's suppose tomorrow is a super day for you, and you accomplish all the items on your list before the end of the day. What should you do next?

In Dennis Waitley's fantastic tape series *The Psychology of Winning*, Waitley encourages us to reward ourselves for finishing what we set out to do. We believe in those words.

In Og Mandino's book, *A Better Way to Live*, he suggests rewarding yourself in the presence of your loved ones, if possible.

Once again, lest you get so caught up in accomplishment that everything else is forgotten, remember the basic human need for reward. When you've finished your list, take a little time to relish the feeling of accomplishment so vital to mental health and well-being. Reward yourself with a cup of coffee or a few minutes of exercising or by reading an article that interests you. **Then** consider what might be next on your list and start again!

Are you convinced of the importance of planning, making time to leverage your day? Has an obstacle been keeping you from taking these steps, that you can now overcome? Does the term-paper story sound a bit too familiar? Have you allowed the urgent to be your tyrant more often than you care to admit?

Reactive And Proactive Approaches To Planning

How you approach planning is one area where, most certainly, the choice is yours—and yours alone. There are two words that describe everyone's approach to planning and to life: you can either be **REACTIVE** or **PROACTIVE**. Just like everything else, 80 percent (or more!) of all people fall into one category: Reactive.

Reactive people wait for things to happen and then respond to them. All their effort and work accounts for less than 20 percent of all that is accomplished. More than 80 percent of everyone you know fit this description. These people watch things happen and often wonder what's happening!

Proactive people comprise the minority—the less than 20 percent who actually achieve more than 80 percent of all success. These are people who take charge of their lives through planning and bold decision-making based on their plans. They make things happen.

The choice: As usual, it's back to you. Where are you now? Where do you want to be? What are you willing to give up short-term for long-term advantages and freedom? Tell yourself NOW:

> **I DO NOT CHOOSE TO BE A REACTIVE PERSON.**
> **I WILL TAKE CONTROL**

Making Planning Work For You

Having convinced yourself of the importance of planning, now take a look at some of the factors that can help you make something out of planning for your own situations.

Two elements work for you here: Time and tools.

TIME

Prime Time and Energy Levels

No one operates all day at the same level of energy. Each person has his or her own ups and downs, and for each person those occur at different times of the day.

We become not what we think but what we do.

People frequently make statements that indicate they have a basic idea about themselves and those around them. You may hear someone say, "I'm a morning person. I like to get up and get moving around quickly." About others you might say, "She's really a night owl. It seems the later it is, the more energy she has."

There's truth in both of those statements. In order to effectively use the time available, you first need to take a look at yourself and your habits. Do you know what (and when) your "Prime Time" is? Find out using the worksheet below:

WORKSHEET—Your Personal Prime Time

Directions: Divide your day into two-hour segments, and you will learn a lot about when you function better. In the graph below, plot an X in the appropriate box for each two-hour segment to indicate whether you have a high, medium or low level of energy during a typical day at work.

TIME OF DAY							
Energy Level	6-8 am	8-10 am	10 am-12 pm	12 pm-2 pm	2-4 pm	4-6 pm	6-8 pm
HIGH							
MEDIUM							
LOW							

Obviously, some days are more typical than others, but did you find yourself noticing some similar tendencies toward energy at certain times of the day?

Once the chart is filled in with the X's in the appropriate boxes, you can graph a typical day by connecting the marks to see how each day has its own natural ups and downs.

Some of the time segments probably don't correspond to the eight hours that constitute the core of your working day. By drawing vertical lines at the beginning and ending hours of your work schedule, you can see how much of that energy flows into the hours you are on your company's payroll.

No doubt, your employer believes that it would be great if some of the "high" energy times actually occurred while you are at work; if you happen to be your own boss, that's probably even more important!

Now, of the times you indicated as "high" energy, pick the one time (a two-hour segment) of the day when you believe your greatest amount of energy and concentration is available. This is called Prime Time, the time when you are at your physical or mental peak. Formal studies have shown the time at which internal (physical) and external (mental) energy is most likely to come together for many people is about 10:30 a.m.

By the way, the informal surveys we conduct during our workshops indicate that about 80 percent of all people experience Prime Time during the morning hours. That means as seminar leaders we have to be exceptionally good after lunch, or people will fall asleep!

The ideal is to do activities that are the most important, those that require the greatest amount of energy and concentration, during your personal Prime Time.

Once you know when your Prime Time occurs, there are three things you should do:

1. **RESPECT** your Prime Time. Don't do the trivial.

2. **PROTECT** your Prime Time. Actually block it off on your daily calendar so the unimportant activities don't crowd into these two hours.

3. **DIRECT** your Prime Time. Schedule the most important things of your day, the ones that require the most energy and concentration, into Prime Time.

Is it possible to change your Prime Time, once you know what it is? Yes! Sometimes your best times are not convenient for others around you. Perhaps your best time occurs outside normal working hours. It's possible to change because the habits you have developed over your lifetime have shaped much of who you are. Habits can be formed, and habits can be changed.

Increased productivity may be as easy as consciously concentrating key activities into certain times of the day, whether you think you have the energy for them or not. Doing this often enough can alter your patterns of energy as new habits begin to evolve.

Is your greatest energy period occurring after work hours? Do you have all kinds of trouble getting started in the morning? Often a change in when you go to bed at night, and when you get up, can make a big difference here. You might not want to try to change everything all at once. Try moving both times ahead 30 minutes at a time and adjusting for the move. After you've done that four times, you will have altered your sleeping pattern by two hours.

Studies conducted by Argonne Laboratories regarding the mental clock that exists in all people support its existence, and habit-changing techniques such as this have been effectively used by many people in overcoming the effects of air travel across time zones (known as "jet lag"). We put ourselves through just such a regimen before any trip involving a change of more than three hours and wouldn't think of leaving it to time and chance!

All of this is leading to a challenge we'd like to issue to you, which is the subject of the next section.

The Challenge That Will Revolutionize Your Day

Even though each person does have different patterns of energy, there is still an idea that you can apply to your daily routine that will make an incredible difference in your productivity, accomplishment and energy during the entire day. Here it is:

> **EVERY DAY, I WILL HIT THE GROUND RUNNING**
> **AND DO THE TOUGHEST THING I HAVE ON MY LIST**
> **THE FIRST THING AFTER I ARRIVE AT WORK!**

Does that sound difficult? It may well be for a while, but after you've developed a strong new habit of doing this, you simply won't believe what it can do for your entire day!

Imagine what a difference it will make to have the most difficult task out of the way at the beginning of your day! While the others at work are trying to figure out where they are and what they're going to do first, you'll have taken on that tough project and be well on your way to completing it! Think of the surge of energy you'll have with that wonderful sense of accomplishment after you've finished. Everything else will be easy. Your day will be a pleasant downhill coast with the "Big One" already under your belt.

Remember a day when you had a tough project that had to be done that day, but you kept putting it off? What a negative energy drain it turned out to be! Anticipation turns to anxiety. Then to fear. Finally to dread. By the time you decided to get going, you were exhausted! And then, it seemed easier just to reschedule the task for tomorrow. All that energy was expended for nothing.

Naturally, the first two hours of your day may not be your best energy-wise. However, it won't be long after you start accepting this daily challenge until things begin to change as you develop new patterns and habits. In fact, you may still find your later Prime Time to still be there, making you ready for another surge of productivity toward the end of the day.

By the way, don't hesitate to reward yourself for the completion of this task or the portion of the task you set out to finish.

The 15 Most Important Minutes Of Any Day

It takes only 15 minutes to leverage an entire working day. Block off 15 minutes on your calendar. Every day. Guard it with your life. No activity on your list requires more protection than does this one.

Use it, along with other planning tools you have (which we'll discuss shortly) to make each day one of purpose, meaning, direction and accomplishment.

While many people choose the first 15 minutes of the day for this daily planning period, we recommend putting it at the end of the previous day instead. Planning at the end of the day has three major advantages:

1. The ideas will be much fresher, since you have been at work all day and are well aware of what you have and have not already accomplished.

2. Doing this at the end of the day will give you a sense of closure on the day. When you've finished your 15-minute

> *Knowledge gives weight, but accomplishments give luster, and many more people see than weigh.*

planning session, you will be able to leave work with a true sense of completion, having accomplished the last item on your "To Do" list. Plus, you will enjoy your free time much more, since you won't be worrying about things you need to remember to do at work the next day.

3. Planning at the end of the day will enable you not only to identify the most important task of the upcoming day, but will allow you to jump in right away the next morning and take on that task immediately. While others are still trying to find the tops of their desks, or drawing that first cup of coffee in the lounge, you can already be on your way to a productive day!

(Even if you don't have all the available information for planning at the end of the day, you will spend less time inputting the newly acquired information the next day by not having to start at ground zero.)

These 15 minutes of planning are critical to productivity because:

- You know where to start.

"THE DAY HATH GOLD IN ITS MOUTH."
          —Benjamin Franklin

- You make the law of momentum work for you, rather than suffering the effects of inertia.

IT'S EASIER TO MOVE IF YOU'VE ALREADY STARTED.

- You know one secret of keeping your life productive: you:

KNOW WHAT YOU ARE GOING TO DO NEXT!

43

We'll talk more about the mechanics and activities of the 15 Minutes A Day shortly, after we've introduced you to the planning tools you have available to you.

THE TOOLS

Each of us has three tools we can use to make planning work for us. While we may use them in somewhat different ways depending on the nature of our work, they benefit all of us. The fundamental point of this section is this:

> **IF YOU WANT SOMETHING TO HAPPEN,**
>
> **YOU HAVE TO MAKE A PLACE FOR IT TO HAPPEN!**

The Appointment Calendar

You make commitments to others each day, and you probably log those commitments on your appointment calendar.

Do you have a meeting scheduled? Put it in the calendar. Meeting a business associate for lunch? The calendar. Appointments to call on clients? A phone call to someone available only at a certain time? An airplane departure time? Yes, you go to the calendar.

There are many, many such tools available. If you haven't recently spent time in a bookstore or office supply store, put this high on your list of priorities, and don't be afraid to spend a little time and money there, if necessary. After all, your planning is worth it!

The basic element of any appointment calendar involves days and perhaps times of the day. Some planning calendars show an entire month on one page; others show a week at a time; still others only one day per page.

The one-day-per-page varieties usually have the day divided into time segments. These segments may be one hour in length, some much less, even as small as five-minute segments.

July

Monday
8 9 10 11 12 1 2 3 4

June 8-12
8 9 10 11 12

The temptation will be to buy the fanciest and most detailed calendar you can find. Resist that desire, at least until you've analyzed your own work and routine enough to determine if that calendar is actually the best one for you.

DON'T AGONIZE. ORGANIZE!

Remember, you don't have to be any more organized than you have to be! Nowhere is this more true than with an *appointment calendar*. If your working day is such that dividing it into five-minute segments (and trying to account for each one) would be chaotic, don't buy that calendar, no matter how nice it may look.

> **SUSAN:** I recently took the position as chairman of a committee at church. People warned me about Sandie, one of the members of the committee. They told me: "You always have to call Sandie the day of the meeting to remind her of it, or she will forget to come."
>
> I decided that all committee members could manage themselves, and decided I wouldn't call Sandie before the meetings. She came to every one, and was always on time!
>
> Several months later, I asked her about her "reputation." She sheepishly dug into her purse and pulled out a small calendar: The kind with one page for each month with a little square for each day. "I finally bought a calendar," she said to me.

Here was a woman in her 40s, who had been in business all her life (much of the time in business for herself), who had finally purchased the first calendar she had ever owned! Sometimes it seems so obvious, but real truth is often disguised in its simplicity.

The Daily Action List

In addition to the appointment calendar, another tool we all need is the *Daily Action List*.

If the appointment calendar is where you list the commitments you have made to others, the *Daily Action List* is where you list the commitments you make to yourself.

On this list, you will write down the specific projects and activities that you need to accomplish on this day. These should be ranked and prioritized (Chapter 8 will explain this further) and listed in such a way that they can be checked off or crossed out after completion.

In looking at this list, if there are items that should be done by someone else, assign those items and get them off your list. Anything with a specific time or deadline can be put on the calendar (including your Prime Time activity and first activity of the day). What will remain after that time is what you have chosen to do that day, based on available time and priorities.

As simple as the *Daily Action List* is, there are three common mistakes made regularly that keep the list from being fully effective.

1. **Unrealistic Time Projections**. If you put 12 hours work on your Daily Action List, you'll end up frustrated even though you accomplish eight hours (or more) of productivity. You've missed out on closure—the feeling of accomplishment and satisfaction that comes from getting a job or list done. As you analyze the items on your list, realistically estimate how long it will take to complete each project. Remember to allow for interruptions, and estimate conservatively.

   Then make sure your list contains only as many activities as time will allow. This can be done simply by estimating the amount of time each task requires and writing the time on the list. It's much better to add to your list again later in the day if you've completed everything on it than to remain frustrated by an unrealistic (and uncompleted) list.

2. **The Calendar Factor Oversight**. Even though you may be at work for eight hours on a given day, those eight hours usually do not represent totally discretionary time. What's already on your calendar? If you have three hours committed on your calendar in meetings and appointments, you no longer have eight hours available to you: You have only five hours. Once again, factor in the time already committed to other people. And be realistic.

HINT: Look for ways to make multiple use of time that has already been committed. Remember the Bowling Ball Theory!

3. **Making the *Daily Action List* More Than It Is.** Wow! Did we ever learn this one the hard way! It happened when we started our first business, in January, 1977. Making a change at the beginning of a year afforded us an opportunity to really begin with style and organization. We both bought a great organizational system and decided no business people had ever been as well organized as we were going to be.

   Each day we started with our calendar on one side of the page, generally filled with appointments, since we found we had to call on a lot of people in the early stages of business. On the other side of the page, we had our *Daily Action Lists*.

   On Tuesday we would start the day updating our calendars, then we would transfer virtually our entire *Daily Action List* from Monday to the Tuesday page. Wednesday we would move Tuesday's entire list over, and so it went for about three weeks.

   Suddenly we became very discouraged—so discouraged from our lack of productivity we started to wonder if we had made a very big mistake going into business for ourselves. We expressed this frustration to a successful friend one evening, and she offered invaluable advice to us.

   She asked to see our organizational tools and within seconds told us, "There's nothing wrong with what you're already doing. You just don't have enough tools." And that was the day we learned about the third organizational tool you simply must have: *The Master List*.

The Master List

In the previous example, what we hadn't learned about was something totally different from the *Daily Action List*. Our problem had been trying to make our daily list serve two functions at once. It was more than just our daily activities—it represented everything we wanted to do, sometime.

> *Wherever anything lives, somewhere there is a register in which time is being inscribed.*

The Master List works as a "project warehouse" where you can store just that kind of item—the things you want to do, eventually, even though you know you won't do them today.

Divide your *Master List* into two categories: Business and Personal. Any time you get an idea of something you want to do, or recognize something that needs to be done, immediately write it on your list in the appropriate category. Then, as you plan the upcoming day, first look at your calendar to determine how much discretionary time you have. Next, look at your *Daily Action List* for the past day. Anything you didn't complete either goes on today's list, or send it back to the "warehouse" if you don't want to work on it again.

THEN (and only then) look at your *Master List* and add to the *Daily Action List* things you want to accomplish on this day (making realistic time estimates, as usual). Once you've moved something from the *Master List* to the *Daily Action List*, cross it off the *Master List*. In this way, you have to remember something in only one place.

This is how we keep our *Master List* to a workable size. We use a three-ring binder to keep the items from our *Master List*, which are divided into work-related and personal-related categories. Each item is also divided into active and inactive areas. As items are marked off the list, if nearly all the items on a page have been crossed out, we remove that page and place it in the inactive section (after we have rewritten the items yet to be done on a current page). As of the writing of this book, we're into our fifteenth year of doing this. Yes, it works!

Saving the completed pages can provide great motivation and input. The completed pages can give you a literal recitation in answer to the question: "What have you been doing recently?" This represents a continual list of accomplishments and keeps a resumé up-to-date. This can also provide valuable information about how much you're doing when additional responsibilities are taken on without others being given up. Upon entering a new job, the list can give you reminders of things you may need to do because you've done them in the past.

Before we wrap this section up, a couple of other planning tips:

Using *The Daily Action List*

- To benefit from the sample *Daily Action List* form below, use the "Time" column in one of three ways:

1. Mark each activity "high," "medium" or "low," based on the amount of energy required, and schedule it according to your energy flow of the day. Don't open the routine mail during your Prime Time, and don't write the most important letter of the month at a low energy period.

2. Actually assign a time of day to each item according to when you want to work on it, once again basing your decisions on energy level. If you use the time column this way, you could also then transfer these items to your calendar.

3. Use the time column to conservatively estimate how long each activity requires, which will enable you to create a realistic, achievable list.

- The greatest writing instrument ever invented for planning is the pencil. A pencil allows you to make changes and corrections. A day planned in ink (or worse, typed or printed) says, "You're not allowed to make any changes." Recognize that change will occur and use your eraser to make necessary corrections and changes, and give yourself a break.

- Remember: Planning is very rarely a solo performance. Few of us are blessed with the opportunity to make our list each day without considering the needs and priorities of others. These planning tools make excellent visuals in proving your priorities and decisions to others, but frequently other people (a boss, for example) will bring things your way that will cause significant changes in your priorities. (We'll discuss this much more in the section on Tracking Priorities—Chapter 9—and Communicating Priorities—Chapter 10.)

```
┌─────────────────────────────────────────────────────┐
│               DAILY ACTION LIST                       │
│                                                       │
│     THINGS TO DO:                        TIME:        │
│   _____    _____     │
│   _____    _____     │
│   _____    _____     │
│   _____    _____     │
│   _____    _____     │
│   _____    _____     │
│   _____    _____     │
└─────────────────────────────────────────────────────┘
```

Making It Work

CONCERN	REASON	STRATEGY
not enough time to plan	don't understand "leverage"	learn: one minute of planning saves 3-4 minutes' work
Daily Action List unfinished	too many activities	prioritize tasks (Chapter 8)
Daily Action List unfinished	unrealistic time estimates	estimate conservatively, allow for interruptions
Daily Action List unfinished	not enough time	count only discretionary, unscheduled hours available
Daily ActionLlist unfinished	contains long-term projects	start to "warehouse" projects
insistent, pressing and imperative demands	small matter left undone has become urgent	pay attention: don't neglect minor details of life
feeling tired, unfulfilled	no mental breaks	reward yourself for finishing projects and lists
difficult to concentrate on tough jobs	low-energy time of day	know your Prime Time, work toughest tasks then
worry about job and tasks when away from work	no plan; activities not written out	plan at end of day for following work day

Putting It To Work

- Planning allows you to leverage your time at three to four minutes saved for each minute spent planning.

- The more time you plan, the more unencumbered time you will have!

- Planning is essential for job and career advancement.

- Decision-making is easier when you have planned first.

- Energy can be directed productively with a well-made plan.

- Analyze your day-to-day operations to identify tasks better left undone.

- Pay attention to minor matters to keep them from becoming urgent.

- When a task is urgent, it takes complete control of your life.

- Reward yourself for completing your activity lists.

- An appointment calendar, a daily action list and a master list are essential to productivity.

- Know your Prime Time, and direct the day's most challenging projects into that time frame.

- Like any developed habit, energy levels during the day can be changed through regular, corrective action.

- Do your toughest job first, and the rest of the day will be a piece of cake!

- Plan tomorrow at the end of today, and enjoy relaxation and freedom tonight.

Check Your Working Knowledge Of Planning

1. What does leverage mean with regard to planning?

2. If you spend one hour planning a project, how much less time will it take to complete the project?

3. What kind of crisis can be eliminated through planning?

4. What activity are you doing every day just because you always have?

5. Why is it impossible to fail when you plan?

6. Describe the Tyranny of the Urgent. When was the last time you experienced this?

7. What is the difference between *important* and *urgent*?

8. Define "Reactive" and "Proactive" styles. Think about five people you work with. Place each in one of these categories.

NAME	REACTIVE	PROACTIVE
a._____	[ ]	[ ]
b._____	[ ]	[ ]
c._____	[ ]	[ ]
d._____	[ ]	[ ]
e._____	[ ]	[ ]

9. When is your Prime Time?

   When is your lowest energy period of the day?

10. What is the "Challenge That Will Revolutionize Your Day"?

11. What are the "15 Most Important Minutes of Any Day"?

MY SLIGHT-EDGE IDEAS FROM CHAPTER 3:

Reward yourself for accomplishment

Plan properly.

Be Pro-active - Make things happen.

Schedule most important activity during "prime-time"

Do toughest thing on schedule; first.

C HAPTER 4

Planning With A Mission

- **A Mission Statement: the first and last step**
- **How to establish your personal Mission Statement**
- **Steps of planning**
- **How goals work**
- **Questions you need to ask about goal-setting**
- **Applying goal-setting to priorities**
- **Path for Personal Productivity**
- **Personal Goals Map**
- **Determining the compatibility of your goals**

In determining your priorities via the planning process discussed in the previous chapter, the same questions will frequently arise.

- What's the best use of my time?

- What's really important to me?

- What do I want?

- What should I do next?

Accurate decisions regarding sequences and priorities cannot be made until you answer these questions. Surprisingly, perhaps, the answers do not come from outside sources or persons, even though many factors have significant control over many aspects of your life.

No, these answers come first from within . . . deep within.

The actual items on your *Daily Action List* are far down on the list as far as the sequential planning process is concerned. Planning actually must begin with both a personal and organizational purpose for existence, which we call a Mission Statement.

Before you think about your Mission Statement, let's think about the question: "Where are you now?"

SELF-QUIZ: Examining Your Goal Orientation

After reading each of the following statements, circle the number that corresponds to whether you agree (3), are not certain (2) or disagree (1):

1. My organization has a Mission Statement	3	(2)	1
2. I know my organization's Mission Statement	3	(2)	1
3. I agree with that Mission Statement	3	(2)	1
4. I have a personal Mission Statement to guide my decisions	3	2	(1)
5. I have specific, written goals for my job	3	(2)	1
6. I have specific, written goals for my career	3	(2)	1
7. I have specific, written goals for my personal life	3	2	(1)
8. My job, career and personal goals are mutually compatible	(3)	2	1
9. If a challenge arose today, I know people who would help me	3	(2)	1

Interpretation time:

22 or more: You know where you're going, and you're getting there!

21-14: With a little more work, you'd be all right

Less than 14: You need to explore what things are important to you and learn to set goals

The Mission Statement: The First And Last Step

If you were to approach your boss today and ask, "What are we doing here?" or, "We opened our doors for business today. Why?"—what do you suppose would happen? Would your boss give you a knowing look, then smile and begin to explain quite clearly the answers? Or would you get that puzzled expression that can only mean "You're obviously not playing with a full deck. The door is over there."?

You probably already know which reaction you would get. But, do you know the answers to the questions asked? The fact that so many offices, plants, agencies and stores are floating aimlessly in a sea of confusion can only tell us most people, and most organizations, don't know. In many cases, this problem has moved past the humorous to the critical.

So we begin by considering important issues philosophers have discussed for centuries: The ultimate meaning and purpose of life. Except, in this case, the discussion is hardly philosophical. It's as necessary to personal and corporate survival as air, food or water are to physical existence.

Thus, a Mission Statement is something everyone, and every organization, ought to have, because it is a **reason for existence**.

When the reason for existence is known, understood, accepted and communicated, things happen, and in a big way. Without it, energy and effort are wasted, and an organization can't last long going around in circles.

A Mission Statement should fit three qualifications—whether it's a personal or organizational statement. The Mission Statement must be:

- Distinct. It should be yours, and belong to nobody else.

- Stimulating. It should stir you to action on its behalf.

- Motivating. It should personally inspire and excite you.

Defined, the Mission Statement is a somewhat short but specific statement that clearly identifies the major purposes of the

> *A company cannot live without purpose, vision, leadership and a mission. A clear overall aim serves as a beacon, helping managers and workers down the line as they search for criteria to make decisions and take actions.*

organization that must be foremost in the minds of all employees at all times. Better defined, it's like the examples that follow.

Examples

We have done contract seminar work for National Seminars, Inc., for three years. We're pretty well acquainted with the operations of many public-seminar providers with national markets, and National truly stands alone at the front because of the simplicity and clarity of its purpose. We have called it "Q.L.R.I." long enough that our associates at National do, too. It stands for:

QUALITY LEARNING FOR A REASONABLE INVESTMENT

That's the Mission Statement. Sure, there's definition and lots of explanation that can go along with it, but if you know that much you've got a pretty good picture of what's going on, and why.

Look at the two parts of the statement. "Quality Learning"—what does that mean? Only that every decision of the organization regarding program and resource content and curriculum is dictated by that objective. New seminar? Change in course content? New publication for purchase at the workshop? New workshop leader? One question only: "Will this provide for a quality learning experience?"

Then, "Reasonable Investment." Believe us, companies in this business don't survive long without this aspect in gear. Each decision made is based on the question: "Will this enable us to provide our product for a reasonable investment?"

The two parts of this Mission Statement must function together. National Seminars might offer the greatest educational experience the world has ever seen, but if no one can afford to attend, no one would benefit. Perhaps costs could be reduced so low as to provide a full-day seminar for a very low price, and only a place the size of the New Orleans Superdome could hold the crowds that would attend. But, if the program was poor, no one would benefit and no one would ever come back. No element can stand alone in the Mission Statement—it must be complete.

Most company mission statements are worthless, because they use abstract superlatives, such as "biggest," "best" and "greatest." None of these words does anything to move the company along in any mission. Try to use concrete company objectives, so progress can be measured.

Part of Johnson & Johnson's Mission Statement goes:

> **OUR #1 COMMITMENT IS TO THE
> DOCTORS, NURSES, PATIENTS AND FAMILIES
> WHO RELY ON OUR PRODUCTS**

Simple enough? Pretty strong and directed, too!

A Mission Statement not only guides in times of prosperity and
success, it also provides leadership in crisis. Remember the
Tylenol® (a Johnson & Johnson product) scare a few years back?
How did the Mission Statement help during this crisis? It
immediately advised employees what to do. The first thing the
company did when the tainted bottles came to their attention was to
pull them from the shelves.

A bold move? Yes. Expensive? Definitely. But it was the only
move that made sense, considering the commitment expressed in
the Mission Statement. Nothing is more important to a
pharmaceuticals company than public trust. Thus, Johnson &
Johnson's Mission Statement reflected this fact. Today, Johnson &
Johnson still rates right at the top of every survey of public trust and
confidence in the product. Johnson & Johnson survived a crisis that
might have killed many other companies and came back to achieve
higher trust levels than ever before.

By the way, who do you suppose made the decision to pull
Tylenol® off the shelves? The Chief Executive Officer? The
Chairman of the Board? Actually, a relatively low-level executive
who happened to be the first to learn of the problem made the call.
With the confidence only a clear, purposeful Mission Statement can
provide, the decision was made immediately at that level.

Mission Statements. We talk about them frequently in our
workshops, and people who work for organizations with Mission
Statements are often quick to tell us (and show us) theirs.

We recently conducted a workshop for Hewlett Packard's
McMinnville, Oregon, plant (a cardiology equipment-

manufacturing facility). Our coffee was served in a mug with the company's Mission Statement printed on the side—a constant reminder of the division's reason for existence:

> "The Cardiology Business Unit (CBU) mission is to become the global, leading supplier of diagnostic cardiology and resuscitation products."

> "The CBU will meet its customers' needs and gain market share by being the low-cost supplier of a broad line of profitable products which offer value through quality and best-in-class performance."

All day, employees of the CBU talked enthusiastically about the ways in which the Mission Statement was making a difference in the quantity and quality of production and the resulting impact on the company's sales figures.

We recently worked with Todd Shipyards of Seattle, Washington, which had recently experienced a long reorganization process, repositioning itself primarily as a ship-repair, rather than ship-building, facility. The company felt a new Mission Statement was needed to reflect those changes in the industry. We worked with all levels of management—from lead people in the paint department to Todd's president, Hans Schaeffer. As we gathered words and phrases that best explained Todd, incredibly strong, creative words flowed from all levels. Probably the most astute, forward-looking statement of all came from a department supervisor who said:

"I don't know why we still have the word 'Shipyard' in our name. With the facilities and craftsmen we have, we can do quality building, maintenance and repair work in virtually any area."

Armed with its new Mission Statement, Todd moves cautiously, but confidently, into the rough seas of domestic and international competition.

Perhaps by now you're thinking, "OK, I can see how and why a profit-making company can and should have a Mission Statement. But I work for a non-profit organization or agency. How can a Mission Statement work there?"

Communicate your mission. Employees need to know their goals.

To answer: Here are two more Mission Statements we've picked up from clients. One is a government agency, one a public school system.

From the Naval Aviation Depot, Alameda, California: "We are a national resource. We provide responsive maintenance, engineering and logistics services in support of our nation's defense. Our mission is to support our customers by continually improving our products and services, while providing the highest quality at minimum cost."

Good grief—this Mission Statement uses all sorts of words we associate with the profit-making sector! Customers. Products and services. Highest quality. Minimum cost. By the way, these terms are all clearly defined so that everyone can understand them, and printed on the back of a plastic-laminated Mission Statement card carried by each employee.

From Prince George, British Columbia, Public Schools: "We are a Public Community Resource. We provide education for our nation's children. Our mission is to provide quality education and services while supporting individual needs and being responsible to our taxpayers, whose money funds our schools."

Every Mission Statement quoted represents a clear, specific definition of purpose that guides planning, decision-making and activity—one that's available to every employee in the organization. Communication of this kind creates motivation and commitment on all levels of responsibility.

Now, a Mission Statement by itself is certainly not a guarantee of organizational success. But, when you realize how a Mission Statement affects motivation and understanding throughout the workplace, is it any wonder why some organizations move ahead and others stall? Why some succeed when others fail? Why a recession forces some companies out of business while others grow? An executive we met recently on a flight commented to us about the possibility of recession:

Winning is an attitude: "First we will be the best, then we will be first."

"We actually welcome a recession, because we're strong and well-positioned. If some of our competitors go out of business, it means we'll increase our market share. And all of our people know and understand this."

What is your organization's Mission Statement? Do you know it? Does it even have one? Now, before you go charging into someone's office tomorrow and begin to rock the boat, please make sure you know the answer to this question:

What Is YOUR Personal Mission Statement?

Just as an organization must have a purpose for existence, so does each one of us. Why did you get out of bed this morning? What forces drive you, compel you to action and productivity? Where is the unique human being known as "you" headed in life?

If a company needs a Mission Statement to help make decisions and set direction, you do, too. Maybe you don't have too much control (if any) over where your employer is headed, but you have the ultimate control over who you are and what you become—not only to your organization but, even more importantly, to yourself.

It's not too late, nor is it one minute too early, to do some serious thinking about what your personal Mission Statement should be. In fact, this is quite possibly the most important thinking you can do in this entire manual to make a difference in how you organize, manage and control your projects and priorities.

Wally Amos, the "Famous" chocolate-chip cookie seller of the same name, put it this way in an interview with Dr. Robert Schuller: "You have to determine exactly what it is you want in life, and make it clear and specific. Then you make all your decisions based on the Mission Statement you develop in answer to that question."

Actually, the process doesn't even have to be all that complicated. In fact, here's an easy way to begin, simply by filling in (after some serious thought) the blanks in the following statement:

_____'S PERSONAL MISSION STATEMENT

(Print your own name here)

My intention in life is to use my _____ (noun) and

_____ (noun) to _____ (verb) _____

(verb) so that _____

_____

_____

_____ (my conception of the ideal world)

Can you do that in, say, 25-50 words? Commit it to memory and to heart? Repeat it to anyone who asks? Use this statement as a guide to important decisions about what's important to you, and the best use of your time?

Just to show you it can be done, we'll tell you our personal Mission Statement, modified only enough to fit into the blanks above.

Jonathan and Susan Clark's personal Mission Statement

"Our intention in life is to use our speaking and writing skills to inspire and equip people in all walks of life to become better managers of themselves and their lives, and, in so doing, have ample time and resources to enjoy the many opportunities, interests and pleasures we have chosen to pursue."

That's it. That's us. It's distinct. It challenges us to action, and it motivates us.

Now, do it for yourself! This is how effective planning and decision-making begin.

Remember To Fine-Tune

Whether it's an organizational or personal Mission Statement, the statement has been established in a world that is constantly changing.

Every three months, review your Mission Statement and make the subtle but necessary changes required to keep it current. Perhaps no fine-tuning will be necessary; but if the Mission Statement is neglected without updating for too long, it will no longer reflect your purpose for existence.

Think back ten years. Where were you ten years ago? What has changed in your life since that time? What would your Mission Statement have been then, compared to what it is now?

If you can imagine the shock that would come from jumping directly from the ten-year-old Mission Statement to a new one, remember it's possible to avoid that through the quarterly fine-tuning process.

After The Mission Statement—The Other Steps

> "IF YOU HAVE BUILT CASTLES IN THE AIR,
> YOUR WORK NEED NOT BE LOST.
> NOW PUT FOUNDATIONS UNDER THEM."
> — Henry David Thoreau

Mission Statement

↓

Goals

↓

Objectives

↓

Strategy

↓

Related Goals

↓

Tactics and Rules

↓

Action Steps

↓

Implementation

↓

Evaluation and Redefining

We defined the Mission Statement earlier in this chapter as the "first and last step" of the planning process. Once the Mission Statement is in place, other steps follow as you move up the ladder to results and accomplishment in your life and organization.

- **Goals:** Targets you must reach in order to achieve the purposes of your Mission Statement.

- **Objectives:** The steps required to reach your goals. You can also call them "short-range goals" (and the previous step "long-range goals"). We won't mind!

- **Strategy:** Key areas you must work on to get you most effectively to your goals.

To make these definitions come alive, let's look at an illustration to show the relationship between the first steps. Consider a professional football team that has a Mission Statement that reads: "To provide a quality entertainment product for the people of (city or area) at a reasonable cost while being well supported by the community and reflecting positively upon the city or area." That's not too hard to imagine.

What kind of goals would be based on the Mission Statement? Well, what is the ultimate goal of every professional team at the beginning of the season? Right! To win the Super Bowl. If you're Canadian, make that "Grey Cup."

Based on that goal, some of the objectives would be: To qualify for the playoffs (should probably win more than we lose!); to win the division and have the home-field advantage all the way to the final game by having the best regular-season record.

Some of the strategies required to reach those objectives might include developing a better running game to go along with our passing attack, to shore up the linebacking in our defense, to improve special-teams performance.

- **Related Goals:** This is an optional step, and what it refers to are the side steps that also might be helpful in attaining the goals. It might be taking a course at night that would make you better qualified to achieve some of your objectives. For our football team, it might be to start a booster club to increase fan enthusiasm (and the chance of winning home games) and help new players feel at home in the city.

- **Tactics and Rules:** Measurement. How will you evaluate what you're doing? What are the boundaries you have to work within? Without a means of measurement, achievement can never be verified, and mileposts never established to show progress.

- **Action Steps:** The *Daily Action List*. What do you need to accomplish today as you move in the direction you're headed?

- **Implementation:** Do it. All you've done so far is think. Peter Drucker says: "All planning must eventually degenerate into work for anything to actually happen."

"If you don't have a destination, you'll never get there. Setting goals is simply a long-term method of keeping track of your time. A goal is a dream with a deadline."

If you want to improve something, then measure it.

65

- **Evaluation and Redefining:** Step back and look at your results and decide what those results mean. Are they directing you toward your long-range goals? How do your results fit with your Mission Statement? Use the **FAR** Method to evaluate and redefine.

> **FEEDBACK**
> **APPRAISE**
> **REVISE**

Feedback lets you have fun! It's information that tells you how you're doing. Many organizations, of course, have their own built-in methods of giving feedback—hopefully more than a once-a-year performance evaluation. If nobody is measuring your performance for you, develop your own methods!

For example, in writing this book, we established goals for ourselves of writing a certain number of pages per day, and we have frequently used the Page Preview menu item on the computer to see how well we've done. And we've never reached the end of a day without printing out one copy of what we wrote that day. It's visual, and very satisfying.

Appraisal is the pivot point—the place where you begin to turn from the past to the future. Lee Iacocca describes such an activity in his autobiography when he talks about a Sunday evening time in his family room at home when he compares the last week's results to his plans for the week, then refocuses his direction ahead to the coming week based on his appraisal.

To do this, you must focus on measurable results, and you must know what the target is. Look at results every day and appraise your progress weekly. Idea: So you don't get caught with short-sighted thinking, you might also want to do this monthly and look at the big picture—with long-range goals and objectives.

Revision is the step that is the least popular (but the most progressive!), because most of us don't like the idea of having to change our strategies or direction. However, the reality of life is that all plans are subject to revision. Goals usually shouldn't change, but perhaps the process should—revision allows for each change as it occurs.

If you are a golfer, this should be easy to relate to. When you put the ball on the tee to drive it down the fairway, you plan for a long, straight shot to the center of the fairway, where you might pull a mid-range iron out of your bag for the next shot. Then the reality: You hook the ball into the trees. The goal is still the same: To play the hole in as few strokes as possible; however, your plan for doing so must be revised based on what has actually happened.

Therefore, when you evaluate and redefine, take a hard look back down at the bottom of the ladder—at the Mission Statement supporting all your plans. Were the results consistent with the Mission Statement? If not, what do you need to do differently next time to produce results more in line with what your purposes are?

This review process certainly isn't always a negative one in which shortcomings are analyzed. Many times the results will please you so much they may actually cause you to modify your Mission Statement to reflect the exciting discoveries made as you evaluate.

As you can see, the planning process begins and ends with the Mission Statement. That's why we call it the "first and last step" of the procedure!

Understanding Goals And How They Work

The major purpose of this chapter is not to teach you about goal-setting; there are lots of wonderful books devoted exclusively to this process. But, we would be overlooking a significant aspect of priority management if we didn't spend some time considering goal-setting and how it works in relation to the "big picture" of personal and organizational Mission Statements.

Goal-setting is work! We'll not downplay this fact, and although you may have heard or read someone eloquently telling you how easy it is to set and achieve goals, we don't believe it. We believe setting goals is a real struggle, but, it's a healthy struggle—one that is absolutely essential for success and survival.

Did you ever watch a butterfly trying to get out of its cocoon? What a struggle it is! In fact, in watching this event, you might be tempted to make it a little easier for the butterfly. You could take a knife and make a small slit in the side of the cocoon to help it get out. If you do that, you have just done the butterfly the ultimate disservice. By denying the butterfly the struggle, you have also denied it the ability to fly!

> **THROUGH THE STRUGGLE TO GET OUT OF ITS COCOON, THE BUTTERFLY'S WINGS ACQUIRE THE STRENGTH TO FLY!**

Is there a message for all of us here? Without the struggle of good goal-setting, you can never develop the strength and resolve to spread your wings and fly—to achieve the targets you set out ahead of you, and to overcome the setbacks and adversity that inevitably come to a person with a purpose.

Many warm, fulfilling stories come to mind about the importance of the struggle associated with goal-setting. It's exciting, for example, to think about people who are many, many years past what used to be considered "retirement" age who are doing everything but retiring!

George Burns recently celebrated his 95th birthday. He's already scheduled a televised extravaganza from the London Palladium for February, 1996, to celebrate his 100th birthday! The great conductor Leopold Stokowski died at age 97. He had already made commitments before that time for conducting engagements three years ahead—engagements he would have been 100 years old to make good!

Insurance actuary figures show the life expectancy of a person who has truly retired, with no goals or ambitions remaining, to be less than two years. The two men above are only representative of many people who discover goals to be not only strength-giving, but life-giving! As long as you'll set goals and commit yourself to them, you may eventually wear out, but you'll never rust out. Do these illustrations convince you of the importance of setting goals and continuing the struggle of setting them?

Rather than a lot of description about the "how" of goal-setting, let us ask you some questions that will give you direction and focus.

Three Questions For Everyone

1. Do you commit your goals to paper? Writing your goals enables you to identify them most clearly, and increases your personal and career commitments. Without writing your goals down, the possibility of achievement drops to nearly zero. Writing your goals:

- Makes them concrete. Your goals are not nebulous clouds floating around somewhere in your head, but entities you can see.

- Reminds you of them. When goals are written, they're never forgotten.

- Gives a sense of urgency and commitment. As you look at what you have written, you are constantly encouraged to action.

- Makes them measurable. Nothing is more satisfying than looking at a list of goals and actually being able to check them off and reward yourself.

- Makes things happen. There's almost a supernatural attraction of written goals to getting results. When Conrad Hilton was a young man, he owned two small hotels (his first hotel was in Cisco, Texas). One day, he read an article about the Waldorf Astoria Hotel in New York, called "The greatest hotel in the world." He clipped a picture of the hotel and placed it under the glass on his desktop. He looked at it every day. Thirty years later, Conrad Hilton owned the Waldorf Astoria!

Written goals represent the difference between results and good intentions. Harry Truman once remarked the worst thing that could be said of a man was: *"He meant well."*

> *Concrete goals are easier to attain. They are a specific aim to achieve and a gauge by which to measure success. Example: "One weekend excursion with the whole family every month" vs. "Spend more time with the family."*

2. Do you strive for improvement, not perfection? Remember the 80-20 rule? When you set your standards unrealistically high or severe, the chance of success disappears.

You can learn a lesson from Japan here. The Japanese have a principle called *kaizen*, which relates closely to the question. Every day, the objective of each worker is to do his or her job a little bit better than the day before. No quantum leaps! No revolutionary changes! Just a little better than yesterday. And tomorrow, the goal is to do a little better than today.

Spectacular? No. But amazingly productive. This is how mastery is achieved. And mastery is not perfection. One can be achieved; the other can't and really isn't even necessary. In the year Tom Kite became the first golfer ever to earn one million dollars in one year, he never made a hole-in-one! Did he have a bad year? No, he was a master of his skill, even though he never achieved perfection!

3. Do you develop strong interpersonal relationships? It is seldom possible to achieve goals without the involvement of other people—the "Lone Ranger" approach is rarely successful.

Good interpersonal relationships imply a connectedness of yourself with others, mutually achieving beneficial objectives. Sometimes your assistance can be important in another person's achieving his or her purpose or Mission Statement. And, you need others as well.

Canadian geese give us a clear picture of how we can function together. As a flock of geese flies, several things are happening. First, the formation is always a V shape. The geese at the head of the V have to fly the hardest, breaking through the air while the others in the formation fly in the draft created by the lead geese. Just behind and inside the head of the V you'll frequently notice some geese not in formation. These are the old and the weak. They can fly longer if they never fly on the edge of the formation. The stronger geese do the work.

> *Perfection is something you never achieve—you only strive for it.*

If you watch long enough, you will also see the lead goose break out of formation and fly to the back of the V, letting another take the point. By sharing the work load, the flock can fly faster and longer as each takes the point position while others rest. If a member of the flock lags behind, another goes back and flies with it. If a goose leaves the formation and goes to the ground, another accompanies it.

There are many lessons about needing each other we can learn by watching geese! How connected are you? Are there people you can call on when help is needed? Are there people who literally block the road to your progress because a relationship is broken or has never formed? Are you willing to rest once in a while and let others fly at the leading edge?

Three More Questions

1. Where are you going? Determine this as far out as you plan. If you can only see 18 months ahead, fine! That's much more realistic than a 20-year vision, for example. However, Winston Churchill once said:

> **"YOU CAN ONLY SEE AS FAR AS YOU CAN LOOK."**

Remember to "look" carefully at both the organizational and personal Mission Statements. This will enable you to see farther.

The more specific you make your goals, the more direction they will provide for you. For example, if your goal is to maximize efficiency by buying an improved photocopy machine, start trying to determine what you have in mind. Size? Services? Paper? Manufacturer? Resale? etc.

> **"LUCK" MEANS BEING PREPARED FOR OPPORTUNITIES!**

Of course, not all goals are easy to measure. A goal such as "strong interpersonal relationships," for example, is pretty hard to quantify. In these cases, you can construct a rating scale from 1-10, with 1

The key to healthy business relationships is being unconditionally constructive. Do only those things that are both good for us and good for the relationship, whether or not others reciprocate.

71

representing the poorest and 10 the ultimate. Then you can estimate where on the scale you think you are, and decide where you would like to be.

If you don't get a rating that is appropriate, you can try describing what you want as vividly as you can. If you find that you can't:

- Qualify it
- Quantify it
- Measure it
- Rate it, or
- Describe it,

Then forget it as a goal, for you'll never be able to attain it!

2. How will you get there? Once the long-range goal has been set, determine some along-the-way objectives. What will be a milepost to mark the progress you have made? What obstacles might you encounter along the way? These produce the strategies we implement to help us reach our goals.

Achievement motivation has become so synonymous with today's culture that we need to be aware of our tendencies here. In executive-leadership sessions, we sometimes challenge people to a simple game of ringtoss. The objective is simple: Try to throw the ring over the post.

As we watch different people take on the task (we set no rules as to how close to stand), it's interesting to note what happens.

- Some people stand so close it's a cinch. They hit the stake several times in a row, but then lose interest.

- Some people stand so far away that achievement is almost impossible. They fail several times, and they, too, lose interest.

- Others stand close enough to make the goal attainable, but far enough away to make it challenging. These are the ones who keep at it! They try and try again, using different stances, methods of release, height of throws. They stay motivated.

Novelist Ernest Hemingway used reinforcement systems to increase his productivity. He kept track on a graph of the number of words he wrote each day; each evening that number either scolded or encouraged the author.

Only a goal that is tough but attainable will attract and keep our interest for very long.

3. How will you know when you've reached your goal? If your goal is not specifically measurable, how will you know when you're there? Determining the actual position, the accomplishment and what it looks like is critical to attaining closure—the completion of our task.

A GOAL DOESN'T BECOME A GOAL WITHOUT A TARGET FOR COMPLETION

This is a great rule to impose on yourself to create even greater momentum. Target dates, like goals, should be realistic. To set realistic target dates, consider each goal from a time perspective. This could be long-range (even a lifetime goal), accomplished in less than a year, or even daily, to make the most of each day. The target makes the difference!

An analogy involving these three questions relates to the last vacation trip you took. When the time came to leave for the trip, did you just put some things in the car, back it out of the driveway and then ask, "Well, where should we go?"

Probably not. We planned our trips for weeks or months in advance, deciding exactly where we wanted to go, and usually accumulating information about our planned destination. Then, we decided how to get there. We got out maps and marked routes. We determined some stopping points on the route. If we wanted to visit an attraction along the way, we scheduled it into our trip. As we drove, there were literally mileposts and signs along the way telling us how we were doing, whether we were headed in the right direction, and how far we had to go.

Finally, when we arrived at our destination, it was obvious. If the goal is the beach, the road ends and the water begins. If the goal is a particular city or attraction, there are lots of signs telling us we made it.

If you can't see the end of your goal as specifically as the last trip you took, you had better review those three questions again.

**WHEN YOU FAIL TO RELATE
YOUR TODAYS TO YOUR TOMORROWS,
YOU HAVE TO START OVER EVERY DAY!**

Yes, Three More Questions (for Managers and Managers-To-Be)!
If you are setting organizational and departmental goals, as a manager or supervisor, you're not finished with goal-setting quite yet.

1. Is this goal worthwhile for the organization? Is it necessary? Will this goal help you achieve your organizational Mission Statement? If you can't answer this question with "yes," maybe it shouldn't be on your list.

2. Is it the right time for this goal? Is it appropriate? This may be a wonderful goal for your organization or department, but is the timing right? Are there other more important objectives at this time? Would energy directed to this goal detract from achieving other goals?

3. Should I be the one to handle this goal? Is it efficient? Even though the goal may be right and the timing right, you still need to ask, "Why me?" Is this the best use of my time and energy right now? Is there someone else who could (and should) be doing this? Is this something I should delegate?

What is the growth trend in your department? The mark of a leader is the growth and development of the people for whom the leader is responsible! What are you delegating? What can you delegate? (There's more on delegation in Chapters 7 and 10.)

To summarize:

**GOAL-SETTING DETERMINES WHAT'S IMPORTANT FOR ME
AND ENABLES ME TO MAKE DECISIONS REGARDING MY PRIORITIES.**

Marking Your Path

Goal-setting is a struggle to be your own person while a myriad of forces are trying to persuade you to do otherwise. Personal productivity is a by-product of this healthy struggle, for you and your organization.

The Path for Personal Productivity Worksheet is one we encourage you to photocopy and use daily as part of your 15-Minutes-a-Day planning session. This can literally function as your roadmap to take you where you want to go.

You'll notice at the top and bottom of the worksheet (see the next page) there's room for two very important Mission Statements: Your own and your organization's. Write your personal Mission Statement (we hope you've already come up with it—if you haven't, please do so before attempting to complete the page) at the top.

Comparing the personal and organizational Mission Statements can tell you a lot: Are you in the right job? The right organization? The right career? What is your primary work value? How does it compare to the organization's values and objectives? What kind of "match" is or isn't there?

If the fit isn't really tight, what can you do to change your personal Mission Statement to align more closely with your organization's? What position should you be seeking within your organization that will enable you to fulfill your personal statement? If the two statements are too far apart, is it time to change organizations?

Note on the Path for Personal Productivity page the statement about re-evaluating your personal Mission Statement every three months. Remember, this is an excellent way to fine-tune your purposes to align them with your needs and your circumstances. Regular re-evaluation enables you to stay on top of the circumstances with a currently valid personal Mission Statement.

The boxes in between the two Mission Statements are for goals— not only work-related, but also personal and leisure-related. We believe it's extremely important to have all three! It creates a sense of balance and fulfillment in all aspects of life and increases the

Path For Personal Productivity Worksheet*

My Personal Mission Statement:

_____

_____

_____

My Long-Range Goals:

Personal	Work-Related	Leisure-Related
_____	_____	_____
_____	_____	_____
_____	_____	_____

My Goals for the Next Month or Year:

Personal	Work-Related	Leisure-Related
_____	_____	_____
_____	_____	_____
_____	_____	_____

My Goals for the Next Week or Month:

Personal	Work-Related	Leisure-Related
_____	_____	_____
_____	_____	_____
_____	_____	_____

My Top Priorities for Tomorrow:

Personal	Work-Related	Leisure-Related
_____	_____	_____
_____	_____	_____
_____	_____	_____

Note: Your personal mission statement should be re-evaluated quarterly. This process helps you maintain a sense of

My organization's mission:

*Photocopy before filling in for reuse later.

likelihood that at any time, at least one of the three areas is showing progress. That enables us to keep persisting in the other areas even though the results aren't evident.

After filling in your personal and organizational Mission Statement, complete the long-range goals section. Set these as far out as you can realistically visualize. If you can only see 12 months ahead, look only that far. If you can see five years out, great! To keep the chart realistic and attainable, don't go further than five years.

You can't set short-range goals until you know what your long-range goals are. After you've established those long-range targets, think about the next month (if your long-range goals are 12 months out) or year (if they are five years out).

Of course, you can't set goals for the next week or month if you don't know where you're heading in the next month or year, so don't do the third box down until you've finished box #2.

Finally—the top priorities for tomorrow. Once again, it's useless to try to determine what these could be without the advantage of seeing the big picture, the one all the way out to the long-range goals. A common mistake in goal-setting and plotting is to start with today and trying to work in an outward direction. It makes about as much sense as getting into the car and driving, trying to figure out where your destination is, based on what you pass along your way.

We suggest you make several photocopies of the Personal Productivity Worksheet while it's still blank to use as work copies. Once you're satisfied with the basic information on the page, then make more copies leaving boxes 3 and 4 blank, because these will change so frequently. Then include these pages in your work pages as a part of your daily 15 Minutes of Planning.

Below are several examples of goals in the areas listed on the worksheet, which we have included only to stimulate your thinking, not as suggestions. Your own ideas will be much better, much more personal and, therefore, much more stimulating to you.

Work-Related

- Get promoted this year
- Become top salesperson in the district
- Pass the CPA examination
- Change careers to better match my Mission Statement with my job

Personal

- Pay off the mortgage on my house
- Develop one new friendship each month
- Take a class in a subject that interests me
- Learn to control my tendency to procrastinate

Leisure-Related

- Join the garden club
- Get my private pilot's license
- Travel to the South Pacific
- Get selected to appear on *Jeopardy!* TV show

Reading The Map

One final way of looking at your goals and mission is the Personal Goals Map. This is a great tool for brainstorming and visualizing your way to success.

The Profound Point to remember as you do this is:

THIS IS LIFE, NOT A REHEARSAL!

It's amazing how many people are going through life as if this were only a rehearsal for the real thing! They wander around aimlessly, with no plan or goal, waiting for the director to tell them to go to the dressing room, put on the makeup and report to the stage for the performance.

Of course, you wouldn't be reading this manual if you were still waiting for the show to start. The good news is, even if you're already in the third act, there's a lot of performance still to go as long as you get started now!

The Personal Goals Map shows you how you can get a better sense of who you are and where you are on stage. You function in many different areas of life, don't you? Is it important to have goals in all the areas listed? We believe it is, and we do so because of our personal experience.

PERSONAL GOALS MAP

Use this map to provide a structure to get you started and stay enroute to meaningful goal accomplishment. When you follow these instructions and pathways, the task of goal-setting will become a valid way to balance life and create an enjoyable existence. You first need to get a clear picture of exactly where you are right now.

SELF-ANALYSIS: Where You Are Now

Directions: You'll need a stack of at least ten file cards for this self-discovery exercise. On each card write: "My name is (your name). I am a (n)_____." It should take only a few minutes to complete each of these ten statements differently. Write down your true feelings without analysis, qualification or censorship. Some of them might be negative: Overweight. Some of them will merely be factual: Stamp collector. Others may reveal positive insights: Sensitive, caring person. The only requirement is to be honest. There are no right or wrong answers.

After you've done all the cards, arrange them in order of importance and number them. Add the statement: "This 'I am' is first because _____." Do this for all the cards in numerical order.

Finally, to learn something about the person who wrote these cards, ask yourself these questions:

- What do I know about myself from reading these cards?
- What things are most important to me, and why?
- Are there things I would enjoy doing with life, but aren't doing now?
- If I had only six months to live, how would I spend my time?

The answers to this self-analysis will not only tell you a lot about yourself, who you are and what's important to you, it will also provide the information that will enable you to apply this statement:

WHEREVER YOU ARE, BE THERE!

This statement serves as a reminder to be aware of where you are at all times. If you can't answer the question, "Where am I now?" it's impossible to determine the directions you want to go.

Then, look out from the center of the circle in the Personal Goals Map all the way to the edge. Be visionary for a while. What kinds of ultimate goals and accomplishments can you see in the areas on the map? Write them into the appropriate section.

After filling in the outside, once again work your way back in to attainable goals (maybe 12 months out), and determine some immediate goals and steps you can take, right now, to move in the direction of the outer edge of the circle.

In our experiences and studies of goal-setting, we've learned some valuable lessons about goals that we now pass along to you:

1. You may have to give up some things to have what you want.

2. You can only do one thing at a time in the present moment. Recognize this limitation.

3. There may be some pain or unpleasantness in the present moment as things begin to change.

4. When you know where you're going and what you want, it's worth it!

Personal knowledge such as this is invaluable in planning and decision-making. Don't put it off!

The Classic Struggle: Compatibility Or Incompatibility

Have you ever poured time and energy into several projects at once only to discover you can't achieve them all? In fact, did the effort required to achieve one of the goals pretty much guarantee you couldn't reach another?

Goal-setting is a healthy struggle that becomes unhealthy when the goals set are not compatible with each other. Examples:

- The hard-nosed business executive loses his or her family in the quest for corporate success.

- The musician chooses career over love.

- The mother is torn between her profession and her children.

- The retired person loses the reason to live.

If you pursue certain goals, it may well mean you have to sacrifice something else to attain your objective. *A Passion for Excellence* author Tom Peters observed that if a person truly wants to be at the very top of his or her profession—the Chief Executive Officer, the best-selling author, the award-winning actor or actress, even Volunteer of the Year—it's highly unlikely that goal can be achieved unless that person is willing to throw every bit of energy in that direction, at the expense of other things in life.

We're certainly not recommending that, but we suggest you count your personal cost as you determine the things you want most. We highly recommend a balanced life (see Chapter 13), with reasonable goals in many different areas of life. It may mean you won't hit the very top in your career, but you'll probably enjoy the journey a whole lot more.

Compatible goals must be written into your plans for success, because achievement (if it occurs) can be pretty empty without them.

Remember, success comes as a series of small accomplishments rather than as a big "break." If you read about an "overnight success" in the business, entertainment or sports world, don't believe it! Most of the opportunities of life are disguised as work, and lots of it.

Copy the planning pages in this chapter right now and begin to make your maps and cut your paths through the woods. You'll be able to organize and manage your priorities with effectiveness you never thought possible.

As we wrap up this chapter, a few final comments:

- We were all meant to be achievers. Life is fulfilling and satisfying only as long as you stretch and strive to achieve in some way. When you set a goal, the energy to achieve it comes from within. It's always there, but it's not released until the challenge of a goal is set before you.

- You are capable of continuing to grow as long as you live. You can continue to learn, to take on new challenges, to discover yourself.

> *"We have to win the world with our sacrifices."*
> — *Churchill*

- Goal-setting fosters career and mental health. Look at the people around you. Those who are going places in their careers and who have enthusiastic attitudes toward life are the ones with goals. If someone is stagnating in a job or looks at everything with a negative or suspicious attitude, you'll know this is a person without a goal.

Making It Work

CONCERN	REASON	STRATEGY
uncertain about purpose of your job	don't know mission	find out and learn company mission statement
indecision about personal priorities	no personal mission statement	develop one today!
unsatisfactory results	unsatisfactory results statement	evaluate and modify steps to produce desired result
no goals	don't know importance	recognize as key to success
goals take too long to accomplish, can't finish	attempting perfection	strive for mastery instead of perfection
can't get assistance or encouragement on goals	people don't want to help	work on developing good interpersonal relationships
goal is unclear	not written or hasn't been quantified	write it down; determine a method of measurement
conflict between career, personal goals	goals are incompatible	choose one and give up other or modify for compatibility

Putting It To Work

- All planning and goal-setting begins and ends with a Mission Statement.

- A Mission Statement must be distinct, stimulating and motivating.

- A personal Mission Statement and an organizational Mission Statement should be compatible.

- If your personal and organizational Mission Statements are not compatible, think about your options.

- If you don't know your organization's Mission Statement, ask!

- If your organization does not have a Mission Statement, write one.

- Know and follow the steps of planning to attain your goals and objectives.

- Revision of your plan is vital to ultimate success in any endeavor.

- Goal-setting is work, but the struggle is essential to strength and resolve.

- Putting a goal in writing helps you achieve it.

- People need each other! Work on developing "connectedness" with others to obtain their help and support.

- Remember the play has already begun. This isn't a rehearsal!

Check Your Working Knowledge Of Mission Statements And Goals

1. What is your Organization's Mission Statement?

2. Does your personal Mission Statement match the one for your organization? If not, what should you do?

3. What is the FAR Method of evaluating and redefining?

4. Who are some people you know who are still thriving late in life because they have goals?

5. Are your goals committed to paper? If so, where do you keep them?

6. What is your primary goal in the reading of this manual?

7. How can you measure a goal like "learn about new developments in my field"? What are some steps that might be necessary to achieve this?

8. a. In which areas of the Personal Goals Map are you going to work?
   b. What will you have to give up or cut back on, at least temporarily, to grow in those areas?

9. Based on your ten or more index cards in the self-discovery exercise, what things are most important to you?

MY SLIGHT-EDGE IDEAS FROM CHAPTER 4:

Mission Statement - Goals, objectives, Strategy.

Controlling Productivity: Part 1

> - **Dealing with human interruptions**
> - **Handling telephone interruptions**
> - **Making meetings effective**

"Watson, come here! I want you."

History does not record the first instance of procrastination on the job. Nor do we have any inkling of when someone's desk first became too cluttered to find anything. Eve was pretty decisive in the Garden of Eden, so nobody really knows the first time indecision led to unproductivity. The first time someone stayed too long in another's office? Your guess is as good as ours.

However, we can pinpoint with absolute certainty the time and place of the first telephone interruption in history. After all, when Alexander Graham Bell invented his contraption in 1876, the first call he made caused someone else—namely, Mr. Watson, his assistant—to change his plans. We don't know what he was doing at the time it rang, but he probably wasn't already headed out the door to see his boss.

Even though the telephone has accomplished far more good than harm to productivity since its invention, we can be certain of one thing: No one has had an uninterrupted moment since the telephone took its place on the desks of the world.

87

Actually, the telephone is only one of many causes for lowered productivity. This chapter (and the next one, too) will be devoted to identifying all the reasons for reduced accomplishment. It contains useful suggestions for helping you take back a substantial amount of the time and energy spent on these unproductive activities.

In this chapter we'll be dealing with the productivity killers that are at least partially caused by other people. Chapter 6 discusses the productivity killers for which we all must accept full responsibility.

Interruptions

- **It happens every eight minutes!**
- **Interruptions are sometimes necessary**
- **Handling drop-in visitors**
- **How to deal with work associates who interrupt you**
- **Control the telephone: don't let it control you**
- **Using telephone time effectively**

Starting At The Top: Interruptions (In Person)

By far the most universally experienced and frustrating productivity problem is interruptions. Interruptions come in two forms: In-person visits and telephone calls.

Studies show that people in office settings are interrupted, on the average, every eight minutes. That's more than 50 times a day.

If each interruption takes out three minutes, that adds up to two and a half hours a day, gone. Gone to interruptions, which seem to happen when we least want them, when we can least control them.

To begin with, one thing we must always keep in mind is:

SOME INTERRUPTIONS ARE NECESSARY!

Unless you happen to be a Trappist monk copying documents by hand, your job involves, needs and requires interaction with other people. To hope for a life totally free of interruptions, then, is not only unrealistic, it is also inappropriate. Just as we frequently require access to other people, so other people need us to be available.

Your goal, therefore, should not be to eliminate interruptions from your life. The goal should be to eliminate the unnecessary ones (and there are many of these, no doubt about it), and learn how to manage those that are necessary so that time is not wasted and schedules forced into changes.

> **"NO ONE EVER HAS MORE THAN 25 PERCENT OF THEIR TIME UNDER CONTROL."**
> —Peter Drucker

Even the most well-planned and well-scheduled day is not immune to drop-in visitors—those people who just happen to be passing by our office or desk and manage to elude whatever barricades we might have erected, ending up in the chair opposite our desk.

In-person interruptors take two forms: Drop-in visitors and co-workers. When the unexpected outside visitor arrives, here are some steps you can take to control the situation.

1. **Screen your visitors.** Is it possible for someone to walk in the front door of your place of business, get on the elevator, walk down the hall and enter your office without passing a single checkpoint? In a very small operation, perhaps nothing can be done here. In a larger organization, several steps can be taken.

   Do you have a secretary? Does your office have a receptionist? Is there someone who can safeguard your territory so it isn't on limits to everyone? Much of this problem can be eliminated by an individual who can ask questions such as:

Stand up for visitors to your office. It's a gracious gesture and it gives you control of the situation. If you choose not to talk then, you can escort the visitor to the door and arrange another time to speak.

- "Could I tell _____ who you are, and the purpose of your visit?"

- "Mr. or Ms._____ is busy at this time. Could I make an appointment for you for a later time?"

If you are the safeguard of your own territory, screen the conversation immediately by directing it with questions such as: "What can I help you with today?"

2. **Meet the visitor outside your office**. If the visit is convenient and appropriate, meet the person somewhere else in the building. Setting up a "neutral" site for the meeting enables you to have more control over the situation. It's often difficult to move a person who has camped in your office, right at your desk. Eliminating access to your office can prevent this.

3. **Confer while standing up**. Nobody should get too comfortable in your office besides you! If you offer someone a chair, and are seated yourself, this encounter can go on indefinitely. Many meetings can be kept brief and to the point if both parties remain on their feet! If the other person is standing and you're not, immediately get up to establish equal ground for the discussion.

4. **Set a time limit for the visit**. Assuming you are agreeable to receiving your drop-in visitor, begin with a very specific time limit. Say something like, "I have only ten minutes to talk right now (and look at your watch as you say it!). Is that enough time, or should we schedule another time when I can spare the time we need?" Note a specific number of minutes, and avoid saying you have "a few" or "a couple of" minutes. After setting a time limit, glance at your watch from time to time. It shows your visitor you are serious about the limit.

5. **Develop rescue signals**. This works best with an informed and aware colleague (whom you would help in the same way when necessary). When another person is aware of your interruption, at a predetermined time this person might enter the room to remind you of something the two of you need to work on right away. Or perhaps a secretary or receptionist could call you after a certain time has passed. These methods create opportunities for you to politely excuse yourself to get back to business.

By the way, the pocket pager is a way by which you can "rescue" yourself! Many units today can be "tested" to make the same sound an actual paging would make. If you can subtly push the right button, you have your own built-in interruption.

Some of these same ideas will work for interruptions from your co-workers, but for these individuals there are several other time-limiting methods available, as well.

1. **Meet with your associates regularly.** A well-planned, regular meeting can eliminate the necessity of some people interrupting you during the day. If a person knows a certain subject will be discussed in tomorrow's meeting, or that a specific time will be allotted for pertinent questions, he or she may not feel it necessary to interrupt you today.

   However, the key word in this solution is *meet*. If you decide to schedule regular meetings, have them. Make them worthwhile. Respect the time within the meeting and others will respect your time outside the meeting. (We'll have more solutions on making meetings effective later in the chapter.)

2. **Agree on an office "quiet time."** Perhaps you can't control interruptions completely all day, but you can set up an hour each day when you don't allow any interruptions. Appointments should not be scheduled during this hour, nor should people answer the phone. This is an hour in which each individual can work productively, without interruption.

   An office "quiet hour" makes the rest of the day something to shout about! Set one of these hours up at your place of business each day. It really works! (Note: You'll find this hour even more effective if you don't use it to plan! In fact, an early hour in the day can actually be the one in which you tackle and complete that top priority project you determined the night before!)

3. **Establish "available" hours.** For years, we've traveled across the country telling managers they need to be accessible to their people. We've preached the "open door" policy from Philadelphia to Paducah to Phoenix.

   It simply means: Be accessible. It does not mean that people have access to you every minute of every day. Establish certain times during the day when you are (or are not) available to your people. Not only can you now plan for certain times of your day with no disturbances, you may be doing your people a favor, too! You'd be amazed how many people say their biggest interruption is their manager.

There's a real serendipity to establishing reception hours. How many times do your people come to you with trivial questions you really wish they'd answer for themselves? If you're not available all the time, folks may solve some of their own problems, or the problem may go away completely. At least they will build up so you can deal with several at one time instead of at several different times!

4. **Go to your colleague's office.** The "home field advantage" simply doesn't exist in the workplace. It's to your advantage to meet someone in their office, not yours. Why? Because you can leave when you're done. It's pretty hard to leave your own office when someone else is still in there!

5. **Block interruptions.** Sometimes the physical aspects of the workplace can create problems. Are your desk and its environs inviting to others? Are you positioned so you make eye contact with practically everyone who walks by? Do you have a comfortable visitor chair right next to your desk? Is it always empty? Do you happen to be located on the way to the office lounge, coffee pot or copy machine?

Simple solutions abound here:

- Move your desk so that you don't have to look at everyone who passes.

- Put your visitor chair at a distance from your desk (you can always invite the right people to move it up closer for better communication).

- Pile things on that chair—your overcoat, packages, purse. Few people will be so brazen as to clear that chair themselves so they can sit down.

- Move the coffee pot. If that's not possible, consider investing in a screen that can block much of the distracting movement. You'll probably be doing some of your associates a favor, too!

6. **Close your door.** While nothing is as inviting as an office with an open door, closing that door sends a strong signal to others: Leave me alone. If periods of concentration are required (such as when you're writing), take advantage of the closed door and its message.

If you have more than one comfortable chair for office visitors, move to a smaller office.

92

To still maintain the "open door" feeling, consider putting a sign on the closed door reading: "Let's talk later. Thanks!" Part of the attitude could be conveyed with a clipboard on which to write messages or questions, or listing the name of who to contact if you're not available.

What's that? You say that would be wonderful if only you had a door to close? True, many people simply don't have that luxury. You may work in an area in close proximity to many other people with no means of shutting out the rest of the world. The employees of Hallmark Cards have solved this problem in a novel way—a nonverbal signal that says "My door (I realize you can't see it!) is closed. Please don't bother me right now." It's a little flag each person has on his or her desk. When the flag is pulled down to half-mast, it's the signal that means "not available."

7. **Find a hideaway**. You can enjoy lots of peaceful, uninterrupted time if you can't be found. When demands press you from all sides, where else can you go to work on them? Is there a conference room that is usually vacant? Another department with an empty desk, where people wouldn't think to look for you? Do you even have to be in the building at all times?

We worked with two men once who headed up a large company and had built for themselves private offices as large and luxurious as any we've ever seen. At the same time, they rented, two blocks away, an 8-by-10-foot cubbyhole of an office in an executive suites building. When they had work that really had to be done, they would invariably escape to their hideaway. Nobody ever found them.

In-person interruptions: We all have them, yet there are many methods at our disposal to help deal with them in acceptable ways. You don't have to lie. You don't have to be rude. But you do have the right to control your time and work, and these techniques can make the difference.

Interruptions (Telephone)

These interruptions are frequently a lot more tricky, because they can't always be screened or prevented. Dealing with telephone interruptions, just like the in-person interruptions, calls for a little creativity and assertiveness. Making the decision to do that can impact control in unbelievable ways!

> *If you are in the midst of a blizzard, you won't see the light of day, much less the sun.*

The telephone interrupts us in two different ways: When it rings, and when we choose to use it for calling. The solutions carry over into both categories.

1. **Decide when you will use the telephone**. You probably wouldn't think of doing your writing at various times during the day. Most people will set aside a specific time for letters and memos and do them during that time. Yet people just as readily respond to nearly any kind of outside stimulus to make a phone call. Just looking at it makes you want to place a call. Thinking about someone you need to contact? If you're not careful, whatever you were doing will be delayed as you pick up the receiver and begin to punch in the numbers.

   Consciously choosing certain times to phone, and ignoring the impulses at other times, gives you much more control.

2. **Group important calls.** Do several calls deal with the same meeting or subject? Make these calls at one time! Get the reference material out just once, put yourself in the frame of mind the subject requires, and go for it!

3. **Decide before the phone rings if you will answer it**. We're convinced Pavlov's dogs were never as conditioned in their responses as most people are to the signalling of the telephone. The responses are never turned off, either.

   Important meeting going on in your office? Deep in thought about tomorrow's speech? Planning a major project? Catching a well-deserved five-minute break with a cup of coffee?

   At home: Are you outside working in the yard? Just sat down to dinner? In the bathroom? Spending quality time with children? Just settled in to watch the television program you've wanted to see all week?

   Somehow, once that phone rings, it becomes top priority. Why? Do you even know who's calling, what the call is about, and how important it is? We have discovered (the hard way) that if the phone rings right in the middle of dinner, it's probably a telemarketer!

   Once we were sitting in a personnel director's office, discussing some management-training programs we were going to be presenting to her organization. Suddenly the telephone on her

If an important phone call isn't being answered, fill out a standard telephone message slip, enlarge it in your copier and fax it to the hard-to-reach person. Your message will stand out among the others.

desk began to ring. Here it comes, we thought; our meeting is interrupted, and who knows when, or even if, it will resume.

But, to our surprise, the phone continued to ring. We asked, "Are you going to answer the phone?" and we'll never forget her response. "I don't know if that call is important or not. I do know what we're discussing right now is important!"

If a caller doesn't get an answer, chances are he or she will try again. Maybe someone else will answer the phone instead. Does your telephone system automatically divert to another extension (or to a Voice Mail system) after a certain number of rings?

At home, we keep our answering machine turned on continually. If no earlier calls have been logged, it doesn't respond until after the fourth ring. That gives us plenty of time to answer if we want to. If not, we still have another chance as we hear the caller logging in. It's amazing how many times the caller doesn't even leave a message!

Now, if one of the most important responsibilities of your job is "answer the telephone," then this advice does not apply to your situation. By all means, answer the phone and don't resent the intrusion. This is a very important part of your job, as your organization's customers or clients rely on being able to contact it.

4. **Have calls screened "positively."** If you have a secretary or receptionist answering the phone, the more information this person can pull out of the caller, the more effectively you can use the telephone.

   Who is calling? From what company? What is the nature of the call? What does the caller really want? Is there someone else who could help the caller? Could the secretary or receptionist provide all the information or answers the caller is seeking?

   The more positive (action-oriented) questions asked, the more likely it is you'll never have to talk with the caller yourself. The caller gets answers and you aren't interrupted.

5. **Make appointments for callbacks.** This is another function of screening calls positively. It often doesn't happen because of the misconceptions concerning telephone messages. What does "take a message" mean? We'll tell you one thing it doesn't mean: A name and a telephone number does not a message make.

> *Telephone image is as important as letterhead. Being screened and not being put through can irritate callers. Develop a standard telephone response and supervise the people who answer calls.*

95

Who called? From what company or organization? What does the caller want? When is a convenient time to return the call? What's another convenient time if your schedule shows a commitment at that first time?

Possibly more time is wasted playing "telephone tag" than in any other single activity at work. This game can be avoided if message-taking is more thorough and complete.

6. **Return calls at appropriate times**. Yes, this means at the designated callback times, but it also challenges you to think about other ways in which a time may be appropriate or inappropriate.

   For example, trying to reach someone at 12:30 p.m. is probably a waste of time, as most are out at lunch then. And consider time zones. If you live in the Pacific time zone, 4 p.m. is a pretty lousy time to think about trying to reach someone in the Eastern time zone.

7. **Use your secretary effectively**. If you have a secretary who is part of a real team working with you, many of the telephone-control ideas are going to involve this person. Part of teamwork involves mutual protection of each other. It involves respecting each person's time and priorities (more on that in Chapter 10).

8. **Get to the point assertively, but with a smile**. A business call can be divided into three parts: the greeting, business portion and ending. Obviously, the purpose of the call, and the most value-effective part, is the business portion. You don't want to sacrifice any time here.

> *Try voice-mail systems because: 55% of all business communication is one-way, with no conversation required. 50% of every business call is not about business. 75% of all business calls go uncompleted on the first attempt. Start phone calls with the important business. That way, if the call is interrupted, you avoid wasting time by having to call back.*

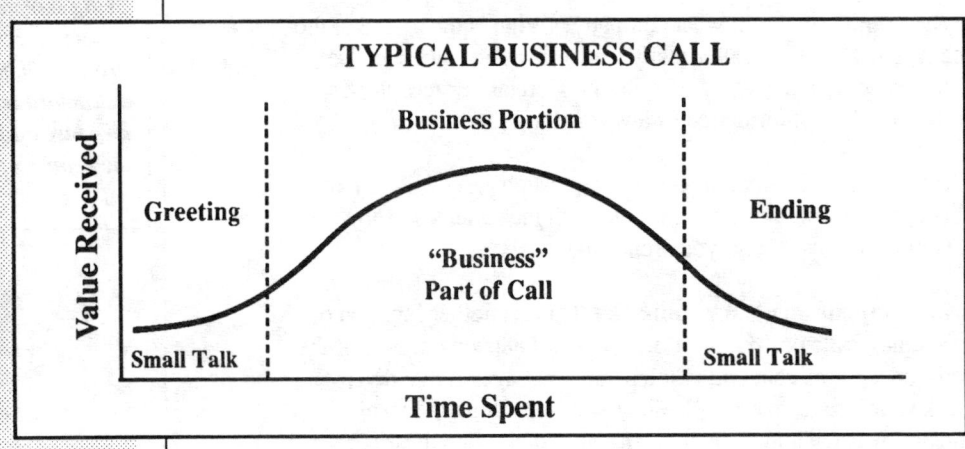

TYPICAL BUSINESS CALL

But, the greeting and the ending . . . what time is wasted here! Small talk, friendly chit-chat, beating around the bush—all sorts of things take place before and after the business part. It's a habit. It's probably related to the fact that we want the caller to be glad he or she called.

Can you hear a smile over the telephone? You should be able to. And this is the very best way to get right in to (and out of) the valuable part of the call. As soon as you know who's calling, smile and say, "Hi! What can I do for you today?" Hear the smile? The caller's glad to have called and you've jumped right over the small talk into business.

Once you feel the business purpose of the call has ended, you can get out the same way. Smile! Ask, "Is there anything else we need to discuss?" If the answer is "yes," perhaps you've misjudged and there's still value to be gained. No problem! When that topic is finished, smile and ask the same question again. Once the answer is "no," that's the time to smile again and say, "Great! It's been nice talking with you today. Good-bye."

By smiling and asking a question at those two critical junctures, you have created a pleasant calling experience and directed all the time and energy of the call to the business purpose for which it was made.

Using Telephone Time Effectively

The telephone is for your convenience, and the better you can control the time spent on the phone, the more convenient it will be. Let's look at some ways to do that.

1. **Plan your calls in writing**. A meeting without an agenda is worthless. A letter or report without an outline won't be effective. Is it any different for the telephone?

   Before making a call, outline the ideas you want to cover. Make a list of questions you want to ask (and leave room to write in answers as you get them). Gather the information and references you need. Clear enough working space on your desk. Have a pen or pencil in your hand as you call.

2. **Focus your concentration on the call**. Here's where the real value of a written outline comes forward. Get to the point. Stick

to it. When you speak, be as brief and concise as you can be. What if you would later have to write out, word for word, the entire telephone call? Would you be more careful in how, and how often, you said something?

Replace the standard two-foot cord on your telephone handset with one that is 25 feet long. You'll be able to walk around while talking, which improves circulation and energy and helps you think.

3. **Stand up to talk.** For many people, the opportunity to make a phone call represents a time to take a break and rest. It's easy to see when this is happening: Is a person leaning back in the chair, feet up, arms at side, cup of coffee nearby?

   If you have consciously decided to use this as a break, fine. But if you want to stick to business, and get this over with quickly, make the call standing up. The same effect of meeting while standing up takes over here: If you're not all that comfortable, you tend to stick to the purpose of the call.

4. **"Time limit" each call.** Decide before you call about how long the business should take. Set a conservative time limit, and stick to it. Measure the call yourself—using the timing feature on the phone system, with a watch that shows seconds, or with something as simple (and effective) as a three-minute egg timer.

6. **Develop a set of verbal gestures to sign off.** Sometimes it's harder to end a phone call than it is to get into the business part. You need to have several possible phrases ready to begin to close a call. The easiest phrases to use are those that indicate your concern over the other person's time, rather than your own. Some of the phrases we like:

   - "I need to let you get back to work."

   - "I've probably tied up your line long enough, so…"

   - "You probably have a lot of important things to do…"

Others relate to the simple fact that the conversation is ending: "Before we hang up, I have just one more quick question…" or "Before you go…"

This is also a wonderful time to "smile" and ask a question, as we described earlier in dealing with the interruptions. "(smile!) Is there anything else we need to discuss? Great!"

There are lots of ideas and solutions for the every-eight-minute distractions to our day. But, we promised we would deal with other productivity killers, so let's go on to another one.

Meetings

- **The real cost of meetings**
- **The value of your own productivity**
- **How to conduct a productive, successful meeting**
- **Dealing with the perpetual latecomer**
- **Can you eliminate some meetings completely?**
- **Making the most of a meeting if you're a participant**

Meetings: A Waste Of Time And Money?

The typical midlevel manager may spend as much as 25-30 percent of the work day in meetings of one kind or another. Yet, in survey after survey, managers universally point the finger at "meetings" when asked to name the biggest time waster on the job!

Can we possibly be spending so much time and energy in an activity that produces so little in the way of results and accomplishment? Sadly, the answer is "Yes." But it doesn't have to be that way, as you will see.

In this section, we will consider the problem of time-and money-wasting meetings first from the perspective of when we are in control: We call and schedule the meeting, and chair the meeting while it is in progress. Then, we will look at meetings from the vantage point of the person attending, without much control of a lot of areas.

Part of the reason meetings are inefficient is that most people have never taken the time to figure out just how much meetings cost. Not only in time, but in money.

Calculating time spent isn't really too difficult, but we often forget the multiplication factor. Sure, the meeting only lasts for one hour, but 20 people were involved. In reality, this meeting cost the organization 20 production hours—one hour for each of the 20 participants.

Annual Salary	Each Hour Worth	Each Minute Worth	One Hour/Day For 1 Year Worth
20,000	11.90	.20	2857.
25,000	14.88	.25	3571.
30,000	17.86	.30	4286.
35,000	20.83	.35	5000.
40,000	23.81	.40	5714.

Figure your own: For each $ 1,000 in salary

1,000	.60	.01	143.

240 working days x 7 hours/day
1680 hours/year

The monetary cost is even more staggering, as the chart shows. As you can see, it assumes some very realistic averages: 240 working days per year (there are actually 260 or 261 days, considering holidays, vacation and sick leave), and seven hours per day (eight hours, one for lunch).

A person earning $30,000 per year is paid $17.86 per hour, based on those numbers, or about 30 cents per minute. (Actually, since most organizations estimate the actual cost of each employee as about 60 percent more than that—work space, materials, benefits, etc.—the true cost is much higher!) This employee is paid nearly $18 for the one hour spent in the meeting (more if you count the extras). If 20 people at roughly the same pay level attend, the dollar cost of this meeting is $360.

Now, a question. What if the meeting lasted all day? What if 200 people attended? What if they averaged $60,000 income per year? What if these meetings occurred monthly? Obviously, the potential for wasted time and money is staggering.

The good news is that meetings are not necessarily unproductive any more than dynamite is necessarily destructive. It's all a matter of application. The calculations and monetary analyses provided have been given so you can be effective.

One Dozen Recommendations For A Successfully Chaired Meeting

1. **Start the meeting on time.** You've called a meeting and invited 15 people. Fourteen of them managed their schedule and time and are ready to begin at the announced starting time.

   Respect the ones who are already there by beginning on time. Only an ineffective leader will make everyone wait for the one latecomer. Moreover, when the latecomer wanders in, don't even acknowledge the arrival, if possible. Most people will get the message that there is a reward for effectiveness, not availability. With forethought and diligence, you can eliminate useless meetings and make the remaining ones move more quickly. You can make the message even more clear if you cover (and decide on) an issue that person was very interested in.

   There are some people who intentionally arrive late because they enjoy making grand entrances and the inevitable fuss made over their arrival. If a "latecomer" frequently disturbs your meeting, and if this person doesn't change his or her ways, you may eventually decide this person doesn't need to be at the meeting.

   Remember: Making a group of people wait for one late person doesn't just waste time . . . it wastes money.

2. **End on time.** When you develop the reputation for starting and stopping your meetings in a timely fashion, people will have respect for you and your meeting. And, they willingly attend and participate, because they know up front just what their commitment to your meeting means.

   Did you ever attend a meeting that was to end at 10 a.m. and ran until 11? What if you had made an appointment to meet with someone at 10:30? What if your accomplishments for the entire day were based on having a set amount of discretionary time available, which was now reduced by one hour? Have you noticed the nervous twitches and concerned clock-watching that occurs as a meeting runs overtime? People have places to go

"You are eternity's hostage — a captive of time."
— Pasternak

and things to do, and permitting a meeting to run over is an infringement on all who attend.

A very effective way of promoting endings to meetings is to use a digital clock in the conference room that runs backward (or timer, like the play clock on a football field or the shot clock in a basketball game). As 60 minutes gradually drops to 20, then 14, then 11, people will pick up their resolve and intensity to discuss and decide.

3. **Have an agenda.** Simple enough, but do you really have one? Specific goals for discussion? A time frame? One with a clear sense of purpose for each item? Are the items clearly indicated as to whether they are "for information," "for discussion" or "for decision"? An "Agenda Planning Guide" has been provided here to help you devise a complete agenda for every meeting.

4. **State clear objectives and purpose.** What are the major goals of this get-together . . . why are you meeting? What do you hope to accomplish? Why should you (or anyone else) attend? How will you know if the meeting has been successful? Just like any goal, the more clear and specific, the greater your chances of achievement.

5. **Notify people in advance of the agenda and their responsibilities.** This is helpful not only to the individual person, but to all meeting participants. Tell someone, "You're going to be talking about (subject), and I've allowed eight minutes for your talk, plus five minutes for questions and discussion."

This enables people to "tool up" for meetings and have with them the necessities, such as charts, exhibits, pencil and paper, background information and data.

6. **Cover the most important agenda item first.** This not only pays respect to the people who arrive on time, it also allows people who may have to slip out before the meeting is over to do so without missing as much. Plus, if you've ever attended a one-hour meeting where the first 45 minutes were spent on a relatively trivial item, forcing more important items either to be rushed through or delayed to another meeting, you can see the value of doing #1 first. A BONUS: People get in the habit of coming on time.

AGENDA PLANNING GUIDE

AGENDA

Start Time

Topic	Time Required	Person Responsible

Finish Time   **Total Time**

FOLLOW-UP REQUIRED

Topic	Due Date	Person Responsible

7. **Make specific assignments.** During a meeting, if a certain job needs to be assigned, make sure it is done at the meeting in such a way that everyone, including the person assigned, knows it. Meetings often end with fuzzy pictures as to who (if anyone) actually took responsibility for carrying out a decision made at the meeting.

8. **Control the discussion.** As meeting chair, you can limit the amount of discussion time on any one subject to keep the agenda moving along. If the purpose of an agenda item is to make a decision, bring discussion to a close and make the decision. If it's still at the discussion phase, allow a pre-set amount of time and control by announcing, "We have time for just one more comment."

9. **Get input before scheduling a meeting.** If a key participant already has a commitment, or will be away from the office, find this information out before announcing a meeting, so that this person isn't put in a dilemma of having to choose. Also of prime input importance here is participant suggestions of topics to discuss, so you don't have to call another meeting after the meeting.

10. **Invite only those who need to attend.** You've surely sat in a meeting where your presence was requested (required?) and wondered why you were there when the topics discussed didn't involve you. Keep your "guest list" to a minimum and re-think it before another meeting in case someone wouldn't need to attend the next time around.

11. **Cut your meeting frequency.** Take inventory of all meetings held regularly. Write down the purpose of each. Is it really necessary? Have some outlived their usefulness? Can any be consolidated? If you're used to meeting every week, make it every two weeks. If you normally meet monthly, try every two months. See if you can't cover just as much in nearly the same amount of time. Half the meetings equals half the cost, half the time, half the preparation.

12. **Cancel unnecessary meetings.** If a meeting isn't absolutely required, don't have it. Consider a reasonable alternative. Can a conference call suffice? Can the job be done by an individual? Bad habits abound here, because "we've always met on the first Monday of the month." Since meetings are an acceptable way to

structure work time, you appear to be productive, but your time may well have been better spent in other activity.

Finally, a last reminder on calling meetings. Don't forget to calculate the cost—in advance. Consider both the time and the money.

As you calculate, think about some popular but costly reasons for meetings:

- To give someone an audience—quite an expensive ego trip!

- To socialize—since we can't afford time off for a party, we have a meeting and pass it off as constructive.

- To allow "pseudo-participation."—"All those in favor, say 'aye.' All opposed say 'fired.'"—Human resources are such a great asset you simply can't afford not to capitalize on them.

Recognize any of these? Count the cost.

Now, consider the anticipated results of the meeting. Is the meeting costly or is it cost-effective?

The Meeting Planning Guide

The Meeting Planning Guide accompanying this page can be used beautifully to plan your meeting, determine its objectives, who needs to attend, what kind of preparation is required and develop an agenda for the meeting.

As you see, it can also be used at the meeting as a way of listing the necessary follow-up required for actions taken and assignments made.

Copy this form and use it any time you are responsible for calling or chairing a meeting. At the same time you fill out this form, do as accurate a calculation as you can concerning the actual cost, in dollars, of the meeting, based on the approximate hourly salary of each participant.

Meeting Planning Guide

Date _____
Called by _____

OBJECTIVE
- What should be achieved
  by the end of meeting

MEETING PARTICIPANTS
- Who can contribute
- Who needs information
- Who would provide support
- Who might assist

BACKGROUND INFORMATION
- Information already known
- Further information needed
- Limitations that exist
— date issue must be resolved
— constraints
— resources available

PARTICIPANT PREPARATION
- Background information
  participants need
- How should participants
  prepare before they come?

LOGISTICS
- Date
- Start time
- Finish time
- Location
- Contact person
- Support material needed
  (e.g., handouts, overhead,
  equipment, etc.)

Regards, Responsibility And Respect If You're Attending A Meeting

- **Regarding** starting and ending on time: Since you have no control, take with you work for "In-Between" Times in case the meeting does not begin on time.

  Establish in advance with the leader of the meeting the time you MUST leave, and LEAVE at the predetermined time, regardless of whether the meeting has officially adjourned.

- **Responsibility:** In advance, find out the agenda and know the objectives and purpose of the meeting. This will enable you to determine your purpose for attending and establish respect for your time. Plus, you will be prepared with necessary information or materials needed at the meeting and won't be caught off-guard.

- **Respect** the agenda at the meeting. You can be sure your important items will be covered because of your advance preparation. Be responsible yourself by directing all comments, questions and discussion to the agenda items only. If there are other things you want to discuss, either set up time for these items to be discussed individually or, if these subjects would be beneficial to all, suggest making them a part of the agenda at the next meeting.

Making It Work

CONCERN	REASON	STRATEGY
angry about human and telephone interruptions	productivity affected	recognize interruptions are sometimes necessary
people just walk into your office	it's possible to do so!	screen visitors; make it difficult to get through
can't get rid of visitor	it's too easy for this person to stay	meet outside office or stand up while receiving visitor
can't get rid of visitor	time not respected	set specific time limit, or have someone "rescue" you
associates require you for information, decisions	your time too unscheduled	meet with them regularly, have scheduled "open" hours
easily distracted at work	heavy traffic near desk	block interruptions by turning desk, moving chair
during important activity, telephone rings	we stop to answer it	decide before phone rings if you will answer it
telephone "tag"	insufficient message taken	get callback information, let someone else handle it
phone conversations run too long	ineffective use of time	smile and ask a question to get to business part of call
unproductive meetings	value of time not known	calculate actual cost of your meeting based on salaries
financial position of your organization	employee time not used as productively as possible	use ideas in manual to boost each person's productivity by only 10%
meeting begins late	some participants not yet in attendance	begin without latecomers
meeting runs too long	ending time not set and stuck with	ending time is as important as starting time
people unprepared for meeting	participants not notified of responsibility	assign in advance
no follow-through	assignments and actions not clearly understood	make specific at meeting and log on meeting planner

Putting It To Work

- People are interrupted more than 50 times per day.

- Recognize some interruptions are a necessary part of your job, and treat them with respect.

- If someone has to get past somebody else to get to you, many unwelcomed interruptions can be eliminated.

- Shorten the time of the interruption by meeting the visitor outside your office, and by talking while standing up.

- Set a time limit to an unscheduled interruption, and stick to it.

- Remember, being available doesn't mean you are at everyone else's beck and call every minute of the day. Schedule "reception" hours.

- If you don't want to meet with anyone, close your door or go somewhere else.

- Determine specific times of day to use the telephone, and group your calls.

- There is no law that requires you to answer the phone every time it rings. You decide if you will, or not.

- Practice the art of real message-taking, i.e., taking down available times for callbacks, purpose of call, etc.

- Develop your own set of verbal phrases to sign off on a phone call.

- Meetings cost money! Use the salary chart to determine the actual invested dollar amount. Using those salary figures, you can identify the value of each hour of your time, and decide how effectively the money has been spent.

- Meeting planners who start and stop on time and who have a preplanned agenda they stick with are respected!

- Not only that, their meetings are always productive!

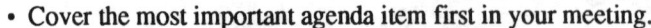

- Cover the most important agenda item first in your meeting.

- Time-limit all discussion and keep control of time.

- Try to meet only half as often, and for half as long.

- Identify meetings that are only habitual and eliminate them.

- As a participant, actively involve yourself in timing, responsibility and sticking to agenda items.

Check Your Working Knowledge Of Interruptions And Meetings

1. How many times a day do you get interrupted? How much time is used in handling the interruptions?

2. Why should eliminating interruptions not be a goal?

3. Why is the "home field" not an advantage at work?

4. Who is your most persistent interruptor? What strategy can you devise for handling this person more effectively?

5. Do you have a scheduled "quiet time" in your office? If not, how could this benefit you?

6. What hours could you schedule in your day to be unavailable?

7. If you don't have an office, what nonverbal sign can you use to establish your work space?

8. What is a telephone message? What is it not?

9. Name the three parts of a business phone call. Where can you cut time?

10. How much is your time worth, per hour, when you are at work?

11. Consider the last meeting you attended. How much do you

think this meeting cost? Was dollar value returned in results for time spent?

12. How can a meeting be ended on time?

13. How can each participant be more effective during a meeting?

14. What regular meeting in your organization could be held less frequently? How much less? Could it be shorter? By how much? How could you do it?

MY SLIGHT-EDGE IDEAS CONCERNING INTERRUPTIONS AND MEETINGS:

_____

_____

_____

_____

_____

_____

_____

_____

_____

C HAPTER 6

Controlling Productivity: Part II

- • Taming the paper blizzard
- • Gaining confidence in decision-making
- • Overcoming procrastination

In the previous chapter, we discussed ways to overcome the productivity killers that are at least partially caused by other people. Now let's look at some other problem areas where we must accept greater responsibility—not only for creating the problems, but also for solving them.

Is it that pile of paper accumulated on your desk (when was the last time you saw the surface of the desk itself?) the backlog of unmade decisions that saps your energy and spirit or the curse of procrastination?

The good news is that you have control to develop the habits and procedures to eliminate these problems. You need not concern yourself with what can't be done; these are areas where you have the power to make a difference.

The Paper Blizzard

- **Where are you heading?**
- **Develop the right mindset for paper control**
- **Handling the paper flow**
- **Using the RAFT process**
- **Four things you should never file**
- **A question to keep from adding to the problem**
- **Creating an effective filing system**
- **Reading for control**

Clutter And Paperwork
(Now, Where Is The Bottom Of My Desk?)

Not only have modern inventions made it easier for people to talk to each other and drop in on each other, they have also created amounts of paper in unheard-of quantities.

It may be mid-summer, but is there a blizzard going on in your office right now? Are you up to your knees in white stuff? To your waist? Neck? Are you trying to dig your way up to the top for a breath of air? More productivity is lost each year to the paper blizzards inside our workplaces than is ever lost due to outside weather forces that keep people from getting to work!

The first proponents of the computer told us we were headed for a paperless workplace. Most of us have recovered from the disappointment of this delusion by now.

Printing processes have become so simple anyone can create a document ready to be printed, and the printer is frequently sitting right on our desks to do it for us. This manual would have been written on a typewriter ten years ago, then the first draft retyped, sent to the editor, who would then also have retyped the manuscript and submitted it to a printer, who would have typed it again. Instead, the process was done once, placed on a 3-1/2" disk, and keyboard time was never necessary again.

Regular mail delivery has been augmented by private delivery services, overnight mail capability, electronic mail and fax machines. Third-class "junk" mail has become a major source of funding and support for the postal service. Databases are bought, sold and exchanged. All you have to do is order by mail once, and suddenly the whole world of direct mail knows about you!

The photocopying process has evolved from one-at-a-time to producing, collating and binding thousands of pages per hour.

In a world where documentation is everything, we are afraid to throw anything away. As a result, filing systems are bursting from the pressure of billions and billions of documents, many of which could never be found even if someone wanted to! It is estimated that 75 to 80 percent of the contents of today's business files are being saved unnecessarily.

As competent business people, we're all expected to be well read and informed as we stay on top of our fields. More books, magazines, trade publications and reports are being published than ever before. The world's information base is doubling every three to four years.

Are we fighting a losing battle? No! Is the battle a fierce one, one that requires great resolve, determination and personal discipline? Yes!

The solutions are part of three major categories of action: Changing the mindset, developing a streamlined process, and knowing how, what and when to file.

Developing The Paper-Controlling Mindset

Mental attitude has much to do with how we control and deal with the storm of paper blowing through our lives every working day.

Are you ready to change your attitude about paper? Let's begin by looking at some rules you'll want to remember every day of your life. Clip these rules out of this manual (or—gasp—photocopy them!) and post them in prominent places around your work area.

IF THERE IS A WAY FOR SOMETHING TO
ENTER MY DESK, THERE ALSO HAS TO BE A WAY
FOR IT TO LEAVE

MY BEST FRIEND IS MY WASTEBASKET
(OR RECYCLING BIN)

I AM NOT A PACK RAT.
I AM DECISIVE ABOUT PAPER!

NOT EVERYTHING MUST BE SAVED

WHAT IS THE PROBABILITY THAT
I WILL EVER NEED THIS PAPER AGAIN?

WHAT CAN I DO WITH THIS PIECE OF PAPER NOW
TO MAKE CERTAIN I NEVER HAVE TO SEE IT AGAIN?

WHEN IN DOUBT, THROW IT OUT!!

> **I CAN'T CONTROL HOW MUCH PAPER I GET,
> BUT I CAN CONTROL WHAT I DO WITH IT!**

> **WHEN THE PAPER BEGINS TO FLOW,
> I NEED TO GET OUT MY R-A-F-T!**

Re-read the above statements. Do you see the mental attitude about paperwork each one helps to create?

Some of the statements may be unclear and make you want explanations. We'll be doing just that as we share practical, proven techniques for managing your priorities better through effective control of paper.

Paper-Control Strategies That Really Work!

First, you can **control the flow of paper coming in**. One way to do this is to have a specific place for it. Whether it's a basket labelled "IN" or simply a designated spot where paper starts when it reaches your office, you need to have a clear and well-communicated location.

By the way, if you have an "IN" basket on your desk, do you also have one labelled "OUT"? If you don't, this may be one of the biggest reasons for your paper blizzard!

Time-and-motion experts have long maintained that paper should flow across the desk. The flow should either be from left to right (if you're right-handed) or from right to left (for lefties). The diagram below shows a desk for a right-handed person.

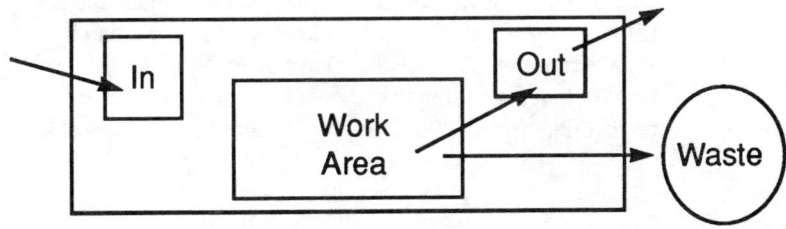

Paper should begin its flow from the upper left-hand corner of the desk to the center of the desk, the work area. From that point it either moves upper right, where it leaves the desk, or lower right, into the properly situated disposal unit.

You must keep paperwork moving. Allowing this work to accumulate for too long spells disaster, so be sure to set aside a regular time of day to go through the new arrivals.

CAUTION: Unless a major factor of your work depends on the daily arrival of mail, resist the temptation to look at mail the moment it arrives. Are you already busy with an important project? Is this a prime-energy time of the day for you? Don't waste it! Most of us can handle sorting and analyzing our paperwork during one of our low-energy periods.

Alec Mackenzie, author of *The Time Trap*, tells us one of the greatest self-management habits we can develop is the habit of "single-handling" items and projects. Time and productivity are continually lost to activity involving the shuffling of paper. That's why, when you begin to look at the paper, you need to ask that question: "What can I do with this piece of paper to make sure I never have to see it again?" The ideal is to handle it just that one time.

Realistically, though, it may not be possible to deal with every piece of paper in a single action. A typical piece of paper is handled eight to ten times; so, if, by asking that question, you could cut the average down to three or four times, you automatically cut the paper blizzard in half.

What can you do, then, to handle this paper only once? The solution is to get your RAFT out and float it in the flow of paper. RAFT is an acronym for the four options you have with all paperwork. You can

- **REFER it.** If this paper should indeed be handled by someone else, then refer it to that person immediately, and get the paper off your desk forever. Is this something you should handle soon, but not immediately? Refer it to your Tickler File (see below). Is it something that should be done sometime but has no real time frame? Put it in your "In-Between" Time folder!

- **ACT on it**. Many papers require only a quick response or action. Why not take that action immediately and be done with it? Do all written questions and requests need a separate response? Write your answer or the requested information on the same page, send it right back and get the paper off your desk so you never have to see it again!

  We had a friend who did this on a regular basis. Once, a person complained to her that this approach seemed a little impersonal. She solved the problem by getting a rubber stamp that read, "This informal reply is to give you an immediate response."

- **FILE it.** If this paper belongs in a file, this is the time to put it there, or at least put it in the area with other paper waiting to be filed.

A major mistake is filing too much. Remember, 75-80 percent of what's in files should never have made it there in the first place. It gets there because our mindset makes us ask this question: "Could I ever, possibly, need this paper again?" We can all think of bizarre and obscure situations when the only thing that could save us is digging that particular paper from the file. So, everything gets filed.

That's why the question should instead be: "What's the probability of my ever needing this paper again?" Of course, for many papers, there are only two probabilities (in the immortal words of baseball great Dizzy Dean): "slim and none." The question makes you look at probability, not possibility. Throw this paper away, and throw it with confidence. In the unlikely event that you might actually need it again, isn't it likely someone else filed it? Did the writer save a copy? Could you ask for another? Face it: even if it's filed, it may well be "misplaced."

- **TOSS it.** Remember, this ought to happen a lot more than it does!

Here are four things that you should never file:

   Routine Memos: They are just that—routine. Read the memo, act on it, remember it, and toss it out.

Meeting Announcements: When you get one, immediately put the date and location in your calendar, and toss the announcement out.

Directives Since Revised: Did you ever get a policy memo, then a week later get the "revised" policy memo? Toss the first one out!

Company Information on File Somewhere Else: Unless you're the person designated to maintain the file!

A classic story on the virtue of tossing out unnecessary paperwork was told to us by a friend who worked for an engineering firm with many foreign clients. He had just returned from three months overseas working on a project. As you can imagine, he returned to quite a bit of mail and paperwork that had accumulated in his absence.

His first day back in the office was devoted to conference and briefings. As he prepared to leave work that day, he determined that going through this paper was his top priority for the next day, so he placed it all in a pile on his credenza, ready to be tackled first thing in the morning.

Unfortunately, his company had recently hired a new cleaning firm. That night, his unorganized pile was discovered by one of the workers. Our friend came in to work the next morning to find three months' worth of paper had disappeared, forever!

Catastrophe! Or was it? The impact of this mistake was not immediately known, but as time passed, he reported the following events occurred: One check had to be re-issued; two people wrote again, wondering why they hadn't received a response to their first letter, enclosing a copy of the original letters "just in case." That was the sum total of the problem created by three months of mail disappearing.

We're not recommending you throw away everything that's piled up on your desk, but remember this story before deciding to hang on to things that are better disposed of.

Finally, you must **make a decision not to add to the problem.** Tom Peters, the "Excellence" books author, once commented that the worst memo ever written "should have been a phone call." Are you choosing the wrong communication medium by putting something in writing? Could this situation be handled more quickly and more effectively over the phone or face to face? Do you really need to have written documentation of the content? If you don't ask these questions, lots of paper will stay in your office unnecessarily.

You can do your part to keep the paper flow from becoming any worse than it already is. Keep these suggestions in mind:

DON'T ADD TO THE PAPERWORK PROBLEM!

AM I PART OF THE PROBLEM,

OR PART OF THE SOLUTION?

Creating An Effective Filing System

Finally, when you do put things into files, how you do it makes a big difference in how effective your system is, and how easily you can locate what's already there.

Here are some proven file systems:

1. Tickler File. This is a reminder file. A well-run Tickler File enables you to make paper disappear from your desk, only to reappear at the exact time you need it. In the meantime, it doesn't clutter your desk or your mind.

The Tickler File we use involves two large, expandable file folders. Into one of these folders we have put 31 individual file folders, numbered from one to 31, to correspond to the days of the month. In the other folder are 12 file folders, labelled with the months of the year. Once the file is set up, it works great to help process paper and keep on top of all the little things that might otherwise slip through the cracks.

Did you get a bill that needs to be paid? Most bills have a grace period of from 10 to 30 days. If you're responsible for paying the bills in your organization, there's no sense in paying it upon receipt if the money could stay in your account a little longer. Put the bill into the numbered folder in your Tickler File three or four days earlier than the day it's due.

Did your boss ask you to check on an order that was made last week and to remind her next Wednesday to follow up if it's still not in? Make a note to yourself to do it, and put it in the Tickler File for Wednesday.

Did you write a letter that has been typed and is now ready to mail, only you don't want to mail it for a few days? Put it in the Tickler File for the day you want to mail it. That day, the letter will resurface and you can send it. In the meantime, it hasn't cluttered your desk or your mind.

Once the Tickler File is established, it becomes a part of your daily 15 minutes of planning. Because you'll replace a folder at the back of the line once you've emptied it, the current day is always at the front. Pull out that folder, take out its contents and add these items to your *Daily Action List*.

Once you've established a Tickler File, you'll no doubt discover all kinds of other uses as well. For example, we have used it successfully to remember family birthdays and anniversaries.

2. Current Projects File. Keep another file where only material relating to current activity is stored, so it is readily accessible either to you or some other member of your work team. Maintain this file in a location easy for all to use!

3. Ideas and Plans File. As you come across things that interest you or bring to mind an idea, have a place to put them. As you review this file from time to time, these plans and ideas will incubate, your subconscious mind will work on them and eventually you'll decide whether to activate the idea (moving it to the Current Projects File) or throw it out.

4. "To Read" File. When those inevitable magazines and papers come across your desk that you need to read sometime, put them in a file designated for that purpose. Keep the file close at hand, because these are great fillers for "In-Between" Time.

If some of this information consists of magazines or periodicals you receive, before putting them in the file, scan the publication, or at least the table of contents. At a glance, you can identify subjects that interest you enough to want to read about them later. Put paper clips around the pages containing the articles, or better yet (if the publication will ultimately be thrown away), tear out only the pages with the articles, and eliminate the rest immediately.

5. Travel File. If you (or your boss) are occasionally out of the office on business or for conferences or conventions, this can be a time saver for you. Set up a separate folder for each trip on your calendar. Put everything pertaining to the trip in that folder: airline tickets, hotel confirmations, meeting agendas, correspondence related to the trip, travel tips on the area you're visiting, etc. If it's all in one place, all you have to do before leaving is take the one folder and put it in your briefcase as you walk out the door.

6. The General File. Finally, everything that doesn't go into any of the other files is a candidate for the General File. Just a few reminders about this file:

- It's probably larger than it needs to be. Have you eliminated the 75-80 percent that shouldn't have been filed in the first place?

- It should be purged periodically to keep it current and manageable.

- Keep an "active" and "inactive" section, and keep moving things to the inactive area. Even tax records have to be stored for only so long!

- Arrange the file either alphabetically or chronologically, whatever method is most appropriate to your situation.

Reading Controls Paperwork, Too!

Richard Saul Wurman, in his book, *Information Anxiety*, writes about the need to read selectively. No matter what field you are in, there are more magazines, books, journals and other publications coming out than you can possibly read, even if life itself were devoted to keeping up.

Since you can't possibly read everything, choose. Pick the one or two publications in your field that you get the most from, and cancel your subscription to everything else. Pick only one newspaper and read it. Make a positive decision not to let yourself be overwhelmed by the sheer numbers of what's out there which could be read. Don't put yourself on guilt trips for what you haven't read.

There are varying levels of reading, depending on the purpose of the reading:

- **SCAN** your material to get a quick overview. Sometimes this is all you'll have to do. Perhaps all you need is one idea or answer. Many times you can determine if there is anything important in the document at all.

  Even if you're eventually going to read or study the document, scanning first will increase reading speed and comprehension. Since human minds have a tendency to want to try to figure out where this is all going, a quick scan of the entire contents (maybe taking only a minute) gives your curiosity the answers it seeks. This will enable you to read with greater speed and comprehension as you concentrate on the material.

- **READ** your document when you need more knowledge and information, or if it's something that requires a response. Remember, if it will help speed and comprehension, don't hesitate to scan it first.

- **STUDY** material that you'll be required to know thoroughly. Just like when you studied for a test in school, you may take notes, re-read the text a number of times, and check yourself occasionally to see how well you've absorbed the information.

No matter what speed you choose—scan, read or study—here's one last tip that will help you.

READ WITH A PEN OR HIGHLIGHTER

Prereading a book, report or memo can improve comprehension

- *For a memo: Preread the signature, the beginning until you learn the purpose and the last sentence to see what the writer wants you to do.*

- *For a report: Preread the title, author and publication date. Then go on to the subheadings, boldface and underlined sections.*

- *For a book: Preread the dust jacket, the table of contents, the first chapter and the first paragraph of every other chapter.*

As you go over the material, mark it for reference in such a way that it's easy to refer to later on. Underlining or highlighting will help you gain that extra "Slight Edge" as you effectively and confidently deal with the paper blizzards of your life.

Procrastination

- **Defining the problem**
- **Three causes of procrastination**
- **The question that overcomes the problem**
- **Putting it off isn't always a bad idea**
- **Seven steps guaranteed to eliminate procrastination**
- **The last-ditch effort**

Procrastination—We've Put It Off Long Enough!

How much productivity do you lose every year because you suffer from the universal energy killer, procrastination? This habit alone costs businesses many dollars and closes the door on countless opportunities.

Procrastination can be defined: "Delaying anything you need or want to do until later, when there is no valid reason for the delay."

There are a lot of psychological implications that may lie at the root of procrastination. Those who study human behavior generally agree on three underlying causes:

1. Fear of failure. This is often expressed as the fear of failing to meet your own, possibly unrealistic, high standards. By putting things off until the last minute, your best efforts (which might not "measure up") are never really tested. What's actually tested is your skill at throwing something together at the last minute. Thus, procrastination avoids a test of your true ability.

2. Fear of success. Success has its rewards, but it also has its dangers, e.g., leaving friends or family or business associates behind on the "fast track" to success. Many people fail at tasks they superficially set out to accomplish while they succeed at maintaining an unconscious status quo in their lives.

3. Fear of surrendering control. Procrastinators often think that every deadline missed is a battle won in the war to maintain absolute control over their own lives. Constantly arriving late or having your late contribution hold up a project's completion are subtle ways of saying, "I'm really the one in control here..."

Other reasons some people procrastinate:

- They imagine they'll have more time later, such as putting things back where they belong.

- They imagine something is not really important, when in reality it is.

- They imagine having no deadlines. "Now that I'm an adult, I can do as I please."

If procrastination is a problem for you, and you're committed to improving your productivity, you can't afford to put off working on eliminating the habit of procrastination any longer. Remember, as an ingrained habit, it can be pretty persistent, but it can be overcome.

Before any problem can be overcome, though, it must be recognized. This is true whether the problem is work-related (avoiding certain jobs or projects), physical, mental or emotional (alcoholism, overeating, drug abuse, etc.). Begin the process of tackling procrastination by acknowledging that it exists in your life.

So, if your office resembles the emergency room at the hospital, acknowledge that procrastination is a problem for you. Define its significance and the result. Then, change it.

Here's a phrase to keep in mind when you suspect procrastination is about to take place. It comes from Alan Lakein's book, *How to Get Control of Your Time and Your Life*. This classic book contributes something that has become known as "Lakein's question," because it is asked so frequently.

Managers can help prevent procrastination by setting a good example. If managers act promptly on business matters, subordinates will follow.

WHAT'S THE BEST USE OF MY TIME RIGHT NOW?

Good advice, isn't it? Post this phrase in a prominent place as a continual reminder of what your priorities ought to be at any point of the day.

After acknowledging and defining the problem, set up for yourself some kind of reward for getting this job done. Make it something that motivates you and is worth looking forward to. An ice cream cone? Some reading time for your favorite novel? A project you'd really like to do? Remember, the "carrot-in-front" concept works not only for animals, it motivates people to performance, as well.

Actually, some people procrastinate because they love that rush of adrenaline—that natural high that comes only from one of those "frantic finishes"! If that's you, define it as your choice so it is a positive action instead of a negative reaction.

It is important that you not confuse procrastination with *planned delayed action*; there are often legitimate reasons to postpone action. Procrastination is the *unnecessary* delaying of a task that should be done now. Waiting makes sense when you must have more information before you can take action or when conditions are simply not right. The Murphy's law that states "Left to themselves, things tend to go from bad to worse" is not always true. Sometimes things get better, instead; hence a delay may be a very positive step!

Here are seven steps guaranteed to permanently end your procrastination once and for all!

1. Ask Lakein's question. "What's the best use of my time right now?" To clarify this question, in its context here, ask, "If I wasn't doing this right now, would I do it at all?" or "Is it directly related to my goals?" This will help you make an immediate appointment with yourself to get organized and get on with prioritizing.

2. Get right in front of your answer. Once you've identified just what to do, get it out of the file and put it on your desk, right in front of you. If the task requires you to be somewhere else in your office, or even off the premises, go to where the task is. Physically put yourself in front of the job.

In most cases, these first two steps are enough to set in motion a series of actions that will lead you to the habit of getting things done. When you know what's most important, and are looking right at it, there's really no reason not to go to work on it. Or is there?

Put it this way: If you're still not working on it, it's because the task is either unpleasant or difficult. If that's the case, move on to the next step.

3. Break it down into small pieces. Too difficult? Too unpleasant? Chop big jobs into more manageable chunks. Taken individually, maybe the steps are not as difficult. Maybe a specific step isn't all that unpleasant.

Unpleasant tasks are like the dinner dishes: Ignoring them doesn't make them disappear and usually makes them even tougher to clean later.

4. Write out a plan and include the steps required. This will give you a checklist to mark off as you achieve each step. Maybe you can start in the middle and do something easier first. Maybe there's a start-up task you can do: Do you have a report to write? Take a piece of paper and list five major points and rank them in order of how you want to discuss them. Correspondence waiting? Address the envelope first. Do you need to settle a misunderstanding with a customer? Look up and write down the phone number as your first step.

Begin your plan now. On the Action Plan below, identify three activities you've been putting off. Then, list one step you could take to get each of the activities started, and set a starting date or time and completion date or time for that step.

WORKSHEET—Procrastination-Ending Action Plan			
TASK	EASY STEP	START	FINISH
1.			
2.			
3.			

5. Go public! Make a commitment to others. Tell other people what you're going to do—people whose opinion of you is important. Tell them when you're going to start it, and ask them to check on you at that time. A little peer pressure can go a long way, as long as there is something in it for you if you win. This gives you both an incentive for reaching your goal and a penalty for falling short.

6. Talk to yourself. If the pressure of others hasn't motivated you, maybe it's time for a heart-to-heart talk: By yourself . . . to yourself. This self-talk can be a positive pep talk, in which you tell yourself that you've got what it takes to do this job; you remind yourself of the reward you've set, and you state how great you're going to feel when the job is done. Positive self-talk is especially helpful if you are looking at a long-term project.

Negative self-talk—that mental kick in the rear we all need from time to time—can also be helpful. The negative approach is not a real self-esteem builder, but it's often great for the immediate short-term project.

We have looked at six steps. It takes only one. And once you reach the step that works, it's not necessary to take any others. However, if you've tried each of the preceding six steps and you still find yourself procrastinating, then perhaps it's time for some drastic action. We call it:

7. The Last-Ditch Effort. Take off your wristwatch. Place it on your desk. Tell yourself: "I'm going to work on this for only five minutes, and then I'm going to stop."

It's not all that difficult to put up with anything for five minutes, and that's all you're committing yourself to. Just five minutes, and then allow yourself to stop. Go ahead and stop after five minutes, too, if you still feel you can't continue your work on the project.

Frequently this kind of experience is like jumping into a swimming pool. To start with, the water's pretty cold, but once you get used to it, it's usually not that bad. If you can do five minutes, you can do fifteen. As long as you're at it, why not keep going? But remember, you're allowed to quit after the five minutes are up. The worst thing that will happen is you've now completed five minutes of work on this project that wasn't done before.

It all boils down to:

> **STOP THINKING ABOUT IT AND JUST DO IT!**

We have a good friend named Moe Schaeffer, who is an old-time Ozark Mountains farmer. Moe isn't educated, school-wise, but he's got one smart head resting on his shoulders. He has a way of putting things that cuts through all the fluff and gets right down to the facts of the matter. We'll quote him a few other times before this book is completed, we're sure. He swears this idea came from a farmer he used to know back in the mountains, but we would rather credit him for it:

> **IF YOU HAVE TO SWALLOW A FROG,**
> **DON'T LOOK AT IT TOO LONG!**

The longer you look at the frog, the worse it would be, right? If you've gotta do it, you might as well get it over with, because it won't get any better. We hope that creates a picture in your mind you won't forget!

Decision And Indecision

- **The time wasted in worrying**
- **Why we put off making decisions**
- **Developing a bias for action**
- **The three questions when indecision strikes**
- **Ready...fire...aim!**

But I Can't Make Up My Mind: The Pitfall Of Indecision

Many an opportunity has been wasted . . . many wonderful events have never occurred . . . jobs and careers have gone down the tubes . . . precious time has been lost, never to be recaptured. All because a decision was not made. Not a wrong decision; just no decision at all.

When faced having to with make a decision, decide whether or not a task is worth doing, and act on it. If it is not worth doing, forget it. Don't let it clutter your life. Simple mathematics can help you determine whether or not a task is worth doing.

Let's say you have a task that will probably take an hour to complete. You put it off for two weeks and worry five to ten minutes each day about doing it. Total up the time worrying, add a little extra time because you let it pile up, plus the original time required and you succeed in turning a one-hour job into a 3-1/2-hour project. One factor not even considered here is the emotional drain that saps energy you need to do your other priorities.

GOOD MANAGERS HAVE A BIAS FOR ACTION!

— Tom Peters

We couldn't agree more with Tom Peters on this one! If you ever hope to have control over your projects and priorities, it's going to be because you are the type of person who gets things done.

The reasons people put off making decisions are many:
- We don't want to make a mistake. As long as we don't decide, we believe a mistake isn't possible.

- We don't want to take responsibility. A decision is a big thing, because its success or failure reflects on us.

- We don't think we have enough information. Sometimes this is true. Other times, it's simply the reason we come up with for failure to act.

- We are looking for the perfect solution. Of course, that means we can never decide, because a "perfect" solution does not exist.

NOT TO DECIDE IS TO DECIDE

If you want to be the kind of person who gets things done, then be decisive and have the courage to act! Don't be deceived into thinking that you can put off a decision indefinitely. By making no decision, you have made one. You have decided not to decide. Unfortunately, the consequences of this decision are usually far worse than making the wrong decision. And often, the lack of decision-making actually forces the consequences themselves. So the scenario below develops.

- "I should really do my term paper, but I've got two weeks. So, I'll go out with my friends tonight."

- The next weekend, the same choice is made.

- The third weekend, there is no choice. The paper is due Monday.

In the final analysis, the circumstances forced the decision. The lack of time now presents an excellent reason for turning in a less-than-perfect product, and the person takes no responsibility for not measuring up or failing.

WHEN YOU FAIL TO MAKE A DECISION, THE DECISION IS USUALLY MADE FOR YOU

This behavior is even more damaging because it becomes a learned trait that follows people all through life. As a student we may not recognize that we have given up control and become a victim—a victim to be forever controlled by life and all its whims and woes.

How do you keep indecision from knocking you out of the game?

Three questions:

1. What's the real problem? This question causes you to analyze what's going on, and why. What is keeping you from making this decision? What, in fact, is the decision? Indecision and procrastination often are close companions at this point.

If you have a hiring choice to make from among five equally qualified candidates, why have you not decided? Is it too hard to identify the best one from the group? Is there an intuitive, gut-level feeling telling you something different from what the facts may be? Do you not want the responsibility of having chosen one of the candidates? Do you actually feel none of them would work well with you? Is this a position you don't even believe needs to be filled? Are you looking for the perfect candidate (he or she is not out there, we promise)?

Identifying the real problem also focuses your thoughts on the real decision, which may not always be the one you think it is. But you have to see it clearly, or you can't go any farther.

2. What are the choices? Rarely is a decision a matter of "either-or." Life is not black and white, but is filled with subtle shades of gray. You probably have many possible choices you could make. List them on a sheet of paper. If you want to devote space to listing the advantages and disadvantages of each choice, do so. Once this information is in front of you, consider the third question:

3. Which is a BETTER choice? Note—the word is "better," not "best." The biggest mistake you can make is to believe there is one option that is clearly the best of many, because work and life are ambiguous most of the time. There simply isn't a best choice, and even if there were, it would be impossible to know that at this point.

If you have several choices, a number of them are probably pretty good. Making a decision is simply picking one of those and going with it.

If you were about to enter a large city, it wouldn't make much sense to call the Police Chief and say that you weren't going to start through town until someone could assure you every traffic light would be green. Yet many people approach decision-making just

> *Overwhelmed by many choices? Eliminate your options systematically. Survey your choices a few at a time, picking the best one; then review your best choices again, a few at a time, until you have narrowed down your options.*

133

that way: If I can't be assured my decision is completely right, I'm not going to make it.

You simply can't see all the way to the end of the road, so go ahead and make a decision based on what you can already see. And, as you travel up the road, continue to do what it takes to make your decision the right one.

CASE STUDY: The M*A*S*H Unit

Who can forget the longest-running situation comedy in television history? For eleven years, M*A*S*H sat at or near the top of the Nielsen ratings. Actors Alan Alda, Gary Burghoff and Loretta Swit became household names. What did the letters in the show's name stand for? (answer at the end)

The show was based during the Korean War in a medical unit just behind the conflict. In the unit were highly skilled doctors and nurses, most of whom had been drafted out of their successful careers into service overseas.

For hours at a time, they had practically nothing to do. Then it all happened at once: The helicopters would start to fly in, bringing the wounded from the battlefront for emergency assistance.

Suddenly the quiet hours were only a memory. Each member of the team moved around quickly, in "controlled chaos," attending to the critical responsibility each had been assigned. Now, there were too few facilities. There was too little time to do the work that had to be done; too few specialists to attend to the needs; and too many wounded people, all at once.

In those situations, decisiveness was an essential key to survival and success. Somebody had to make life-and-death decisions. The most important decision involved categorizing the wounded into three categories:

- Those who would probably die, no matter how much was done for them.

- Those who would probably survive, even if nothing were done right away.

Don't fall into decision-making traps. Not all decisions are big decisions. Don't turn a problem into a crisis. Consult others. Admit a mistake.

- Those in between the two extremes. The ones for whom immediate attention would have the greatest impact on their chances for survival. These are the ones the M*A*S*H unit worked on.

Unless you're literally out on the battlefront, the decisions you have to make are probably not nearly as gut-wrenching. But, there's a very important lesson to learn from the M*A*S*H unit.

Look at your priorities. Do you have too many? Is there too little time and resources? It's time to decide:

- Are there some projects you are putting lots of effort and energy into that are probably going to die eventually, no matter what you do? Pull the plug. Let these activities die. Put no more time and commitment here.

THERE ARE THREE TYPES OF PRIORITIES: THOSE THAT WILL MAKE IT, THOSE THAT WON'T AND THOSE THAT MIGHT. I PUT MY ENERGY WHERE I MAKE THE DIFFERENCE!

- Are there some activities that will undoubtedly survive very nicely even if you never did another thing personally? Let go of these, too. Set them free. You'll never regret it!

- What's left? Just like in the Mobile Army Surgical Hospital (there's your answer to the question at the beginning of the story), the priorities and projects remaining are the ones where you have the greatest impact on their success. These are the ones that make a difference—your priorities. List them, arrange them and plan them. And then accomplish them, knowing you've chosen correctly!

There's one more lesson here. Richard Hooker, author of the novel on which the movie and television series M*A*S*H were based, worked for seven years on the book, but it was rejected by 21 publishers. The 22nd publisher, Morrow, decided to take a chance on it. Only then could it become a best-seller, a blockbuster movie and a highly successful 11-year television series!

Making It Work

CONCERN	REASON	STRATEGY
too much paper	right! there is too much!	develop a paper-controlling mindset
paper backs up on desk	no place for it to go	develop a controlled flow of paper across your desk
too much paper in files	try to save everything	ask question about probability, not possibility
creating more paper than necessary	put everything in writing by habit	ask "Is this necessary?"
small paper projects frequently overlooked	misplaced or lost on desk	start a Tickler File
not enough time to read everything you get	probably is too much	scan things quickly and decide promptly
can't keep up with business or the field	too much information available	choose carefully, then read selectively
frequent procrastination	fear of failure, success or of surrendering control	understand your reason and acknowledge it
frequent procrastination	love the adrenaline rush	go on to the next section!
frequent procrastination	poorly developed work habits	apply as many of the seven steps as necessary
worry about upcoming task	reluctance to act/decide	calculate worry time, add to length of job, just do it
delay in decision-making	real problem unidentified	determine real problem, then act
delay in decision-making	want perfect solution	list options, pick one of the better ones—can't be perfect
can't see all obstacles	can rarely see all the way	make a decision, and then make it be the right one

Putting It To Work

- We are living in an age where paper is easily created and circulated.

- If you develop the right mindset about paper, you can control it.

- Set up your work area to ensure a smooth flow of paper across the desk.

- You can't control how much paper you get, but you can control what you do with it.

- A great habit to develop is that of handling paper only one time.

- Effective paper management requires you keep in a decisive posture.

- Ask yourself "Is this necessary?" before creating a document.

- Read selectively.

- You must acknowledge your procrastination before you can change this well-ingrained habit.

- Frequently ask yourself Lakein's question: "What's the best use of my time right now?"

- Sometimes a delay can be positive if you need more information, conditions are not right, or the matter could resolve itself.

- Procrastination sometimes occurs because the task is either difficult or unpleasant, or both.

- Break large tasks into smaller steps to overcome putting them off.

- Just beginning a task puts you halfway to completion!

- If you have to do something, just do it . . . don't dwell on it.

- Good managers have a bias for action!

- Remember, not to decide is to decide. Have the courage to act.

- Identify the real problem if your decision seems unclear or uncertain.

- Make your decision based on what information you have, and continue to make it the right decision as circumstances develop.

- Select a better choice, instead of seeking a "best" choice.

Check Your Working Knowledge Of Paperwork, Procrastination And Decision-Making

1. How much paper in the typical file should actually be there?

2. What question should you ask to keep from saving everything?

3. If you have an "IN" basket, what else should you have?

4. What great self-management habit helps control paperwork?

5. What are the four options you have with every piece of paper?

6. What four kinds of documents should never be filed?

7. Before you start to put something in writing, what question should you ask?

8. Why is it important to scan something before you read it?

9. What are the three underlying causes of most procrastination?

10. Which one do you relate to the most? Why?

11. What is the most creative way in which you procrastinate?

12. What is Lakein's question?

13. Is: "Left to themselves, things tend to go from bad to worse" always true? Why not?

14. Which two steps are generally all that is necessary to eliminate the problem of procrastination?

15. If those two steps don't work, what is really the problem?

16. What are some of the reasons people put off making decisions?

17. Which of those reasons affects you most often?

18. What is the biggest consequence of not deciding?

19. How many "right" choices are there?

MY SLIGHT-EDGE IDEAS CONCERNING PAPERWORK, PROCRASTINATION AND DECISION-MAKING:

_____

_____

_____

_____

_____

_____

_____

_____

_____

*C*HAPTER 7

Am I Trying To Do Too Much?

- **Determining self-overload**
- **Is this actually important?**
- **Giving other people the chance**
- **Reinforcing your priorities**
- **Things you should never do**
- **Being flexible and allowing changes to occur**
- **The most powerful word in any language**
- **How to say "the" word and mean it**
- **How to give alternatives**
- **A memory phrase**

This chapter should be one of the shortest ones in the manual, but for many it may be the most important. We all need checks and balances to manage life's resources and responsibilities, and that's what this chapter is all about.

Each person has a different reason for reading this manual. You may be overloaded with responsibilities and demands. You may feel incapable of effectively organizing and managing all your projects. You may be hoping for a mixture of ideas and solutions that, blended together, can restore a feeling of control. You know your life is not perfectly balanced, and want to bring balance to it.

It's possible that all these concerns about your time boil down to one simple fact:

YOU MAY BE TRYING TO DO TOO MUCH!

The best organized schedule, the most well-planned *Daily Action List*, the most effectively applied list of "10 steps" or "12 ideas" cannot change your situation if you are simply trying to accomplish more than you have time to do. Could this be true of you? To find out, you need to analyze your current situation. Begin with the following worksheet.

Self-Quiz: See For Yourself—Is It True, Or Isn't It?

Check yourself on these questions to see how overloaded you may be. Read the statements and circle the number that best describes your response: (3) agree (2) not sure (1) disagree

1. I feel totally responsible for group projects.	3	2	1
2. I believe the job is always done best if I do it myself.	3	2	1
3. I am unable to satisfy my family's needs and requests.	3	2	1
4. I am involved in many things I wish I could get out of.	3	2	1
5. I feel guilty because I can't devote enough time to some jobs.	3	2	1
6. Any time I join a group, I get a leadership position.	3	2	1
7. I am so busy I don't have time to eat, sleep or relax.	3	2	1
8. I have trouble deciding what's really important.	3	2	1
9. I hardly ever say "no" when I'm asked to do something.	3	2	1
10. I don't want to let anybody down, so I usually agree to help.	3	2	1

How you did:
In this quiz, a high score is bad, not good.

24 or more: You're on a collision course with disaster

23-15:   You deserve more of yourself than you're getting

less than 15:   Congratulations! No one controls your life except
you!

Are You Really Trying To Do Too Much?

How can you determine if self-overload conditions already exist?
What can you do to change those conditions? The answer is easy:
If you feel overloaded, you are overloaded. The recognition is there
. . . you see yourself in the picture we painted a few paragraphs ago
. . . and you want to do something about it; that's why you're
reading this book.

If you don't feel that you're presently overloaded, you may fear that
you're heading that way . . . fast. Your question then is: "How can I
keep this from happening to me? Especially since I am the kind of
person who makes a commitment to give all that I have to achieve
my goals."

Whether you've already reached the breaking point or see the point
approaching fast, to avoid certain demise you must take a long, hard
look at all of your commitments and activities. You must be honest,
and you must be realistic. You deceive everyone including yourself
by acting as if the conditions didn't exist.

There are four specific steps you must take to assure you're not
taking on too much.

STEP #1: Is This Important? As you consider your grocery list
of activities, projects and commitments, look at each one and ask
this question:

IF I WERE NOT ALREADY DOING THIS, WOULD I
CHOOSE TO GET INVOLVED?

Isn't hindsight wonderful? Isn't it possible to look at certain
responsibilities and say: "If I had only known then what I know
now, I would never have gotten involved!"? Activities have a way
of innocently creeping into our lives. Once we have opened the door

to them, even just a crack, they are likely to walk in and take over. These activities, the ones to which we say "No, I would not have gotten involved had I known," are the first ones we want to get rid of, get out of our lives. The sooner the better.

CASE STUDY: More Than He Bargained For

Jim North, a personnel director for a small manufacturing firm, began attending meetings of a local organization of personnel directors. The group meets monthly for breakfast and sponsors an annual all-day workshop on a Saturday.

Although Jim enjoyed the association with other professionals in his field, he found it difficult to attend the breakfasts every month. He frequently got his most productive work done early in the day, and sometimes the meetings seemed to have only marginal professional benefits, since a number of the members had known each other for years and seemed mainly interested in the meeting as a social occasion.

Jim was surprised when Gerry Duckworth, a member he knew only casually, called one day and asked if he would consider running for vice president of the organization for the upcoming year. When Jim asked what the position involved, Gerry said, "Oh, you really don't have to do anything. We just need someone to hold that office since our charter calls for it."

Jim told himself he should know better, but agreed to have his name placed in nomination. As it turned out, his was the only name in nomination, and he was elected to the office.

A few days later Kathy Cornell, the president, called Jim and told him there was a lunch meeting scheduled later that week for all the officers of the organization. Jim thought, "An officers' meeting sounds like *doing* something. But, since I'm vice president, I'll attend."

When Jim went to the officers' meeting, he discovered that the vice president had numerous responsibilities, including planning the programs for the breakfasts each month and heading up the annual new-members campaign. Kathy excitedly told the group she had just learned her corporation was sending her across the country for three months to oversee the opening of a new office. This meant Jim would function as president for that time, as well.

Keep a sign opposite your desk that says, "Is what I am doing or about to do getting us closer to our objectives?"

Suddenly Jim realized, "This job's a lot bigger than I was told it was. If I had known I would have this much responsibility, I would not have agreed to serve as vice president." Jim began to envision the additional hours and energy required (which he really didn't have) to serve an organization of questionable value to him, and felt overwhelmed. He also found himself feeling resentful that the importance of the job had been misrepresented to him.

QUESTIONS:

1. What was Jim's biggest mistake?

2. If you were Jim North, what would you do?

What Actually Happened

Jim quickly reassessed his own priorities, and determined this new responsibility didn't fit into them. He analyzed what impact giving up that much additional time and energy would have on the activities he had already committed to. He wondered how much more he could do in those areas if he were to direct the same time and energy to his priorities.

At the end of the meeting, he asked Kathy to stay for a few minutes. Jim said, "Kathy, if I had realized the scope of the vice president's job in this association, I would never have agreed to serve. I'm sorry I didn't ask more questions when Gerry called, and I realize this will put the association in a temporary bind, but I'm going to have to resign from the office."

Kathy reluctantly accepted Jim's resignation, but thanked him for his candor and honesty at the beginning, rather than agreeing to handle the responsibility and then not doing the job. She appointed another vice president before the next meeting and made the announcement in the chapter's newsletter.

For a few months, Jim felt a little uncomfortable at the meetings. A few people teased him about "chickening out" of the job, but the teasing stopped. When the election of officers came around next year, Jim reflected gratefully on his decision, realizing he had been wise to put his efforts into his priorities.

Analysis

Jim could have decided to make the best of his position and plan great programs and spearhead an enthusiastic member campaign. Maybe he would have even gotten more out of the meetings and his opportunities to network with the other members of the chapter.

But sometimes people simply spread themselves too thin—trying to do too much and please too many people. When you identify your priorities by asking "What's important to me?" it is often far more satisfying and rewarding to redirect additional time and effort to previous commitments than to add even more activities to an already jammed calendar.

Put yourself in this story. Change the situation to one of yours. Wouldn't you really rather be out from under this responsibility than trying to juggle it and fit it in with other more important matters? Won't it feel good when that commitment is no longer on your list? The benefits you'll get from relieving yourself of burdensome, unnecessary tasks will undoubtedly outweigh the consequences.

Checks and balances for Step #1: Remember, for any project that you're already involved in or are thinking about taking on, ask yourself this question: "Can I make a strong personal commitment to invest my time and abilities in this purpose, project or pursuit?" If the answer is "I cannot make a full commitment," then it's best not to start it, or if already involved, to find a way out.

STEP #2. Delegate. The way to phrase this question:

DO I PERSONALLY HAVE TO DO THIS?

What's your answer? If it's "yes," go immediately to Step #3. If it's "no," you have just discovered the greatest leveraging fact of all time:

> **THERE IS NOT ENOUGH TIME IN ONE LIFE TO DO
> EVERYTHING. THERE IS ENOUGH TIME AVAILABLE
> TO GET EVERYTHING DONE IF YOU EFFECTIVELY
> MANAGE THE TIME OF OTHER PEOPLE.**

If this is a work-related task, and you have a supervisory or management-level position, there is probably someone in your department who is ready to assume a little more authority and responsibility. Pass this responsibility on to someone else. (See Chapter 10 for some specifics on how to delegate!) Give someone else the opportunity—not only does it give this individual the chance to grow and develop skills, it will make you more effective as a manager. A good manager never tries to do it all, because it's just not possible.

What if you're not in management and you have no one to delegate to? You're the one someone else is always giving that "opportunity to grow"? Your boss won't let you delegate? Don't give up hope, yet. Chapter 9 will discuss ways you can establish and track priorities and negotiate changes in expectations that can allow the release of certain responsibilities.

Everyone can practice delegation with commitments we have made outside work. Have you been the secretary of your bowling league for years? Have you been a leader in a certain club or organization since you started? Are people counting on you to head up the school carnival again? Are you so busy after working hours your family and friends never see you? Review all of your commitments. Is it time to step aside for a while and let other people develop some of their leadership potential and try some of their ideas? Could you remove your name from the ballot this time around? Could you bring someone in to help you, in an official capacity, that would make your life easier? Do you have a vice-president who doesn't really do anything? Would that organization continue without your involvement? Is it actually more important to you than to anybody else?

What kind of answers are you coming up with? Only you know the answer to "Do I personally have to do this?". Would you feel a tremendous burden was lifted off your shoulders if people didn't

A detailed, written account of how you spend your days is essential to mastering your time.

depend on you for this any longer? If you're answering "yes," then delegate.

Checks and balances for Step #2: Does a "do-it-myself" attitude dilute your effectiveness?

> **DEVOTING A LITTLE OF YOURSELF TO EVERYTHING MEANS COMMITTING A GREAT DEAL OF YOURSELF TO NOTHING**

STEP #3. Put your efforts into your priorities. What is really important to you? What do you wish you had more time and energy to pursue, but simply can't because of other commitments you've made?

> **WHEN AM I GOING TO SCHEDULE THIS INTO MY LIFE?**

Remember the last time someone told you about a new organization, or a new activity, and as that person described it, it sounded so interesting? Couldn't you almost already see yourself involved?

Before jumping in with both feet, take a hard, realistic look at your schedule and ask exactly where and how you intend to schedule this into your life. When you're deciding whether or not something will fit into your schedule, use this rule of thumb: Estimate how much time you think it will take, and multiply by 1.25.

- If you think a meeting will take one hour, allow one hour and 15 minutes on your schedule.

- If you think it will take four hours to prepare a presentation, schedule five hours.

- If the committee meets once a week, plan on five times a month.

- If the task is totally unfamiliar to you, estimate the time and multiply by 1.5 instead of 1.25.

Another rule is: Schedule only 50 percent of your time. Already 100 percent booked? You're not alone. Since most of us have already filled nearly all of our allotted time, in order to add a new activity, something has to move out. Are you prepared to do that? What activity would that be? Better yet, what really is most important to you—your true priority? This is the time to recommit yourself to what you really believe is important, and direct unscheduled time in that direction before adding something else.

Checks and balances for Step #3: These services should remain "unscheduled":

1. All low-priority items. (Unless the high-priority items have been completed.)

2. Any task that when completed is of little or no consequence.

3. Anything you can delegate to someone else. For example, household repairs and improvements—beware! You may immerse yourself in a project only to find that you don't have the time, training or tools to successfully complete it. You may even complicate the problem. You run the high risk of pouring your time and energy into a bottomless pit and ending up empty-handed. It reminds us of a sign we saw in a repair shop once:

LABOR CHARGE: **$20 PER HOUR**

IF YOU WATCH: **$25 PER HOUR**

IF YOU TRIED TO FIX IT YOURSELF FIRST:
                  $50 PER HOUR

---

4. Anything done just to please others because you fear their condemnation or want them to be indebted to you.

5. Thoughtless or inappropriate requests for your time and effort. (Think about this one. Aren't there people constantly trying to do this to you?)

6. Anything others should be doing for themselves.

STEP #4. Be flexible. This admonition reminds us that life isn't going around in the same groove all the time. Things change. Interests change. Commitments change.

Once in a while, you will make a conscious choice to become involved in a new area. That's normal. You've done that many times before, and will do it as long as you live. Since we all have exactly the same amount of time, as we let one activity in, another receives less time and attention. Remember some of the activities you were involved in ten years ago? Are there some activities you didn't even know about then that are major parts of your life now? Once again—it couldn't be more natural and it actually may be better.

Checks and balances for Step #4: Remind yourself to be flexible enough to recognize new opportunities and interests, allowing changes to take place. That's part of what makes life so fulfilling and interesting. To restore a true sense of balance and sanity, practice developing these capabilities daily:

- Mental prowess:

> **"ALL THE GENIUS I HAVE IS THE FRUIT OF LABOR."**
> — Alexander Hamilton

- Creative urges:

> **"IF PEOPLE KNEW HOW HARD I WORKED**
> **TO GET MY MASTERY,**
> **IT WOULDN'T SEEM SO WONDERFUL AFTER ALL."**
> — Michelangelo

- Responsive senses:

> **"LOVE ALWAYS AND LAUGH OFTEN."**
> — Norman Cousins

The Power Of A Positive Two-Letter Word

There's a word in our language that is very short. It's very positive. It's easy to pronounce, and no one ever misspells it. It's pronounced the same, or nearly so, in many other languages. It can make the difference between success and failure. It can free us from stress and pressure. It can give us control of our lives. Yet this little word is not used often enough. People avoid it at all costs, and often the cost is very high indeed. The result: Ineffective performance, spiritless effort and utter frustration.

We need to bring this word back into our vocabulary. The word is:

Try saying that a few times. Again. Again. Doesn't it feel great! As good as it feels, say it a few dozen more times. Loudly. Emphatically. Put an exclamation point at the end!

There. You've said it! The more you say this word, the more control you will have over your life, its projects and priorities.

Nancy Reagan's famous phrase including this two-letter word was coined for the purpose of preventing drug abuse. It bears repeating here.

> **JUST SAY "NO!"**

This word can prevent abuse of another kind as well: schedule and time abuse. This abuse is perhaps introduced by others but eventually brought upon ourselves.

Our friend Martha recently returned to the workplace for the first time in many years. She had a boss who was very appreciative of her considerable talents and abilities and showed her appreciation by adding more and more responsibilities to her full schedule. Martha enjoyed the work, but the load became too heavy and she suddenly got that overwhelmed feeling.

She expressed concern to a mutual friend, Jeff. "I just can't seem to say 'no' to her."

Jeff replied, "Martha, first put your tongue against the back of your upper teeth. Begin a nasal 'n-n-n-n-n' sound. Got it? Now, open your mouth to form a circle and slowly blow air out. 'O-o-o-o-o.' Then, just put those sounds together!"

People ask us to do things. They make requests—sometimes unreasonable demands. We don't have any idea how to honor the commitments we've already made, much less add others to our heavy list. But, because we don't say "No!," we end up trying to do them anyway.

Here are five steps that will make it much easier for you to say the word "no" positively.

1. Listen! This in itself is a lost art. We mean really listen. Don't just hear the words, but get a clear picture of what is being asked and what it involves. Ask questions if you're not certain. The more thoroughly you understand what someone is asking you to do, the better your response can be. Don't distract your concentration to "What am I going to say?" You're entitled to take a minute to think about that before you have to respond. Listening is a very positive step because it gives mutual respect both to the speaker and to you, the listener.

2. Stop. Pause. And think. Humans have an almost deathly fear of silence in communication. Re-learn the art of quiet contemplation, and use it after a request has been given.

There's an old adage that those in the sales world have learned about asking for the sale:

THE NEXT PERSON WHO TALKS, LOSES!

In other words, the sales person gets a Slight Edge by managing the silence for 5-10 seconds. The buyer will fill the silence, giving the sales person more knowledge before a commitment is made.

Control your impulse to speak. This is your opportunity to consider what has been said and, even more importantly, to consider what you're going to say in reply.

3. Decide immediately. Once you've determined you are going to decline, tell your listener: "I'm going to have to say NO." Then pause and control your impulse to continue talking. That's it. Such an easy statement can save so much time and energy. But when it gets to that point, most of us chicken out. Instead we say:

> **"I WANT TO THINK ABOUT IT!"**

or:

> **"LET ME GET BACK TO YOU ON THIS"**

or:

> **"MAYBE"**

Have you heard yourself saying these phrases before? Inside, you're mentally kicking yourself. Your stomach is tying up in knots. You don't want to do it. That classic noncommittal answer gets you ultimately committed to "yes," not to "no."

How many times has your answer ultimately been "yes"?

Many of us just don't know how to refuse a request placed against our time. So we say yes for two very negative reasons: We are afraid someone else will have a lesser opinion of us, or a request for our help indulges our own egos by giving us a false sense of importance and power.

When you say yes because of a need for approval, you are saying that someone else's opinion of you is more important than your opinion of yourself. Saying yes to indulge your ego is the ammunition of martyrs and victims, not the essence of leadership!

Shortly after Norman Vincent Peale published his best-selling book *The Power of Positive Thinking*, he suddenly was in great demand as a speaker. From all over the country, offers poured onto his desk at Marble Collegiate Church in New York. He had many more opportunities than he could possibly fill, even if he had actually wanted to, which he didn't. But "no" was a hard word for Peale to say, too, and he found himself putting the requests off. He didn't accept them, but he didn't turn them down. Only after his delays had put the organizations who had asked him in such a bind that the only fair and honorable thing to do was to accept did Peale realize: "It was much easier to say 'no' in the beginning than to end up doing something I didn't want to do in the first place."

Sounds like Dr. Peale learned that overcommitment inevitably leads to procrastination . . . and, quite possibly, failure. Saying yes to everything decreases the chances of successfully completing even one thing.

One of the reasons we dislike saying "the" word is we don't want to let somebody else down. To get a clear perspective on things, let's reverse the positions for a moment. If you were going to ask somebody to do something for you, wouldn't you expect to hear "no" a few times? You'd probably even make a list of potential prospects for this job so that if the one declines, you have others you can turn to.

Yet when somebody asks you, the tendency is to think your answer is going to make or break the situation for that person. Why wouldn't that person have other names on a list, just like you would? Rarely, if ever, are you somebody else's last resort or only option. That person is expecting that you may say no. And, if you truly *are* their last resort, then it may well be an inappropriate request of your time and effort. Even if you're last, it still isn't your problem unless you choose to make it so! In fact, if everyone else has declined doing the task, there may be a good reason for their reluctance to say yes: The task may be too time-consuming or just not worthwhile enough to pursue.

4. Have reasons. If the answer is no, I don't have to tell you why. Yet, there is a benefit in being aware of the reasons for your decision. Look at it this way. You should know the reasons why you are turning down the request. It might be beneficial to the other person to know what your priorities really are, so they have a better understanding of the situation.

> **"PEOPLE ARE USUALLY MORE CONVINCED BY REASONS THEY DISCOVERED THEMSELVES THAN BY THOSE FOUND BY OTHERS."**
>
> **– Blaise Pascal**

The reason for saying no is most valuable to you, as a way of reinforcing what is important. If you don't want to give your reasons, or believe that it would be better if you just kept your reasons to yourself, there's still one thing you should do:

> **YOU DON'T HAVE TO GIVE REASONS,**
> **BUT MAKE SURE YOU KNOW THEM!**

5. Offer alternatives. Is there another way to do this job that doesn't involve you? Are there other people who might be better able to provide the service you've been asked to handle? Could you offer a counter-proposal if you think the request is valid? "I can't sit in for you at the meeting this afternoon, but I'll be happy to answer your phone while you're gone."

Could you possibly suggest an alternative that would allow you to help without taking on such a major time commitment yourself? For example, perhaps someone has just asked you to head the company picnic next summer. There's no way you have the time and energy for a job as big as that. You know you simply can't do the job. So, why not say, "I'm honored to think you would trust me with such a big job, but I'm going to have to say no. However, please tell the person who takes this responsibility I'd be glad to serve on the entertainment committee."

In 1968, newly elected President Richard Nixon asked Art Linkletter to serve the United States as Ambassador to Australia. Linkletter had traveled extensively in Australia and owned property there, but he couldn't see himself in the cocktail parties and political rituals of a job in which he wouldn't have any power, but merely serve as a front for Washington. He also knew you couldn't turn the President down flat.

He said, "Mr. President, what would you rather have me do: Go and be our representative in Australia, or attempt to save thousands of young people from the ravages of drug abuse in this country? I have lectures, films, books and fund-raising activities scheduled for this next year. I believe I'm more effective outside the government, so why not just put me on a commission to fight drugs?"

The President agreed. How could he say anything negative about the efforts to fight the drug problem? Linkletter later wrote:

"Being an ambassador didn't fit in with my goals, and no was the only answer I could give Richard Nixon. But the way I did it points up something important about the method of turning an offer down. It's not always necessary to give a direct negative answer. There are many ways of saying no without actually saying it. In this encounter with Nixon, I merely offered him another choice, which I knew he would accept."

It all comes down to this:

> **WHEN I KNOW WHAT'S IMPORTANT TO ME,
> IT'S EASY TO SAY "NO" TO SOMETHING ELSE**

Considering what's important, it's a good idea to have a direct response, that can be memorized as a way of stating your priorities.

> "____(fill in name)____, there's nothing I would like better than to do what you propose, but you know my rule: I don't do anything unless I can do it well. And I can't do that now because there are too many other things on my schedule that must be done first."

A direct response like this does not keep your asker hanging, and it's stated in pleasant terms for his or her welfare as well as for your own.

Summary: Remember—if you have to say no, follow the steps listed in this chapter. Especially Step #3, Decide Immediately. This is your Slight Edge! The longer you wait, the more you are likely to replay it in your mind, wasting valuable mental, and sometimes physical, energy. Just say no . . . quickly, decisively and pleasantly.

> **"I HAVE FOUND THAT THE GREATEST HELP
> IN MEETING ANY PROBLEM WITH DECENCY,
> SELF-RESPECT AND WHATEVER COURAGE
> IS DEMANDED IS TO KNOW WHERE YOU
> YOURSELF STAND. THAT IS, TO HAVE IN WORDS
> WHAT YOU BELIEVE AND ARE ACTING FROM."**
> — William Faulkner

Making It Work

CONCERN	REASON	STRATEGY
frustration with group or activity	it was more than you thought it would be	begin taking steps now to back out of this job
not enough time to do really important things	too involved in low-priority projects and activities	reconsider priorities: commit yourself to them
too large a share of the responsibility	trying to do it all	identify tasks for immediate delegation to others
no time for something you really want to do	too much time taken up by other projects	let something out to make room for your new activity
inability to say no	don't know how	learn and apply the five steps in this chapter
often get roped into jobs you don't want to do	forced into situation where only answer is yes	decide immediately and say no
pressure to agree to a request for help	don't want to let someone else down	offer alternatives, realize you're not the only hope

Putting It To Work

- Recognize the possibility that you're trying to do more than you can really do.

- If, knowing what you now know, you would not have gotten involved in an activity, begin to look for ways to drop it.

- Remember: Your first obligation is to look out for yourself, your interests and your priorities. No one will do this for you.

- Develop the habit of asking, "Do I personally have to do this?"

- Take a serious look at your schedule before agreeing to accept new work or responsibilities. If someone won't wait, say no immediately.

- In planning, always allow about 25 percent more time than you think you'll need for getting things done.

- If you can afford to give someone else the job, do it!

- Be alert to the changes in your life. Recognize this as part of growth, and make room for the new activities that arise.

- Practice saying the word "no." Have a friend or spouse help you by asking you for things it's easy to say no to.

- Use the power of silence after you've been asked to do something.

- If your ultimate intention is to say no to a request, turn it down immediately. This is a favor to the asker, as well as to you.

- Be ready with alternative suggestions; they keep you from feeling as guilty when you have to say no.

Check Your Working Knowledge Of Overload

1. What question should be asked to determine if an activity is important?

2. Do you recognize yourself to be in an overload situation?

   If so, what activity or activities can you eliminate?

   When will you begin the elimination process?

3. What are some of the benefits that come from delegation?

4. What is truly important to you? How can you direct your energy to this activity or project?

5. In estimating time required for a project, what multiplication factor should you use?

6. When was the last time you said "no" to a request?

   How did you feel about saying it?

   What would make it easier to say "no" next time?

7. What is the advantage of silence after you've been asked to do something?

8. What phrases do you find yourself using instead of saying no?

9. What did Norman Vincent Peale discover about putting off an answer?

10. Why is it important to know reasons for declining a request?

11. When is it easy to say no?

MY SLIGHT-EDGE IDEAS FROM CHAPTER 7:

_____

_____

_____

_____

_____

_____

_____

_____

_____

CHAPTER 8

Doing Things On Purpose: Determining Priorities

- The importance of commitment
- The $25,000 idea — analyzing key functions of your job
- Growth goals — priority planning
- The A-B-C ranking priority system
- Hogs and speeding tickets
- The forced-choice priority indicator
- Automatic top-priority projects

When people are determining and ranking priorities, they say things like: "I'll try to get that done," or "When I have a chance, I'll put it on my list of priorities." These statements accomplish nothing—eliminate them from your speech! You need to quit trying and choose . . .

I SHOULD EITHER DO IT OR NOT DO IT!

As far back as the early 1900s, Victor Pareto explained why a priority system was so important in securing effectiveness. As you recall, his rule, when applied to setting priorities states that 80 percent of the value of a group of items is generally concentrated in only 20 percent of the items. In other words:

**YOU CAN BE 80 PERCENT EFFECTIVE BY
ACHIEVING 20 PERCENT OF YOUR GOALS!!**

If you have a *Daily Action List* of ten items, you can expect to be 80 percent effective by successfully completing only the two most important items on the list. How's that for good news??

The main idea is that to be effective you must concentrate on the most important items.

"KEEP YOUR COMMITMENT TO YOUR COMMITMENT."
— **Dr. Robert L. Lorber**

It's your commitment to your commitment that you need to concern yourself with. People say diets don't work! Diets work just fine—it's people who don't work at them. People say "to-do" lists don't work! "To-do" lists work just fine—it's just that people make the lists. People break their commitment to lose weight, and people break their commitment to prioritizing.

Ivy Lee was a management consultant who helped Bethlehem Steel in 1904. Mr. Lee made an unscheduled visit to Bethlehem's President, Charles Schwab, and said, "Mr. Schwab, I have an idea that I believe will increase productivity at Bethlehem Steel, and I'm going to share it with you. Since I've just dropped in on you today, I don't expect you to pay me. So, here are my conditions: Use the idea yourself first. If it has any value for you, then share it with your people. If you feel the idea was worthwhile, and you want to pay me for it, then pay me what you think it was worth."

"Sounds like I can't lose," said Schwab. "What's the idea?"

"Simple. At the beginning of every day, list in ranked order the six most important things you have to do. Then go to work on number one, and continue to work until you're finished.

When you've finished the first task, re-evaluate the other five items to make sure nothing has changed the ranking. Then go to work on number two. When it's done, re-evaluate, then work on number three.

If the day ends and you haven't finished all six, don't worry. You wouldn't have gotten all six done using any other method, either. And, you did, in fact, do the most important things on your list.

Even if the day goes by and you don't even finish number one, remember, you were still working on the most important thing you had to do."

Schwab thanked him and Lee left the office. Several months later, Lee received a check from Charles Schwab for $25,000 (this was 1904!!), along with this note: "Thank you very much. This has been the most important idea I've received all year."

Later, as the story of this meeting began to make its rounds in business circles, people would often come up to Schwab and say, "Why did you pay so much money for such a simple idea?"

Schwab's answer was always the same: "I paid as much as I did because that simple idea has made the difference between where my company was then and where it is now—the most profitable private corporation in the United States!"

Pareto said it. Ivy Lee said it. Lorber said it. It's not a new principle, but it's one that merits considerable attention:

> **EITHER DO IT OR DON'T DO IT...**
> **BUT, YOU DECIDE!**

Choose what's important to you and do it first.

To be the best you can be, don't adopt impossible standards. Nobody can have everything. No one can do everything. Nobody can please everybody.

This chapter includes several forms and charts that will help you always know the answer to important questions like: How important is this? What should I be doing right now? What did I really accomplish today? But, before you read any further, stop and do a quick self-evaluation of how your goals match up to your present situation.

SELF-ASSESSMENT: Do You Keep Your Commitment To Your Commitment?

Choose one response to each question:

ALWAYS, USUALLY, SOMETIMES, INFREQUENTLY, NEVER

1. Do you set goals?

   Comments:

2. Have you analyzed your present commitments?

   Comments:

3. Have you inventoried how you plan spending your time, and how you actually DO spend it daily?

   Comments:

4. Do you ask yourself, "What's the best use of my time, energy and skills?"

   Comments:

5. Do you know your calendar of appointments?

   Comments:

6. Are your goals and objectives in writing? (Or do they turn out to be wishful thinking?)

   Comments:

7. When working on a project, do you stay focused until you complete it?

   Comments:

How many "always" responses did you have on your self-assessment? If you're like most people, there probably is room for improvement. Don't be concerned with how you answered the self-assessment today—what counts is what you're committed to do to make tomorrow's results better.

The following tool can give you insight into your overall commitments and activities. In fact, when it's complete there will be enough data on the following chart to give you many hours of thought, reflection and decision-making for your priorities, as well as help in answering the questions on the preceding self-assessment.

> *"I got up this morning with nothing to do; I've been busy at it all day, and I'm only half done!"*

Key Functions Chart

Key Functions	a. Time Spent	b. Skill Required	c. Personal Satisfaction	d. Results (Personal)	e. Results (Organizational)

Directions

STEP ONE: Key Functions—List in the left column what you think are the five most important functions of your job, i.e., what are the five major responsibilities for which you earn your paycheck? Don't try to list them in any particular order—you'll rank them in several ways after the five items are written in.

STEP TWO: Time Spent—Thinking about those five key functions, in Column a., rank them in order based on total amount of time you spend on each function. The function on which you spend the most time is #1. The item you spend the next greatest amount of time on is #2, and so forth down to #5, which will be the item on which you spend the least time.

STEP THREE: Skill Required—Which of the five job functions require the greatest amount of your personal skill and expertise to perform? In Column b., rank it #1. Rank the others in sequence down to #5, the function which requires the least skill and expertise.

STEP FOUR: Personal Satisfaction—Which function do you enjoy the most, i.e., what gives you the most personal satisfaction in doing? In Column c., rank it #1. Rank the others in sequence down to #5, the one you like the least.

STEP FIVE: Results—Results can be rated one of two ways. First, which job function produces the greatest results as far as your organization is concerned? Rank them from 1 to 5 that way. Next, rank the functions in relation to the activities that give you the most personal benefit from a results standpoint. (These may be the same, but they may be different.)

Key Function Analysis

What can you do with all these numbers? Actually, they can be interpreted a lot of different ways. They should provide a source of analysis and some direction as you look at your job and what is important.

If this were an ideal world, every column in your Key Functions Chart would be exactly the same as all the others—the rankings would be identical all the way across the chart. Since that's not the case, let's explore some possible implications for the rankings you've made:

- If there are any two columns we would want to make certain matched up, we would pick (a.) and (d.). It just seems logical that a person ought to be spending time on the activities that are going to produce the greatest payoff, be it personal or organizational. If this is not the case, you may want to analyze your time commitments on the job.

- In comparing (a.) and (b.), if these two columns are significantly different (by "different" we don't mean just off by one number here and there, but that the numbers are considerably different from each other—possibly a difference of 3 or more), a question you might want to ask is: "Is this function necessary?" If you're spending the greatest amount of time on a job function that is only #5 in terms of skill required, why are you the one doing it? This function might be delegated to someone else, freeing up your time for activities you have trained and studied to do.

- Looking at (b.) and (c.), if these two columns DO match, congratulations! You have just succeeded in turning a *hobby* into a *career*. If, on the other hand, what you like to do and what you do well are not rated similarly, perhaps you might want to consider re-evaluating whether you're in the right position.

- If columns (c.) and (d.) do NOT match, be careful! This could be a good sign you are *headed for burnout*. If the activities that are greatest in terms of results and payoff are things you truly don't enjoy, then you are never going to be satisfied. Something must change eventually, and this may be an early warning sign. Research consistently states that you must have at least 20% of your day doing what you really enjoy or productivity drops drastically.

These are just a few things you might begin to look for as you analyze the numbers and ask: "What do these mean?" The potential insights are numerous. Just make sure you come to some conclusions about the meaning of your rankings.

A Systemized Approach To Time And Priority Management

Your initial response to these questions gives you a "things as they are" overview. Now, what you need is a system. To start, here are two questions to test the use of your time and priorities. Your answers will help you personalize your own organization system.

DON'T AGONIZE. ORGANIZE AND PERSONALIZE.

- Is this the best use of my time?

- Is this the right time to be doing it?

To test the use of your time and priorities, and evaluate your answers to the two questions above, here are five specific goals you can set for yourself right now.

Test Your Use Of Time And Priorities

WORKSHEET Goal	Target Date	Completion Date
1. I will invest 30 minutes listing the things I am already committed to.		
2. I will invest 15 minutes each day listing the different ways I am presently spending my time.		
3. I will invest 30 minutes reviewing my calendar or appointment book for the past month.		
4. I will invest the time necessary to compare my goals to the actual way I am spending my life and to my present commitments.		
5. I will invest enough time alone to write three short-range goals and three long-range goals for my life.		

Are you willing to commit yourself to these short but vitally important activities? If so, establish a target date in the appropriate box for completing each of the five goals listed above. When these five goals have been achieved, they will enable you to prioritize your activities from both a practical and a realistic position while taking into account your present lifestyle.

If, from time to time, things are not as you would like them to be, here are some additional tools to help you develop a balanced, realistic action plan that will help you move from

HERE & NOW ->->->->-> PLANNING ->->->->->-> THERE & BEYOND

Prioritizing Process Planning

SELF-ASSESSMENT: Effective-Living Chart

Directions:

1. Look at the "Possible Life Areas" column for the items listed. Not all of these areas may apply to you personally.

2. If you are already committed to an item on the list, put an "X" in the "Presently Committed" column.

3. If you are involved in something but are not really committed to what you're doing, place the "X" in the "Doing, Not Committed" column.

4. Determine in which of these areas you should be setting specific goals by putting an "X" in the "Targeted for Goals" column.

POSSIBLE LIFE AREAS	PRESENTLY COMMITTED	DOING, NOT COMMITTED	TARGETED FOR GOALS
Career/ Occupation			
Employer			
Finances			
Others:			
God			
Spouse			
Children			
Relatives			
Friends			
Business Associates			
Others:			
Education			
Skill Advancement			
Community			
Civic			
Hobbies			
Relaxation			
Recreation			
Physical Health			
Emotional Well-Being			
Family			
Education			
Home			
Investment			
Car			
Transportation			
Retirement			
Others:			

NOTE: You may want to do this chart and then share it with others
involved in the various activities, noting agreements or
disagreements on the areas of commitment or the need to set goals.

SELF-ASSESSMENT: Present-Commitments Chart

Directions:
Make a list of your present commitments, including personal,
family and work commitments. These might include family
activities, job responsibilities, finances, hobbies committed to,
activities planned with friends, educational classes—anything for
which and to which you have made a commitment. Determine
which commitments are yours alone, and which are jointly shared
by you and other members of your family or work associates. An
example is provided:

PRESENT COMMITMENT	WORK	PERSONAL	FAMILY
$100,000 loan to United Mortgage		X	X
Weekly breakfast w/Tom Smith	X		
Community Church trustee board		X	
Weekly dinner out with spouse			X
Annual income tax return		X	
Office collection for cancer fund	X		

> "IT'S NOT ENOUGH THAT WE DO OUR BEST.
> SOMETIMES WE HAVE TO DO WHAT IS REQUIRED."
> — Winston Churchill

PRESENT COMMITMENT	WORK	PERSONAL	FAMILY

SELF-ASSESSMENT: Your Time Investment

Directions:
To help answer the question: "Is this the right time to be doing this?" fill in the chart below. List anything that comes to your mind—at home, with your business, with your family—anything. Include job activities, personal activities, family activities and leisure activities.

MY TIME-INVESTMENT CHART

ACTIVITY	ENOUGH	TOO LITTLE	TOO MUCH
• Personal Activities			
Eating		X	
Sleeping	X		

MY TIME-INVESTMENT CHART

ACTIVITY	ENOUGH	TOO LITTLE	TOO MUCH
• Job Activities			
Planning	X		
Reading		X	
Working at home			X

MY TIME-INVESTMENT CHART

ACTIVITY	ENOUGH	TOO LITTLE	TOO MUCH
• Leisure Activities			
Exercise		X	
Television	X		
Spectator sports			X

MY TIME-INVESTMENT CHART

ACTIVITY	ENOUGH	TOO LITTLE	TOO MUCH
• Family Activities			
Paying bills	X		
Religious activities			X
Shopping	X		

Once again, this chart is only an example. Here's one of your own to use (and photocopy to re-use, if you'd like!).

TIME-INVESTMENT CHART—PERSONAL ACTIVITIES

ACTIVITY	ENOUGH	TOO LITTLE	TOO MUCH
• **Personal Activities**			
• **Job Activities**			
• **Leisure Activities**			
• **Family Activities**			

When you have completed the list, analyze and evaluate each item. What is your opinion regarding the time investment you make in each activity? Is it enough? Not enough? Too much?

Do A Weekly Time Inventory

To verify the above activities, keep track of everything you do for an entire week, in 30-minute time frames, from the time you get up until you go to bed. Make a real effort to fill this in, every box, every day, for a week.

Why do this? Very few people think about time this much, or follow it this closely. We get used to having one hour just flow into the next, moving from one appointment or activity to another, letting circumstances dictate our pace and schedule. This kind of inventory is the best way to discover what you are really doing with your time, and will help you determine the best choices for how to use your time most effectively. You will probably be surprised at the results! You'll find you're spending much more time on some activities than you imagined, and perhaps a lot less than you think in other areas. That's all the more reason to try it for a week and see for yourself. You'll need at least seven copies of the blank form here to complete a week.

WEEKLY TIME INVENTORY		Day _____		
TIME	DAY 1	DAY 2	DAY 3	DAY 4
6:00 am				
6:30 am				
7:00 am				
7:30 am				
8:00 am				
8:30 am				
9:00 am				
9:30 am				
10:00 am				
10:30 am				
11:00 am				
11:30 am				
12 noon				
12:30 pm				
1:00 pm				
1:30 pm				
2:00 pm				
2:30 pm				
3:00 pm				
3:30 pm				
4:00 pm				
4:30 pm				
5:00 pm				
5:30 pm				
6:00 pm				
6:30 pm				
7:00 pm				
7:30 pm				
8:00 pm				
8:30 pm				
9:00 pm				
9:30 pm				
10:00 pm				
10:30 pm				
11:00 pm				

Review Your Appointments And Regularly Scheduled Meetings

The following is a sample page from an appointment book:

Monday 12:15 Lunch with Tom 7:30 Board Meeting	**Friday** 7:30 Pizza with kids
Tuesday 7:30 Breakfast with Sam	**Saturday** 8:00 Dinner with Smiths
Wednesday 12:30 Lunch with Betty 2:00 Project presentation	**Sunday** 8:00 Plan for week w/Jonathan
Thursday 8:00 Tennis match	

SELF-ASSESSMENT: Appointment and Scheduled-Meeting Review

Directions:
Refer to your calendar, and use the current week, or the most recent "typical" week if this one was unusual, to complete the chart below. Fill in the chart with all the nonwork activities you were involved in for the past week. In addition, if an activity occurred during working hours, but was outside your normal responsibilities, list it on the chart.

Monday	**Friday**
Tuesday	**Saturday**
Wednesday	**Sunday**
Thursday	

Applying The Inventories—Short-Term

Directions:
Once you've had a chance to complete all the forms up to this point in this chapter (remember, it will take seven days to finish the daily inventory sheets for one week), review the forms along with your written goals in Chapter 4. From your seven daily inventory sheets, check off the items that you feel could be associated or identified with specific goals. Put an X beside the items that apparently have nothing to do with your goals.

Then, ask yourself:

1. Did I do things not related to my goals?

2. Which activities were time-wasters that could be eliminated?

3. Are there any "hidden" goals I noticed and want to add to my list?

4. What activities could be reduced, eliminated or delegated?

5. Were these activities I wanted to do, or things someone else wanted me to do?

Applying The Inventories—Long-Term

Directions:
Set aside a week each year and re-take this inventory. Make it the same week each year, if possible, or at least around the same time period each year. You might want to use a recurring week that would remind you to do this each year, such as the last week of your organization's fiscal year or the first full week of the calendar year. Expect your goals to change from year to year. It's truly a process. To be effective, you must continually set your goals, review your priorities, make your plans, and then start putting all you've committed to into action.

You will find an improvement in your effectiveness after making a conscious effort at prioritizing. Bad habits will be readily uncovered and can be eliminated before they become too deeply entrenched.

Practice using these planning tools—they will give you a great chance of developing beneficial habits.

> **"THE CHAINS OF HABITS ARE TOO WEAK TO BE FELT UNTIL THEY ARE TOO STRONG TO BE BROKEN."**
> **– Samuel Johnson**

Another Very Important Question

- Is there a way I can:
    a. Standardize this?
    b. Delegate this?
    c. "Batch" this?

This question represents a real *organizing* tool.

> **"ORGANIZING IS WHAT YOU DO BEFORE YOU DO SOMETHING, SO THAT WHEN YOU DO IT, IT'S NOT ALL MIXED UP."**
> **– Christopher Robin (the A. A. Milne character)**

In doing something (anything!) ask yourself these questions:

- Is this something I've done before? Likely to do again?

- If I could take time now to set up a format I could use over again, would it be a good idea?

- Could I put it in such form that other people could use it, too?

- If it's a written document, is now the time to create once and forever a "boiler-plated" version that could be used many times in the future?

Before you start something is the time to decide whether or not the task can be delegated. There's probably no better time than now to teach the process to someone else. The more people who can do

177

anything, the less likely you are to have to do it yourself. In determining whether you should "batch" an activity, decide whether it could be combined with another related project. While you have the materials out, what else requires the same things, e.g., if you have to make a trip to the mailroom, what else could you do as well since you're going to be up and around, anyway?

The A-B-Cs And 1-2-3s Of Priorities

Ranking the activities on your *Daily Action List* with the letters A, B and C is a useful step in setting priorities. In considering each item separately, assign a letter priority as follows:

- "A" priority items are the ones that are urgent. They should have been done yesterday. If they're not done soon, big trouble is around the bend. If they have a specific date for a deadline, it's probably today.

- "B" priority items are still important. They may even have a definite deadline, but these activities are not as critical as the "A" priorities. If one of these items weren't completed today, the world would not come to an end.

- "C" priority items have no time frame. These may even be small and relatively unimportant (perhaps even potential "In-Between" Time activities). Energy and attention need not be devoted to these—at least right now.

In using the A-B-C priority ranking system, you avoid attempting to assign absolute priorities to your projects and activities. Instead, you divide them into the major categories of A-B-C. For practice, here's a sample list of 15 typical goals you might have. Go through these, using the A-B-C technique, and rank them according to your estimate of their relative importance.

WORKSHEET: A-B-C Priority Ranking

PERSONAL GOALS	PRIORITY
1. Read one book per week	
2. Maintain membership on only three committees	
3. Invest 15 minutes daily on Action Plan	
4. Invest 15 minutes daily in inspiration (spiritual, etc.)	
5. Take a class on how to get along with difficult people	
6. Learn to fly an airplane by the end of next summer	
7. Take 10 tennis lessons in the next six months	
8. Compliment at least one person per day	
9. Make contact with a manager from a competitor company	
10. Reorganize work area by the end of the month	
11. Buy a personal calendar and appointment book	
12. Increase daily exercise to lose five pounds next month	
13. Take family members to a favorite restaurant this month	
14. Spend 15 quality minutes daily with my "significant other"	
15. Write a Slight-Edge idea to practice each week	

By the way, it's sometimes a good idea to watch the "C" priorities for a while to see what happens to them. Things don't tend to stay at "C" level. These activities either move up the chart to other letter rankings, or they drop off the list completely—because they resolved themselves, someone else did them or they never really needed to be done, anyway.

There are some activities that don't merit a ranking at all. Remember, just because an activity has been presented to you to complete doesn't mean you're obligated to do it. If something is a complete waste of time, keep it off of your priority chart.

Now that you've had some practice with a sample listing of activities, look at the chart below. Photocopy the chart before you begin writing, so it can be used over and over. First, put your *Daily Action List* on the chart; write in each project or activity you plan to do for the day. Then, consider each item on the list based on the prioritization criteria discussed above and rank each item A, B or C.

WORKSHEET: Personal A-B-C Priority Ranking

DAILY ACTION LIST	PRIORITY
1.	
2.	
3.	
4.	
5.	
6.	
7.	
8.	
9.	
10.	
11.	
12.	
13.	
14.	
15.	

Your *Daily Action List* has just become more useful, because now
you have separated the items into categories of importance. This
will help your decision-making throughout the day because you
recognize what you're doing, and what its relative importance is.

Unfortunately, the ABC Prioritizing System does not tell you what
task to do in what order—which means if you have 15 items, there
might be five A's, five B's and five C's. Since you can only do one
thing at a time, if five items have the same importance, which do
you do first?

Here's where the numbering system comes in. If you do have five
"A" priority items on your list, consider only those five items.
Which one is most important? Even if they are all critically
important, you can only do one at a time, so you must choose which
it will be. When you've determined which one it is, this becomes
your A-1 item.

If there are still more tasks left, choose again: Which is the next
most important item? That becomes A-2. Continue to rank these
until you have assigned a numerical order to all your "A" priority
items. Do the same thing for the "B" and "C" priority items on your
list. But don't delay doing A-1 by taking your time ranking the B's
and C's. When you've done this for all items, rewrite your *Daily
Action List*, this time putting each item in ranked order of
importance (A-1, A-2, A-3, B-1, B-2, etc.).

Now you have your way of determining "What's the best use of my
time right now!" Right? Well, in a sense you do, and you don't.
Since most of us work as well as live with others, there are other
people who'll influence both what should be done and when it
should be done. The solution involves getting these other people—
whether family members or co-workers—to work with you to make
a "group" action list.

You could do this in three ways. Have each person individually
rank all of the goals in A-B-C terms and then compare and discuss
lists. Or, you can take an oral vote on each item as you consider
them together, assigning "A" priority only to those on which there
is total agreement. You could also assign or delegate the priorities
within the group (and with the group's approval) to the best agreed-
on person for the job.

It's not too soon to impress upon you the most important thought concerning all ranking and priorities—the one that makes certain you stay in control. Not someone else, and certainly not the List.

> **ANY PRIORITY LISTING IS ONLY A GUIDE IN HELPING ME MAKE THE RIGHT DECISIONS**

You see, lots of other factors, many of them common sense, enter into play here. It's important that you understand that it is poor management to become a slave to a list! The best list still just gives you information you can assess to come to the right conclusions about what to do, and why.

For example, there's a phone call on your *Daily Action List*. It's short, and may take only ten minutes. It's not the A-1 item on the list. But, if the only time of day your party will be available is between 8:30 and 9:00 this morning, when should you make the call?

Any item on your list is subject to all sorts of other factors besides an absolute-priority ranking. Time, conditions and circumstances (sometimes you just need a "breather") all are part of the decisions. But if you don't know the priority of an item, it's easy to make the wrong choice. That's why the ranking has to come first!

The following Work Action Plan chart is one you'll want to photocopy and use daily—you may even choose to use the chart when making your *Daily Action Plan*. There's room to list the activities of the day (see separate categories) and rank them, first by A-B-C, then by 1-2-3. At the top you can list the top five things you have to do for the day. A nice feature of the chart are the check-off boxes that allow you to check off the items as you complete them.

Work Action Plan

Top Priorities Today

☐ 1.

☐ 2.

☐ 3.

☐ 4.

☐ 5.

Activities	Rank	Best Time
☐ Call		
•		
•		
☐ Write		
•		
•		
☐ Meet		
•		
•		
☐ Analysis		
•		
•		

The "Best Time" column can also be used in a number of ways: (1) you can list the energy levels—High, Medium or Low—required to do each task and perform it according to your energy curves; (2) you can assign specific times of day to each item (like the phone call in the illustration); or (3) you can estimate how long each activity should require to ensure a realistic *Daily Action List*.

Naturally, you're going to have some days when everything is a top priority—when you believe you couldn't possibly choose one task over another as more important, or when you've started on the most important task of the day, then something "more important" comes up.

Obviously, you can't do ten things at once. You must be focused and directed. It reminds us of another one of Moe Schaeffer's sayings:

> **YOU CAN'T CATCH ONE HOG**
> **IF YOU'RE CHASING TWO**

Simple, profound and true again. If you want to get one thing done, then pursue only it. Do this one at a time, and soon you'll have "caught" all the loose hogs.

SUSAN: I was recently driving down Interstate 5 in southern Orange County, California, enroute to San Diego late on a Sunday night. The traffic in that section was heavy, as Southern California traffic always is, but was moving fast. I was driving in the left lane of the freeway at the same speed as all the other traffic in that lane—about 70 MPH.

I couldn't believe it when the car behind me turned on its flashing lights to pull me over to the side! The police officer walked up to my car, told me how fast I was going, and issued a speeding ticket to me.

I thought this was extremely unfair, because I had been traveling at the same speed as all the other traffic out on the road that night. Sure, we were all above the 55 mph limit, but I had to drive as fast as the others to stay in the flow.

When the officer handed me my ticket, I asked him, "Why did you pick me to pull over and ticket? Didn't you see that everybody was going the same speed?"

I'll never forget what he said to me:

> **"LADY, I CAN STOP ONLY ONE CAR AT A TIME!"**

What a marvelous lesson in priority management! And it only cost me $96.00 to learn it!

> **THE DIFFERENCE BETWEEN SAGES AND FOOLS IS THEIR CHOICE AND USE OF THEIR TOOLS**

An excellent way to focus your energy and thinking involves using the Priority Indicator. This indicator was developed for use as a counseling tool for people who had been through a substance-abuse program and were ready to return to the outside world. One of the biggest problems these people had was an inability to make decisions. Many, many choices faced them, and most were ill equipped to make good choices. Compounding the matter was that many of these individuals even had difficulty distinguishing the trivial from the important. In order to help them in decision-making, the Priority Indicator was designed. But its best use, by far, is with lists of things to do, when the items are all of seemingly equal importance. This "forced-choice" indicator forces a choice to be made between options. What's nice about it is that no matter how many items are being considered, one need choose between only two at a time.

The Priority Indicator has two parts: On the left, there's a series of numbered blanks. This tool can be used with as few as three items to a virtually unlimited number (in a while we'll tell you a trick you can use in case the list is too long). All the items from the list go in these blanks, in no particular order (that's what the tool itself will determine). On the right, there is a series of numbers, ever increasing in size. The numbers are considered in groups of two—the one number over the other in each case.

Looking at the illustration below, suppose you did have five items on your list, and each one seemed to be A-1 in importance:

- A report that was due yesterday

- A phone call to a client who is very unhappy about something

- Planning and developing a departmental budget for the upcoming year

- Developing of a marketing letter concerning a new product to accompany your mailing list

- Monthly receipts to be posted and deposited

Priority Indicator

Topic	Scale			
Report				
Phone Call	①			
	2			
Budget	①	2		
	3	③		
Marketing Letter	1	2	3	
	④	④	④	
Receipts	1	2	3	④
	⑤	⑤	⑤	5

My A-1 priority for tomorrow is __Marketing Letter__

The five items are listed in the illustration and numbered in the same sequence we have described them above. The circled numbers in the example correspond to the following choices.

First, there is no group of numbers next to #1. You can't compare something with itself! Next to #2, the numbers 1 over 2 tell us to compare only #1 and #2 with each other. Don't worry about anything else on the list. Just ask yourself: "Which is more important—1 or 2?" Circle the number you chose. In the example, we chose #1, the report, over #2, the phone call.

Then, move on to #3. This time there are two sets of numbers off to the right, because now you have two choices. You will compare #1 with #3 and choose which one is more important, then compare #2 with #3, again circling your choice in each instance. We chose #1 when we compared it to #3, and selected #3 when we compared it to #2. Next to #4 are three sets of numbers: 1 and 4, 2 and 4, 3 and 4. Make each comparison and circle your selections. You can see our choices in the illustration.

Next to #5 are four sets of numbers, because you must compare this new item with everything else already on the list. After you've made these four choices (by circling, as we did), the selection is finished.

The final step, once all choices have been made, is to go back and count how many times you circled each number on the right hand side and write that total on the lines to the left of each number. The one you circled most often (in this case, four times) is your true #1 priority item. The remaining items can be ranked in priority order based on frequency of selection, and the one you chose the least times (none) is last on the list. In our illustration, we determined, by counting how many times we circled each selection, that the marketing letter was the most important of the five activities we compared.

This doesn't necessarily mean the #1 priority item is the one you're going to work on first! Don't forget, any ranking like this is only meant to be used as a guide. Other outside factors and your own common sense will help you answer, "What's the best use of my time right now?"

WORKSHEET: The Priority Indicator—Practice

_____ _____   1. _____

_____ _____   2. _____ $\frac{1}{2}$

_____ _____   3. _____ $\frac{1}{3}$ $\frac{2}{3}$

_____ _____   4. _____ $\frac{1}{4}$ $\frac{2}{4}$ $\frac{3}{4}$

_____ _____   5. _____ $\frac{1}{5}$ $\frac{2}{5}$ $\frac{3}{5}$ $\frac{4}{5}$

_____ _____   6. _____ $\frac{1}{6}$ $\frac{2}{6}$ $\frac{3}{6}$ $\frac{4}{6}$ $\frac{5}{6}$

_____ _____   7. _____ $\frac{1}{7}$ $\frac{2}{7}$ $\frac{3}{7}$ $\frac{4}{7}$ $\frac{5}{7}$ $\frac{6}{7}$

_____ _____   8. _____ $\frac{1}{8}$ $\frac{2}{8}$ $\frac{3}{8}$ $\frac{4}{8}$ $\frac{5}{8}$ $\frac{6}{8}$ $\frac{7}{8}$

_____ _____   9. _____ $\frac{1}{9}$ $\frac{2}{9}$ $\frac{3}{9}$ $\frac{4}{9}$ $\frac{5}{9}$ $\frac{6}{9}$ $\frac{7}{9}$ $\frac{8}{9}$

_____ _____ 10. _____ $\frac{1}{10}$ $\frac{2}{10}$ $\frac{3}{10}$ $\frac{4}{10}$ $\frac{5}{10}$ $\frac{6}{10}$ $\frac{7}{10}$ $\frac{8}{10}$ $\frac{9}{10}$

_____ _____ 11. _____ $\frac{1}{11}$ $\frac{2}{11}$ $\frac{3}{11}$ $\frac{4}{11}$ $\frac{5}{11}$ $\frac{6}{11}$ $\frac{7}{11}$ $\frac{8}{11}$ $\frac{9}{11}$ $\frac{10}{11}$

_____ _____ 12. _____ $\frac{1}{12}$ $\frac{2}{12}$ $\frac{3}{12}$ $\frac{4}{12}$ $\frac{5}{12}$ $\frac{6}{12}$ $\frac{7}{12}$ $\frac{8}{12}$ $\frac{9}{12}$ $\frac{10}{12}$ $\frac{11}{12}$

_____ _____ 13. _____ $\frac{1}{13}$ $\frac{2}{13}$ $\frac{3}{13}$ $\frac{4}{13}$ $\frac{5}{13}$ $\frac{6}{13}$ $\frac{7}{13}$ $\frac{8}{13}$ $\frac{9}{13}$ $\frac{10}{13}$ $\frac{11}{13}$ $\frac{12}{13}$

_____ _____ 14. _____ $\frac{1}{14}$ $\frac{2}{14}$ $\frac{3}{14}$ $\frac{4}{14}$ $\frac{5}{14}$ $\frac{6}{14}$ $\frac{7}{14}$ $\frac{8}{14}$ $\frac{9}{14}$ $\frac{10}{14}$ $\frac{11}{14}$ $\frac{12}{14}$ $\frac{13}{14}$

_____ _____ 15. _____ $\frac{1}{15}$ $\frac{2}{15}$ $\frac{3}{15}$ $\frac{4}{15}$ $\frac{5}{15}$ $\frac{6}{15}$ $\frac{7}{15}$ $\frac{8}{15}$ $\frac{9}{15}$ $\frac{10}{15}$ $\frac{11}{15}$ $\frac{12}{15}$ $\frac{13}{15}$ $\frac{14}{15}$

If you've completed your practice worksheet, you probably now know that it is still possible for more than one item to be ranked in the same priority. So what should you do? No problem, really. It may be final proof that two or more items are truly equal in importance, and the choice is yours as to how to list them. The longer the list of items you compare, the more likely you are to have some ties.

Incidentally, if you have a three-way tie, it's probably because your choices ended up going around in a circle. You picked #1 over #2, #2 over #3, but then chose #3 over #1. (It's kind of like the game we used to play as children called Rock, Paper and Scissors. Remember it? The rock broke the scissors, the paper covered the rock and the scissors cut the paper.)

Another factor you've probably been wondering about is the number of items that can realistically be compared. The form shows room for 20 items. Is that workable? Good question, and the answer is yes. Obviously, the more items you try to compare at once, the longer your list of numbers and the more choices you'll have to make. Twenty is about our personal limit, however. What we like to do if our list is even longer is to arbitrarily divide the list in two, complete two Priority Indicators, and then take the two rankings and mesh them together.

Something else that may be helpful to note here: When prioritizing items, this system works best if the items are unrelated. We call this Absolute Priority, because one item is in no way dependent on another. There is another kind of prioritizing called Time or Sequential Priority, which is really more like a scheduling technique than a prioritizing tool.

In Time Priority, ranking items isn't necessary because the calendar does it for you, e.g., you'll have your 10 a.m. appointment before the 2 p.m. meeting.

In Sequential Priority, things have to be done in a particular sequence because they are dependent on each other. In construction, you must pour the foundation before you shingle the roof. One is not more important than the other, but one definitely comes first in the sequence, and your ability to complete one activity is dependent on the completion of the other. The Priority Indicator isn't appropriate for this kind of prioritizing; this is when a PERT or GANTT chart is actually a more useful tool (see next chapter). Information from these tools can also help you establish the most productive work day possible.

Remember, any ranking of priorities is done to give us control over our activities, not vice versa. And the role of common sense in producing good judgment cannot be overstated. These tools will be helpful any time you need to communicate your priorities to someone else, and can even help you say "no" to someone when your priorities have been established.

Now, before we conclude this chapter, even after all the determining and ranking has taken place, there are still four types of projects we often don't even have to rank: These are automatically top priority!

Throw Away The Charts On These!

If any of the four items that follow shows up on your list, save your paper and your brain power, because there's a good chance they'll automatically become top priority.

1. Your boss's pet project. If your boss is in love with a certain project, better put it on the top of your list, too. There's probably not much sense arguing about it; you'll normally end up having to do it anyway.

EVEN IF THE BOSS IS WRONG,

THE BOSS IS ALWAYS RIGHT!

---

2. Something you've never done before (with potentially far-reaching outcome or consequences). If you're headed off into uncharted territory, there'll be a lot of questions that you won't have the answers to. Do you know how much time it's really going to take? Do you know all the materials or information you're going to need to complete this job? Are you certain you won't need someone else's help on part of it? Do you know all the obstacles you will encounter? Is this project within your ability to complete?

Since you won't always know the answers to these questions, this activity will require lots of attention and will possibly become top priority. Plus, this could be something your organization has never done before—truly unique, and a way to really increase your value as an employee.

3. A high-visibility project. Have you just taken on an assignment that will really put you in the spotlight when you successfully complete it? Will this look absolutely fabulous on your resumé? Will this facilitate a promotion or a raise? Or, if you fall on your face on this one, will everybody see it? High visibility is often accompanied by high risk: Will this very thought scare you into keeping this project on the top line? Then make this project top priority.

4. Anything vital to the needs of your customers, peers or subordinates. If you work in a customer-oriented business or job, you know that if you don't take care of the person paying your bills, you won't have a job for long. But for nearly all of us, there are people within our organization who sometimes depend on us for contributions only we can make. If you've committed yourself to one of these, it belongs at the top of your list.

It doesn't make much sense for your subordinates to be twiddling their thumbs working on "C" priority activities because they're waiting for you to finish your part of their "A" priority project. If someone else needs it, raise its priority accordingly.

The four project categories that automatically take top priority represent a real safeguard for your job and continually test your "political" savvy in the workplace. In Harvey Mackay's best-seller, *Beware of the Naked Man Who Offers You His Shirt*, the author counsels:

- Do what it takes to set you apart from the crowd.

- Make them need you.

- Always do more than you visibly promise.

- Make the boss right, and you'll never be wrong.

The good news regarding the automatic top-priority categories is that by sensibly placing these things in the correct priority, you make yourself invaluable to your organization. And, because of your consistent, visible ability to manage and organize your priorities, you will have the opportunity to say "no" even more often than before.

191

Making It Work

CONCERN	REASON	STRATEGY
you try an idea ,but it doesn't work	lack of commitment	realize a commitment is to **do** something, not just try
difficulty determining importance of activity	no way to measure	use the measurement tools in this chapter to determine priority for whatever you do

Putting It To Work

• Making a commitment to do something, rather than just trying to do something, is the key to accomplishing what you want.

• Applying the 80-20 Rule to priorities, you can be 80 percent successful by achieving only 20 percent of your goals.

• To be productive, work on things in ranked priority order.

• Considering the numbers in the Key Functions chart will give you many insights into yourself and where you put your energy at work.

• Getting things done first means making a commitment to plan, organize and prioritize.

• By comparing what you actually do with the goals you have set, you can determine if your energy is pointed in the right direction.

• Recording and studying your activities for a period of time can be very insightful in showing your effectiveness, or lack of it.

• Look for ways to standardize, delegate or batch regular activities for better organization and control.

- Ranking your priorities will help you in decision-making throughout the day, as well as help you determine the most productive use of your time at any given moment.

- Never surrender control to your priority list. It's only a guide.

- Two great habits of self-management is finishing the things you start, and handling a thing only one time.

- Doing a forced-choice priority indicator will provide you with an absolute priority ranking.

- If your boss is in love with a project, you'd better be, too.

- If you've never done something before, its unknown characteristics make it top priority.

- Put any project with high visibility (and high risk) at the top of your list.

- Remember the needs of your customers, peers and subordinates when ranking the activities on your own list.

Check Your Working Knowledge Of Priorities

1. Why is it not good enough to "try" to do something?

2. How can you be 80 percent effective on your job?

3. What were the two most important insights you gained from the Key Functions chart? How are you going to apply those insights? When?

4. Have you committed yourself to goals for analyzing your activities and time usage for greater future productivity?

5. What personal activities did you determine you were spending too little time doing? Too much time?

6. When are you going to do your Weekly Time Inventory?

7. What are some activities on your job you could standardize? Delegate? "Batch"?

8. What is your A-1 project for tomorrow? When is the best time to do this? (Review Chapter 3 if you're not sure.)

9. Why should you never allow a priority list to control you?

10. Why should a high-visibility project be top priority?

11. Why could something you've never done before be top priority?

12. Will you commit yourself to applying the charts in this chapter until their daily completion becomes a habit? When will you begin?

MY SLIGHT-EDGE IDEAS FROM CHAPTER 8:

_____

_____

_____

_____

_____

_____

_____

_____

Tracking Priorities With Flow Charts

- **PERTing your way to success**
- **Backwards is better!**
- **Getting your feet wet**
- **Early warnings**
- **Planning projects involving multiple steps and people**
- **The worksheet**
- **Determining the Critical Path**
- **GANTT (bar) charts**
- **Which chart should you use?**
- **Benefits of flow charts**
- **Keep smiling!**

Imagine you're a scientist working with NASA on the Space Shuttle program. You are the person responsible for planning the next launch. You have all of NASA, its suppliers and resources at your disposal. Any person you ask will do exactly what you want him or her to do. You don't actually have to do any work yourself on the project. You're responsible for only one thing: Developing and implementing a plan covering all the steps that must take place before the launch date.

Sound like an easy job? How many factors do you think you'll have to consider? Let's see, there's the weather. The orbits of the satellites your shuttle is going to connect with several thousand miles over the earth. The selection and training of the astronauts. The experiments that will be conducted during the flight. The landing site, the people and equipment that need to be there. The actual rockets that will launch the shuttle spaceward. You'll need to take care of the newspeople who will report on the event . . . and controlling the crowds of spectators. Is the job big enough for you yet?

Of course, these factors only scratch the surface of the literally thousands of steps and thousands of people (millions of hours) who'll have to work on the project, in complete coordination, so that everything comes together at one time and the launch is a complete success. If you're ready to turn in your resignation before this job even starts, you'll understand why the world owes the space program a debt of gratitude for the flow charts and tracking processes that were developed to enable just that kind of activity to take place successfully.

Self-Quiz: Where Am I Now?
A Flow-Charts Quiz

Read the statements that follow and circle the number that best describes your response: (3) agree; (2) not sure; (1) disagree:

• I currently know the status of all my projects	3	2	1
• It's easy to communicate jobs and deadlines to others	3	2	1
• If a project falls behind, I know it right away	3	2	1
• If a project falls behind, I know why it happened	3	2	1
• If I have time problems, I always know well in advance	3	2	1
• I regularly use flow charts in planning projects	3	2	1
• I usually think backwards when I plan out a project	3	2	1
• I build a cushion in my schedules to allow for emergencies	3	2	1

What it means:
19 or more: Pass the big jobs your way!
18-13: With a little luck, you often get it done, and on time.
less than 13: People shouldn't put their hopes or money on you!

How The PERT Process Began

The PERT chart owes its beginnings to the Polaris missile program of the mid-1950s. The basic concepts devised by some brilliant minds at that time are now used by people everywhere, in all walks of life. By the end of this chapter, you will be able to use these concepts, too.

When multiple projects have to take place, involving multiple steps and people, you can turn to the information presented here to bring it all under control. Once you learn it, it's not only productive, it's fun! Let's begin.

A Simple PERT Introduction

PERT is an acronym that stands for "Program Evaluation and Review Technique," the lengthy name originally applied by the Polaris scientists to their tracking process.

A PERT chart, even the most simple one, involves four elements:

- **Circles**—in which completed activities are written

- **Lines**—showing the direction of progress and indicating work in progress but not yet completed

- **Dates**—completion targets, i.e., deadlines

- **Names**—of people to whom various responsibilities have been delegated

There's one other element that distinguishes the PERT chart from other methods of planning:

WITH *PERT*,
IT'S BETTER TO THINK BACKWARDS!

Not only does this process offer us new methods of presenting the planning we have done, it forces us into a new thinking pattern as well!

In a typical planning process, we ask ourselves "Where am I now?" and then proceed to think in a step-by-step sequence until we eventually reach the end. PERT reverses the process. In PERT we ask:

> **"WHAT PRIOR ACTIVITY OR ACTIVITIES MUST BE COMPLETED BEFORE THIS ACTIVITY CAN BEGIN?"**

We continue to ask this question for every activity, in effect, doing our thinking in reverse.

The principle is more logical than it might sound at first. For example, have you ever watched professional golfers on television? Golfers nearly always think backwards (good golfers, that is). A professional golfer approaches the tee to play a par-5 hole (one in which the target is to play in five strokes or fewer). These are the longest holes on the course (which is why more strokes are required). But, to a pro, the long holes always represent the best chance to go under par, to play the hole in four strokes (a "birdie") instead of five.

Before that golfer ever hits the ball, a backwards thought process occurs first. "Where is the flag located on the green today?" Then: "Where should my ball land on that green to give me the best chance of a reasonable putt into the hole on my fourth stroke?"

Once that question is answered: "Where does my ball need to end up on the fairway to give me the best approach shot (the third stroke) to that part of the green? Where does my second shot need to be hit from if that's where I want the approach shot to be? What club do I need, and how should I drive the ball off the tee, to put myself in that position?"

So, backwards thinking really does work! There are some other advantages, as well:

- Thinking backwards makes you work a little harder—and concentrate more.

- Sometimes you can see things going backwards that you miss going the other way. Kind of like the highway patrol car behind the billboard. You can't see it going one way, but it's pretty obvious going in the other direction.

> JONATHAN: I spent six years as the editor of the National Collegiate Athletic Association's (NCAA) rules and guide books for college sports. That was where I first became familiar with the PERT process.
>
> We discovered (and applied) PERT for two major reasons: We published 26 books annually, and they came out at different times of the year. On any given day, between 15 and 20 of these books were at some stage of production. PERT was the only way we could track them all, stay on top of our tight publication schedules, and keep small tasks from slipping through our fingers.
>
> In addition, we required input from a lot of sources for our books. Each rules book had a rules committee for that sport that met yearly to discuss and make rules changes and forward the changes to us for publication in the next year's edition. We had lots of trouble getting the changes back from the rules secretaries on time, because their thinking was, "If this book isn't coming out until October, why do you have to have the changes in June?"
>
> The PERT charts we made supplied the visual evidence we needed to show the committees just how many other steps were involved in production, and how long each step took. Only then did we get the full cooperation we needed!

Try Something Easy First

For most of us, a simple illustration can get us started here; then we'll graduate to one that is a little more complex.

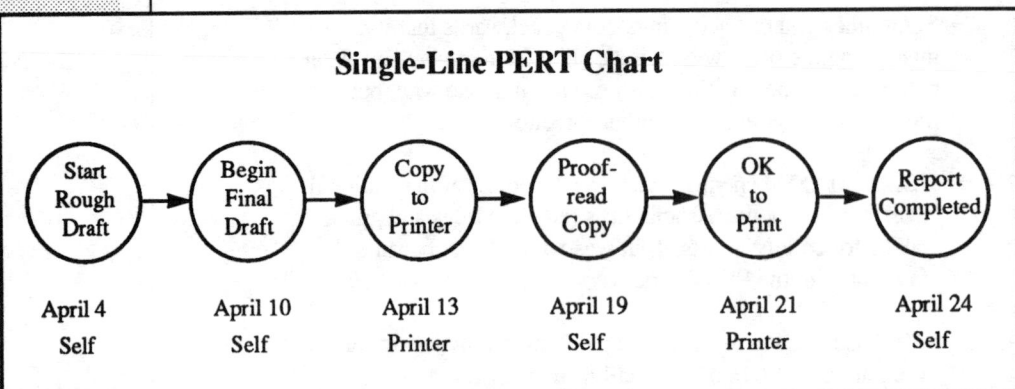

The first illustration is a single, straight-line chart. It is made up of only one series of steps leading to a completed project, each one taken in order with nothing happening elsewhere. The diagram you see above already has the information filled in. This project is a report, with a deadline date of April 24. The last step, the right-hand circle, is labelled: "Report Completed." The deadline is shown, and we've indicated ourselves ("self") as the person responsible for this step.

How did we get all the rest of the information? By working through the project backwards. The question you always want to ask is: "In order for this step to be accomplished, what had to happen just before that?"

This particular report, we decided, is so important we'll secure the best production help available. We're going to have the copy professionally typeset and printed, and thus, the last step before completion reads: "OK to Print," meaning we've given the typesetter permission to proceed with printing the final manuscript. We delegated the printing to the printing company, of course, and the company informed us it needs three days after getting the typeset manuscript to provide us with the finished product. Therefore, the date for giving this "OK to Print" must be no later than April 21 (still leaving us three days to get it on the 24th when we need it).

What had to be done before we could give the press OK? Possibly a lot of things, but we've simplified this example down to

"Proofread the Copy." We delegated this step to ourselves, once again, and determined it will take two days to complete this step. Therefore, our starting date for this activity must be no later than April 19.

As you can see, the only completion date on the PERT chart is the final date at the right end. All the other dates are "start" dates. You can infer from this that the completion date for the previous step is the same as the start date for the next step!

We know the dates we're using are going to cross over weekends. To make it easier, we'll assume no weekends and all working days.

Once again, thinking in reverse, what has to happen before we can start proofreading? Well, at some time the copy has to be typeset so we CAN proofread. Let's call that the previous step, to be done by the printer, who told us to allow six days for this step. This means, as you see, the copy must go to the printer (the start date) no later than April 13.

The copy has to be written. Do you think we ought to have two drafts? We did, which is why the next step to the left reads: "Begin final draft." We allowed three days for finishing the final draft. We must begin, therefore, on April 10.

Finally, before the final draft can begin, there's going to be a rough draft. We've estimated six days to do this. We have to start on April 4 to reach our deadline of April 24 for the finished product.

We now have this entire project broken down into a straight line of six steps, each with a starting date and a person responsible assigned to the step. Does this look like it would work? Does it seem reasonable?

Two interesting points here. Suppose we were to put our plans for this report down on paper as we have done, working our way back to the start date and determining we needed to start on April 4, but then find that today is April 6. Would you call this "a time problem"? We would. But there's very good news. We found out that we had a time problem at the very beginning of the project. Unfortunately, we usually discover a time problem at the very end.

If we knew about it right away, wouldn't we have many more options available to us in overcoming this time problem? What could we do today to make up the two lost days in the schedule? Could we delegate out some more work? Could we delay some other project to give us more time on this one? If we got more help, would that make a difference? Could we go to the person who will receive this report and get a two-day extension?

So, even when you have a problem, it's easier to overcome if you've done this kind of planning up front.

Another important thought: Be realistic. Do yourself a favor, in fact, and even try to build a little extra time into your plan. It's frustrating when the first time things don't go as they should you end up in time difficulties, so add some cushion into your plan.

Now for some personal practice to get familiar with the process. Using the blank form below, think of a project you recently completed, or need to finish, that represents basically a single straight line of steps that you have control over (try to think of a small project, with six or fewer steps). Work from right to left, just like we did, and determine in each case what "had to happen first" before your next step could be taken. Estimate some time lines here and indicate the names for any delegated tasks (if you wouldn't handle a step yourself). It's not important that you use all six circles; just use whatever you need.

Worksheet: PERT—Personal Project

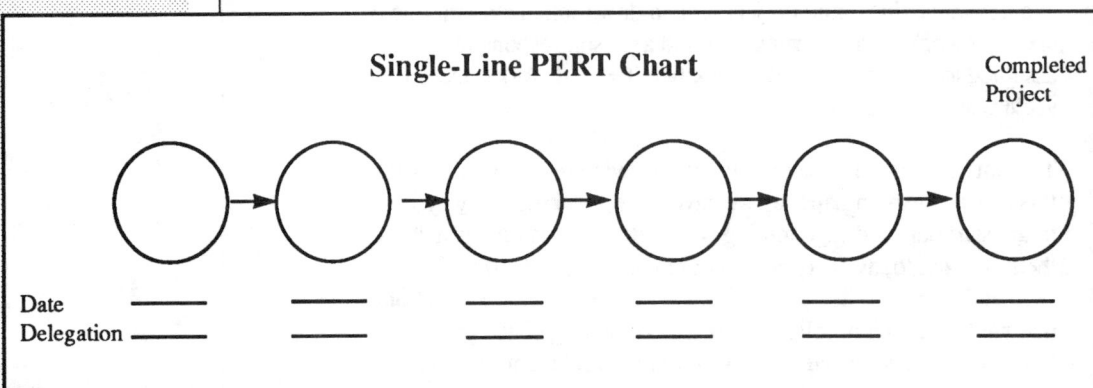

Time To Move On To A Bigger Project

For our next example, we'll use the production cycle of one of the books published by the NCAA: Official NCAA Ice Hockey Guide. This was a combination of two books, actually: The playing rules and a fan publication containing schedules, records, stories and photographs. Once again, the information is already filled in so you can see the steps we'll describe here. Also, although we worked the planning process through from right to left once again, it is easier to explain going the other direction, so that's the way we'll go.

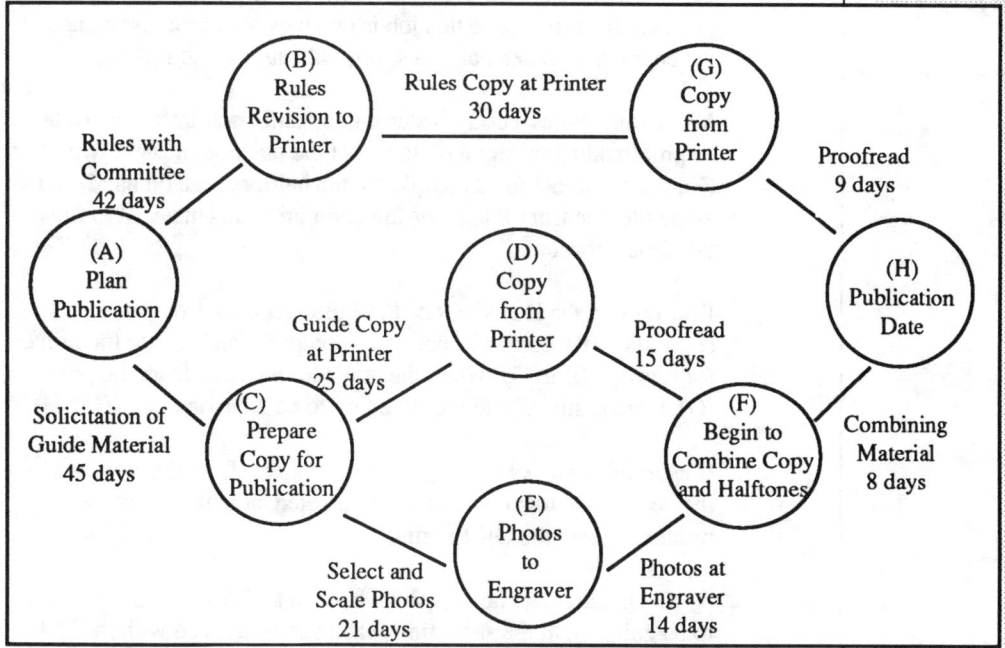

The first project deadline given was the publication date (H on the diagram): The book always had to be out by late September because officials' clinics were held then and the season began by early November.

On the left end is the planning time (A) for the publication. We already know the rules will make up half the book, so our first step was to make up workbooks for the committee to use at its annual rules meeting (this occurs along the line running from A to B, where changes to the rules will be made).

Next time you have a meeting, ask everyone to bring two ideas to make their department more productive or ideas for helping the company as a whole. It makes the meeting more productive and encourages people to think.

In the meantime, we must send out mailings to solicit all the other material for the Guide part of the book. From each member school we need last year's records, next year's schedule, photos, preseason prospects, etc. This process is going on along the line from A to C.

Finally we reach a deadline for information, after which we will not be able to use material (C). Once that deadline is reached, we begin to prepare copy to send it to the printer (C to D).

While the printer has the copy, however, there's still a lot to be done. We can begin selecting and scaling the photographs to use in the book (C to E). Once this job is done, we will send the photos to the engraver to make halftones for publication (E to F).

Meanwhile, typeset copy is starting to come back from the printer, so proofreading is begun (D to F). At the junction of these two lines (F), the proofreading is completed, the halftones are on hand, and along the line from F to H we are combining this material to finish the Guide portion.

Don't forget the Rules! Once the Rules get back from the committee (B), copy will need to be prepared and sent to the printer for revision (B to G). When the revisions are back from the printer (G), there is still a little proofreading to be done on these (G to H).

If everything works out as planned, at letter (H) all the elements of the book come together and are completed, at which point the printer is given the OK to print.

As this illustration shows, even when a lot of different things have to be going on at the same time, each can be tracked with the PERT chart.

The PERT Worksheet

Unless you want your PERT chart to be a big, useless mess of lines and circles, it helps to do some preliminary thinking about just what is happening—what steps might occur and which activities must precede each step in the process.

A linear worksheet is a good way to start, because it allows for lapses in thinking and also provides an easy way to assemble the material in a logical order prior to drawing out the PERT chart.

NOTE: Before beginning the following exercise, copy the PERT Worksheet so you can use it again and again.

Exercise: Developing A PERT Worksheet

Directions:
1. At the top of the sheet, write in the name or description of the project you're planning and put today's date (or your anticipated start date) in the blank.

2. At the bottom of the page, write a detailed description of the completed activity—what it will be, what it will look like, or anything that gives you a clear picture of what form this project will take upon completion. If you know the deadline for the project, place it in the blank provided.

3. Complete the "Activity" column by starting your list at the bottom of the page, writing in the final activity required before the project is completed. Then, using the backwards-thinking process, work up the page, listing the activities in reverse order. You may not use all the blanks if your project does not require too many steps. (Remember the question you'll want to keep asking as you plan backwards: "What prior activity or activities must be completed before this activity can begin?")

NOTE: No doubt you'll occasionally overlook some steps, but don't worry. The blanks in the chart are wide enough to allow you to insert other ideas that come to mind later.

4. Start at the top of the list and letter the activities alphabetically along the left side, beginning with "A" as the first activity. If you get through the entire alphabet, continue with "AA," "BB," etc.

5. Fill out the "Preceding Activity" column, again starting at the bottom of the list. Use the letter you have assigned to each activity

to identify it, rather than writing the activity out again. If your thinking has been fairly clear and complete up to this point, much of this step will be easy. For example, if the last activity is "T," probably the activity just above it on the list ("S") would be listed as the preceding activity, and you'd write "S" in the blank. Sometimes more than one activity must precede a specific step (which will be represented by a branch in the PERT chart), so you may write more than one letter in the preceding activity column.

6. Estimate the time required for each activity, and put the number of hours, days or weeks in the "Time" column.

7. When you have completed all parts of the PERT Worksheet, you will be able to take this information to draw a PERT Chart, using lines and circles to show all the activities visually.

PERT Worksheet

PROJECT _____

_____

_____ START DATE _____

_____

ACTIVITY	PRECEDING ACTIVITY	TIME
_____	_____	_____
_____	_____	_____
_____	_____	_____
_____	_____	_____
_____	_____	_____
_____	_____	_____
_____	_____	_____

COMPLETED PROJECT _____

_____

DEADLINE _____

The Critical Path Method (CPM)

The Critical Path Method was developed separately from PERT, but as it is used today, is usually not actually a separate flow chart. Instead, it becomes a part of a PERT chart. The Critical Path is defined as:

> **THE ACTIVITY LINE THROUGH A *PERT* CHART**
> **THAT TAKES THE LONGEST TIME TO COMPLETE**
> **IS THE "CRITICAL PATH" ON YOUR PROJECT**

Considering the example we did earlier (condensed version below), there are actually three ways (paths) by which we can go from A to H, from beginning to end. We can go A-B-G-H, we can go A-C-D-F-H or A-C-E-F-H. By applying the days required for each activity-line segment in each path, we can determine the Critical Path.

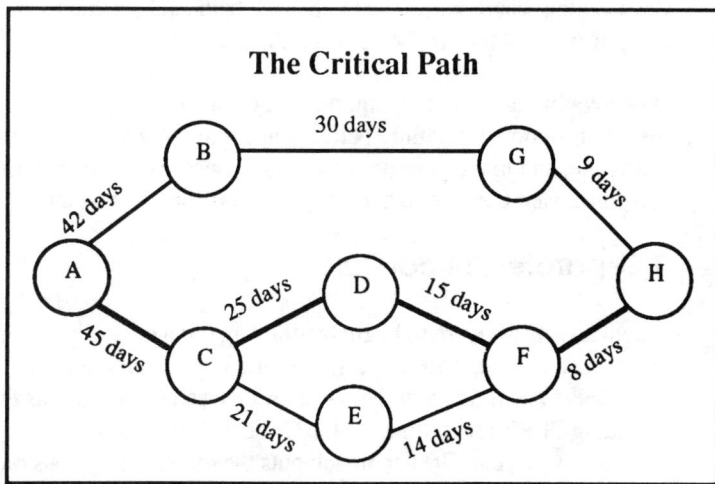

The Critical Path

We've condensed the actual time each of the steps in the chart would take in this simplified version. By adding the segments A-B-G-H, we come up with 81 days. Going A-C-D-F-H totals 93 days, while A-C-E-F-H adds up to 88.

Therefore, in the illustration, the Critical Path is the A-C-D-F-H. We've drawn this line heavier than the others to demonstrate its importance. This is the critical line because we cannot afford to lag behind on this line. Any delay along this line will result in a delay in completion, unless we are able to make up the time later in the project.

If one step along the A-B-G-H path takes a day or two longer than we planned, it's not any real problem, because we had 12 days to spare along this path (this doesn't mean we want to intentionally waste any days, of course). If we suddenly found ourselves 13 days behind on the A-B-G-H path, or 6 days behind on the A-C-E-F-H, it would be a problem. Adding 13 to the original 81 days on A-B-G-H makes 94. Adding six days to the original 88 days on A-C-E-F-H is 94. Either event would mean there is now a different Critical Path, and the completion date will be pushed back if something isn't done.

The Critical Path's most important function is to help you establish your priorities. Any activity along the Critical Path is a high priority. Each day as you complete your 15 Minutes of Planning, any flow charts associated with your activities need to be present. Determining where you stand along each path enables you to assign true priority rankings to the items on the *Daily Action List*.

In developing the Critical Path, please be realistic: A plan with no cushion is doomed to failure before you begin! Try to allow some extra time, and make your time estimates conservative. Remember, you don't want the plan to control you—you control the plan.

A Separate Critical Path

In actuality, if we were to begin by drawing out a critical path only (without an existing PERT chart), we would go about it a little differently. The illustration below shows the same activities as the preceding PERT chart drawn in the Critical Path Method:
As you can see, the CPM approach puts the greatest emphasis on the process of the activities, rather than on the completion of the activities. In the first illustration of the Ice Hockey Guide plan (on page 203), the completion events were listed inside the circles, with deadlines and delegations next to the circles. The lines between the circles represent the particular activity going on, but not yet completed, and we merely added the total number of days between deadlines and indicated them along the lines, to come up with our total days for each path.

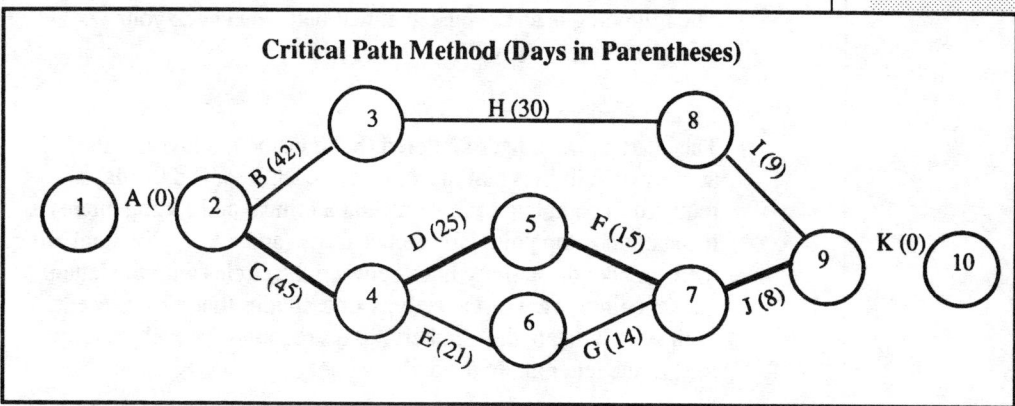

Critical Path Method (Days in Parentheses)

In doing only a Critical Path, then, the major focus is on the activities (not their completion) and how much time each step will take. Therefore, the information we need will appear along the lines, not inside the circles. The circles are numbered only for identification of start or finish events, not for the activity itself (the activities, as you see, are lettered). In addition, there is sometimes the appearance of an "instant" activity (which takes no time) at the merger of various paths along the project.

WORKSHEET—CPM Exercise

ACTIVITY	PRECEDING ACTIVITY	DAYS
A	-	0 (start)
B	A	4
C	A	5
D	A	3
E	D	2
F	C	3
G	E	2
H	B	7
I	H	4
J	F, C	3
K	I, J	0

The following is an exercise that will help you check your understanding of the CPM.

Directions:
The chart shows a list of lettered (but unnamed) activities, the activity or activities that must precede each step, and the days required to complete each. Draw out a critical path, using circles as the start and stop points for each activity (and eventually numbering them). Label the activity lines between the circles with the letters above, being aware of the activity or activities that must precede each step. Indicate the number of days required for each activity next to the letter along the activity line.

When you have finished, determine what the critical path is for this project, and how many days it will take. Also, determine how many "cushion" days you have when following other paths. You'll find the answer to this problem at the end of the chapter.

The GANTT Chart

The GANTT chart, named for its creator, Henry Gantt, also gives us a visual display of activities associated with a project, but presents the information in a different fashion.

Possibly the main weakness of a PERT chart is that the focus is on an activity, rather than a time line. This doesn't mean you can't control time using a PERT chart, but sometimes impending time concerns aren't as clear as you might like them to be. For instance, imagine you're looking at a PERT chart consisting of eight parallel steps at this phase of the project, and today is August 26. How can you identify quickly just what is the most important thing to be working on today? You can usually figure it out, but this is often easier done with a GANTT chart.

The GANTT chart differs from PERT; a GANTT chart is a time line, not an activity line.

Look at the following illustration. As you will see, the GANTT chart is a bar chart in which the separate activities are listed along the left side, with an actual time line across the bottom. This

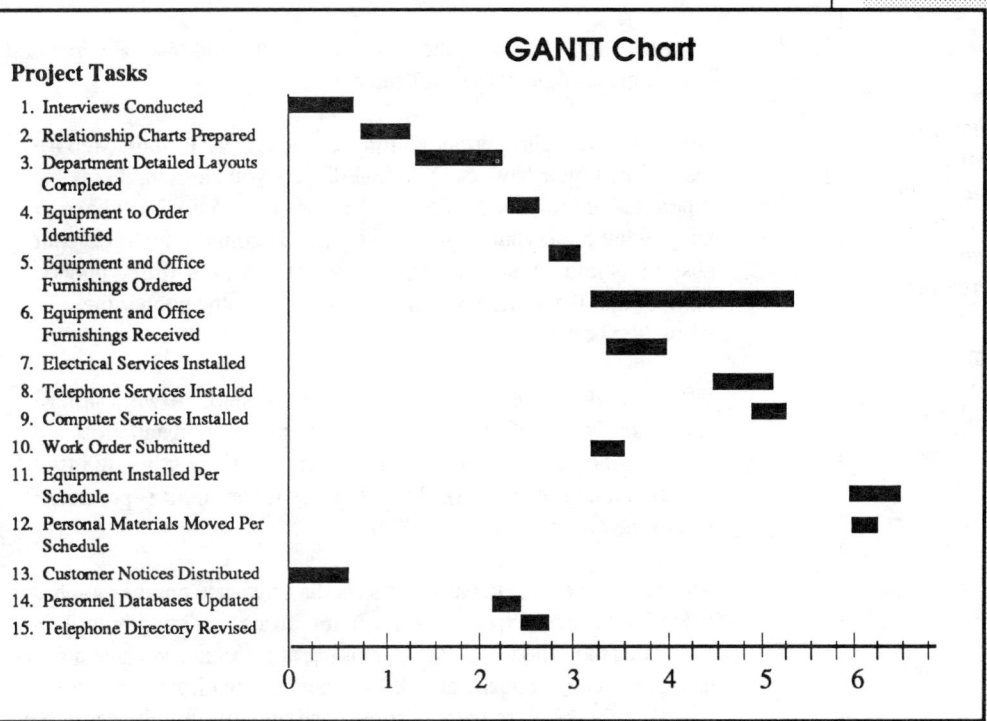

GANTT Chart

Project Tasks

1. Interviews Conducted
2. Relationship Charts Prepared
3. Department Detailed Layouts Completed
4. Equipment to Order Identified
5. Equipment and Office Furnishings Ordered
6. Equipment and Office Furnishings Received
7. Electrical Services Installed
8. Telephone Services Installed
9. Computer Services Installed
10. Work Order Submitted
11. Equipment Installed Per Schedule
12. Personal Materials Moved Per Schedule
13. Customer Notices Distributed
14. Personnel Databases Updated
15. Telephone Directory Revised

particular project (an office relocation), you will note, is planned to take just a little over six weeks to complete.

In doing the plan this way, the many steps are listed. Then bar lines are written in—not only to show exactly how much time each step should take (the length of each line), but to demonstrate exactly when this step needs to occur (the position of the line relative to the time line at the bottom of the graph).

The example here is of a COMPLETED chart, because the bars are solidly filled in. When the GANTT chart is begun, the bars are empty rectangles. They filled in as progress is made.

You can learn much about how this project has been planned, and how realistically, by considering some of the information on the chart. The first six numbered steps seem to represent a series of events, one does not start until the previous step is completed. In analyzing further, you'll see this makes perfect sense; after all, you would want to interview people to learn what they wanted before you could determine who needed to be located next to whom in the new office setup for maximum work flow and communications efficiency. You can't order the equipment until you've decided

211

what to order. (Actually, these first six steps could also be expressed in a single straight-line PERT chart.)

Note a few other important features of the GANTT chart. Step #13 reads "Customer Notices Distributed." As you can see, this is scheduled at the very beginning of the process. You don't have to know what the layout of your new office is going to be to let your customers know you're going to move, your new address, phone number and the anticipated move date. In fact, the sooner they know, the better.

In the middle of the chart are several related steps. A work order is submitted (#10) before the electrician comes in to install electric services (#7). Once electrical services are in, it's possible to install the telephone service (#8). When the phones are in, it is possible to install the computer services (#9).

What if the electrician calls and says that, because another job has taken longer than expected, work in the office can't begin until two days after the scheduled date? Looking at the chart, you see a four-day gap between steps 7 and 8. You can tell the electrician you're still all right, because there is some cushion built into the chart. You might not tell the electrician there are four days, only that you're adding one day to the completion date.

Likewise, at the very end, there is another four-day gap during the sixth week when apparently nothing is scheduled. Great planning! This is to allow for some unexpected delays that still won't affect the actual completion date for the project (which, because of the termination of the old lease, might be inflexible).

By the way, you may not actually want to show this slack time in any external distribution of this flow chart. Work has a tendency to expand to fill the time available, so even though there are four extra days scheduled in here, it may be unwise to show this cushion to others.

With a GANTT chart as part of a daily planning session, you have clear pictures of just where you are on the calendar and where you need to be based on the project you're undertaking. On any given day, the bar lines will be empty, filled or partially filled depending on what has actually been done. In determining what's the most important priority for the day, it may well be the one that has fallen slightly behind schedule, particularly if the other steps are progressing well.

Quality is not costly. It is less expensive to get things done right the first time than to set up a system that checks for errors after the fact.

Once again, the flow chart's visual information helps in decision-making as we plan our day!

The GANTT chart is not without its drawbacks, which is why it's not used as often or as widely as PERT. While it is excellent at demonstrating the time orientation of activities, it simply does not do a very good job of showing how the activities relate to each other in terms of what will precede or follow a specific activity on the chart.

In addition, changes on the GANTT chart are much more difficult to include once the chart has been completed. The effects of missed deadlines or unforeseen activities cannot be easily incorporated. A PERT chart can be easily modified because the dates and time lines are not the critical function of the chart.

Which Chart Should I Use?

Good question! Which one seems to be more comfortable for you? Which chart will better communicate to others the priorities and deadlines? Which one works best for your kind of projects and activities? Perhaps the answer will be both charts. Most project-management software available today is capable of giving us the information in either form. And, depending on who might be using the chart and why, maybe both are better than either one.

An electrical engineer attending our workshop one day told us his company used both charts. They would use a PERT chart in making proposals and selling their clients, because it gave such a clear picture for someone outside the daily activity of the project. But, they used the GANTT chart internally for their own planning, scheduling and communication.

Summary Of Advantages—
PERT And GANTT Charts

PERT Chart:

- Clearly shows relationships between activities
- Easily understood by someone outside the project

- Deadlines and delegations can be specifically indicated next to each step

- Critical Path may be easily identified and shown for planning and prioritizing

GANTT Chart:

- Time line at bottom shows relative length of project activities

- Empty bar lines can be filled in to indicate progress to date

- Unscheduled time readily identifiable if needed to be used

- Vertical line representing current date clearly shows potential problems

The Benefits Of Flow Charts

We've alluded to some of the real advantages of these planning methods throughout the text—the benefits are numerous and touch on many areas of work and relationships.

In summary, PERT, CPM and GANTT charts:

- **Show the interrelation of activities.** A picture is truly worth thousands of words. As you (or anyone else) can see, graphic techniques help others visually understand why a certain step is important and how it relates to other aspects of your project. Without a flow chart, it is often very difficult to explain the necessity of a certain step or time line.

- **Aid in communicating with others.** The importance and value of dates and delegations is underscored by the flow chart. Once people see how they are part of an entire picture, they're more likely to understand why it's necessary for them to complete their portion of the project within the deadline they've been given.

One of the best communications benefits of flow charts occurs when you have a peer or superior who comes up with great last-minute ideas like "How about pushing the completion date for this project up by one week?" Don't argue, but don't accept! Immediately get out your flow chart and use it to communicate what needs to be said. If the new deadline is important enough, what other concessions need to be made? What other project needs to be delayed? "I'll be happy to get this done seven days earlier, if you can help me figure out where I can make up the time." This is an opportunity to negotiate with clear and open communication.

Other benefits of using flow charts are:

- **Flow charts help you keep track of large projects with many steps.** It's very difficult for anything to be overlooked when it's a part of a large plan displayed in a flow chart. Perhaps only one person has the complete plan (and knows all that is going on and who's doing what), but nothing is lost on the master chart.

- **Flow charts help you turn large steps into small ones for delegation.** Perhaps you can't totally turn a phase of a project over to someone else, but as your flow charts divide the project into specific, individual steps, it is often easier to identify particular activities that can be delegated. And, flow charts demonstrate the value of what's being assigned, helping you delegate more effectively as you can show the people you're delegating to just how their part relates to the entire project.

- **Flow charts help you reduce time and cost by identifying trouble spots as they occur.** Never again will you suddenly have to divert large groups of people, or great amounts of money, to deal with unexpected crises. Big problems simply don't sneak up on you with a well-planned (and well-executed) flow chart. You can effectively manage your time, your people and your money in ways you never thought possible!

- **Flow charts give you immediate knowledge of the impact on your deadline.** If a step takes two days longer to complete than planned, you can look at a flow chart and know instantly if this is a problem and, if so, how much a problem it may be. Did the delay occur on your Critical Path? Is the delay creating a new Critical Path? You won't have to guess—you'll know.

Thanks to flow charts, you will never close to the deadline for a project discover you're three weeks behind schedule, and not know how it happened. In fact, when a project is finished, a great wrapping-up step can be to review the entire flow chart, analyze what happened and why, and retain this knowledge to make the next flow chart even more accurate and effective!

215

Computer software that can handle flow charts is abundant and generally very good. Some of the programs we're familiar with include PERT Master, MacProject, InstaPlan, Time Line, Microsoft® Project and AMS Time Machine. The bigger and more complex your plan is, the more useful a computer program can be for you. Your local software store can show you some of the programs available, and will help you try them out to determine the one that is best for you and your computer.

With a program, you can continually update your charts with input as activities are completed and deadlines are met or missed. The revised version is always as clean and neat as the original. Many programs will create a "red flag" as deadlines near or problems develop. Some even use information from multiple flow charts to point out potential problem areas. For example, if, on three different flow charts, you assigned 84 hours of work to one person in one week, some programs will alert you to this problem.

A word of caution: The first few times you develop a flow chart, it may have some weaknesses. If you've never done a certain project before, some of the dates may be guesswork. That's why you can learn so much from flow charts you have finished, and why your ability to plan with accuracy will improve the more you do it.

Practice Your Flow-Charting Skills

To celebrate the birthday of a friend, you have decided to host a dinner in her honor on Saturday night, dinner to be served at 7 p.m. Because you want the gathering to be relaxed and informal, the main course for dinner will be spaghetti. It is now 10 a.m. on Monday.

On the next page develop either a PERT or GANTT chart to plan this event. Do a PERT Worksheet first to identify all the steps required, how long each will take or how much lead time you must allow. At this point no one has been invited. The menu isn't finalized, and you haven't looked in your pantry recently. You want to do something special for the honored guest. Every activity will center upon precisely 7 p.m. Saturday, when at that moment (if your plan works!), everyone will sit down and you will serve the now-prepared food. The hot food is hot and the cold food is cold. Good luck!

NOTE: After you've completed this exercise, turn to the end of the chapter, where we ask you a few questions about your chart and whether you thought to plan for certain steps that were necessary to the success of your event.

A Parting Comment On Planning

To keep a sense of perspective and humor, it may be helpful to have "Clarks' Murphy's Laws" in mind when managing your project.

1. Projects progress quickly to a 90 percent completion factor, and then stay at 80 percent forever.

2. When things are going well, something goes wrong.

3. If the content of the project changes often, the rate of change will always overtake the rate of progress.

4. A poorly planned project will take three times longer to complete than expected; a well-planned project only takes twice as long to complete.

5. Members of the project team will ignore your progress reports because the reports portray the limited progress that has been made.

6. When you know you've thought of everything, you haven't.

Making It Work

CONCERN	REASON	STRATEGY
project not in control	project too big	plan and display it using a flow chart
missing activities	overlooked in planning process	think backwards for better concentration and clarity
difficulty with people not finishing jobs by deadline	haven't bought it, don't understand importance	demonstrate with flow chart relationship of activities
activity falls behind schedule	amount of time not properly estimated	with early warning, use flow chart to negotiate changes
constant pressure to finish steps or project	no float time in flow chart	estimate generously, build cushions into time schedule
flow charts messy and disorganized	steps overlooked or not anticipated when planning	complete PERT worksheet before making flow chart
many activities appear to be top priority	true priorities not known	identify Critical Path of project to know priority
difficulty in seeing time relationships of steps	base of PERT chart is not time, but activity line	develop GANTT (bar) chart to better see time connection

Putting It To Work

- Flow charts were devised to keep track of large, multi-step projects involving many people.

- Thinking backwards is a more effective planning process when using a PERT chart.

- In thinking backwards, always identify the activity or activities that must be completed prior to the beginning of the activity in consideration.

- Include dates and delegations in your PERT chart, so that all relevant information will be on display in the chart.

- Use flow chart information to negotiate for schedule changes or for more assistance.

- Complete a PERT worksheet prior to drawing out your PERT chart for maximum clarity and neatness in the finished diagram.

- Count the number of days required for each possible path from beginning to end of your PERT chart to determine the Critical Path for your project.

- Always make activities along your Critical Path top priority.

- In determining time frames for each activity, estimate conservatively to allow for some cushion if unexpected events slow you down.

- Use a GANTT chart to show the time relationships of activities in your plan.

- Study your flow charts after a project has been completed to learn how to plan the activity more accurately the next time you do it.

Check Your Working Knowledge
Of Flow Charts

1. What are the four elements that make up the PERT chart?

2. Describe a situation (not golf!) where thinking backwards would be advantageous:

3. Why is it not a disaster if you encounter a time problem in a PERT chart?

4. What can keep a PERT chart from totally controlling our schedule?

5. What is the Critical Path of a project? Why is this top priority?

6. What is the value of a PERT worksheet to the planning process?

7. When is a bar (GANTT) chart more helpful than an activity (PERT) chart?

8. Name the six major benefits of using flow charts in the planning process.

MY SLIGHT-EDGE IDEAS FROM CHAPTER 9:

_____

_____

_____

_____

_____

_____

_____

_____

_____

Answer To Critical Path Problem:

The critical path runs A-B-H-I-K, and takes 15 days to complete. Path A-C-F-J-K requires 11 days (four days of cushion). Path A-D-E-G-J-K will take 10 days to complete (with five extra days). See illustration below.

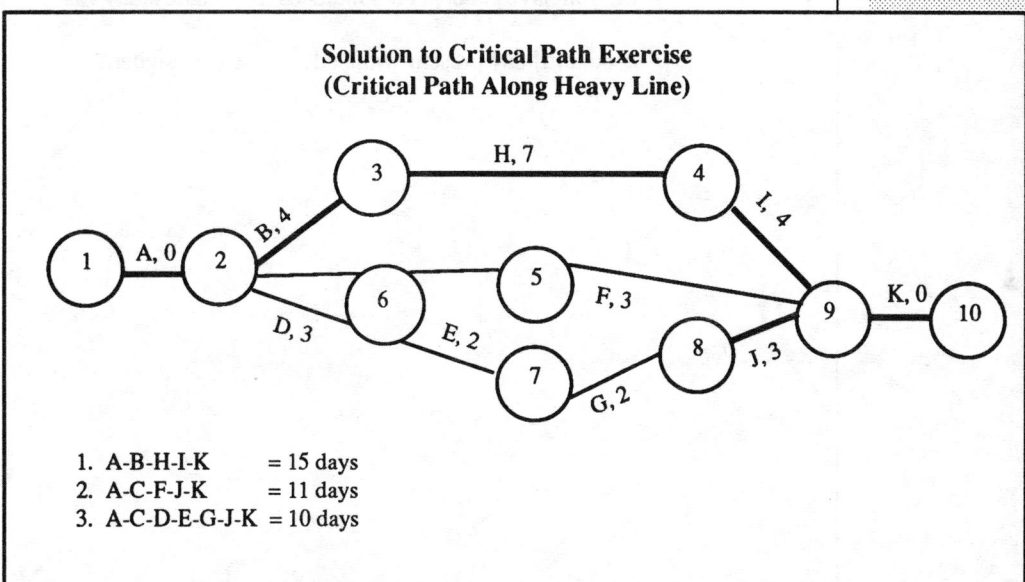

Solution to Critical Path Exercise
(Critical Path Along Heavy Line)

1. A-B-H-I-K   = 15 days
2. A-C-F-J-K   = 11 days
3. A-C-D-E-G-J-K = 10 days

Spaghetti Dinner Exercise

There are many factors that may have become a part of your flow chart. Of course, there are no "right" or "wrong" answers per se, but if something was overlooked, it could prove embarrassing or detrimental to the atmosphere of the evening. Here are a few questions to check how thoroughly your evening was planned:

• Did you consider projects not specifically related to the meal itself, but very important to the success of the evening, such as cleaning the house and getting dressed?

• Did you remember: To set the table? To start water boiling for the spaghetti?

• If it's after dark, did you turn on the outside lights?

• Did you consider seating assignments?

- How will you serve the meal: Family style? Buffet style? Restaurant style?

- Did you decide to have background music? Did you select the music you'll play? Did you turn on the equipment?

- Do you have candles (and matches) for the birthday cake?

- Is the birthday present wrapped? Is the card signed?

Communicating Priorities

- **The Best Defense**
- **Effective listening techniques**
- **Are your words clear, concise, simple and direct?**
- **Being assertive—the key to good communication**
- **Making sure your priorities match your boss's**
- **The 8-minute meeting**
- **Dealing with interrupting bosses**
- **Handling more than one boss at a time**
- **Getting commitment to your plans**
- **One very important question**

If there's a part of priority management that is more difficult to master than effectively communicating priorities and asserting the validity of your own list, we don't know what it is! The better you can be in these areas, the easier life is going to be, the less stress you will have to endure, and the more control you're going to have over your entire situation. The following phrase is taken from sports, but it certainly applies in priority management as well:

THE BEST DEFENSE IS A GOOD OFFENSE!

The 1991 Super Bowl was a perfect illustration of this truism. The New York Giants, through two long time-consuming drives, were able to keep the potent Buffalo Bills' offense off the field for nearly an entire quarter during the game.

If you don't have the ball, you can't score, and if the Giants' offense (through ball control) had been just ten seconds less effective at keeping the Buffalo offense on the sidelines, the Bills could have run one or two more plays and possibly scored, and won. Few Super Bowls live up to the name and the expectations. This one did, and teaches us that valuable lesson of football, life and managing priorities.

To rephrase the defense-offense thought:

IF I HAVE MY OWN PRIORITIES IN ORDER, IT WILL BE EASIER TO PROTECT MY PRIORITIES

Did you ever notice that certain people have almost a "halo" around them all the time? If you really believe somebody is good in an activity and has control, the mystique of that power and control is evident to virtually everyone. The mystique that is associated with people who have effectively planned and prioritized their lives is the same. If others think that you are in control of your schedule and calendar and know exactly what you are doing and why, they probably won't challenge you. Keeping your own priorities and schedule, then, is a matter of protection: Protecting them from less-organized folks who would just as soon share their disorganization with as many people as they can. Do you know somebody like that in your organization? It's even possible that person is your boss.

So, how do you stand strong when others are trying to get you off track? We suggest following this "game plan":

1. Study the priority-management techniques contained in this manual.

2. Apply them until they become a part of you.

3. Develop good, strong self-management habits that allow you to control your own life instead of surrendering control to other people or situations.

Follow this plan, and you'll never lose a game!

This chapter is divided into several subjects, all tied together to improve your communication skills so your priority list belongs to you, and nobody can take it away. We'll discuss the subject of effective listening; clear communication; personal assertiveness to take control; making sure your priorities match your boss's; how to satisfy multiple bosses when you have multiple priorities; how to preserve your own priority list when others try to change it; and how to get others to commit to your plans.

Self-Quiz: Communications Skills

Respond to the statements below, indicating (by circling the appropriate number), whether you agree (3); are not sure (2); or disagree (1) with each statement:

1.	When listening to someone, I always understand what I hear.	3	2	1
2.	I always give lots of verbal feedback when I am listening.	3	2	1
3.	People like to talk to me because I listen so well.	3	2	1
4.	Others tell me how clearly and concisely I speak.	3	2	1
5.	People rarely ask me to clarify something I've said.	3	2	1
6.	I have little trouble getting people to do what I've asked.	3	2	1
7.	It's easy to be assertive when someone tries to use me.	3	2	1
8.	I know my boss's personal mission statement.	3	2	1
9.	At this moment, my priorities match my boss's.	3	2	1
10.	My boss and I meet regularly to go over priorities.	3	2	1
11.	I rarely have a conflict with my boss over what's important.	3	2	1
12.	It's easy to get others to commit to my plans and help me.	3	2	1
13.	I never put something on my "To-Do" list unless I ask "why me?".	3	2	1

Total up your score:

29 or more: You have great communications skills—on to the top!

28-18: You sometimes miscommunicate. Don't worry— we all do.

less than 18: Can it be the whole world's against you?

Listen Your Way To Productivity

Some studies estimate that productivity could practically double if only people would listen—really listen—to each other! Good listening habits are simply not taught and, thus, not developed. Most of us have had classes on how to write, read, speak and lead, but few of us have ever truly studied the subject of listening.

The consequences of poor listening are many:

- Unclear instructions
- Poor communication
- Wasted meetings
- Unnecessary mistakes
- Continually rewritten memos and letters

Think about a typical conversation at work. When you are listening to someone else talk, what are you probably doing at the same time? Most of us would say we're thinking of what we're going to say when it's our turn to talk. In fact, what many people consider "listening" is merely programming their ears for their turn to talk as soon as they don't hear anything else coming out of the other person's mouth. Therefore, all the other person has to do is breathe, and we have now taken command of the "talk" module of communication. (By the way, the other person is no less guilty of doing the same thing. He or she is probably formulating the next comment for when you're through!)

In a conversational situation, there are actually eight kinds of communication going on all at once:

Listening is a skill that can be developed.

- *Do not anticipate what others will say.*
- *Do not allow outside interruptions (phones, etc.).*
- *Do not assume what you hear is all the news, rather listen "between the lines" and ask questions.*

226

- What you mean to say
- What you actually say
- What the other person hears
- What the other person thought they heard
- What the other person means to say
- What the other person actually says
- What you hear the other person say
- What you think you heard the other person say

It's no wonder communication can be so confusing!

Here are three things everyone can do to improve listening.

1. Make eye contact with your speaker. Looking someone else straight in the eye pretty much demands you give the speaker some attention. It makes you aware of who that person is, and what he or she may be saying. Even looking at the mouth occasionally increases your awareness of what the person is saying.

Occasionally, you may find someone will not make eye contact with you. If so, look away at a fixed point for 5-10 seconds. When you return your glance the other person will, too.

When listening to someone, be sure not to look all around or up and down appearing indifferent, exasperated or unsure of yourself. Concentrate instead on a fixed point. This gives the individual back personal space and enables him or her to come to you again. Resist the urge to stare, though; it invades the speaker's space and increases the problem.

2. Keep good body posture. Whether you're standing or sitting, you can put yourself into an erect body posture with the head and spine straight, which opens up the listening channels. Keep your head still and straight, arms in toward your body and hands relaxed with open palms. Can you really give attention when you're slouched, leaning or slumped in a chair? Picture yourself with the relaxed power of a panther—unhurried, smooth movements, but ready to spring in an instant.

Listening effectiveness is directly related to the alertness that has to be present when you put your body into an attentive posture, so give it a try.

3. Give lots of verbal feedback. Even if you are working on listening, what the other person says is one thing and what you may hear (or interpret) is another. As you listen, feedback will tell the speaker your understanding of what is being said, making sure you understand. It's also a way of letting the speaker know you are listening.

This can be done by repeating some of what you're hearing, even by saying something like, "What I'm hearing you say is (and repeat what you think you heard). Is that it?" or "Let me see if I've got this straight...," or "Are you saying...? Right?" At this point, the answer will either be "yes," which means your listening was effective, or "no," which then enables the speaker to repeat and reinforce just what he or she did mean by the words.

Sometimes silence or exact repetition of a statement helps, too. Verbal feedback is particularly helpful when there is a cultural difference or strong emotions, or if the speaker is unclear or confusing.

> SUSAN: When I worked in the collections business, many times I heard the statement, "I can't pay my bill." I quickly learned to respond: "You can't pay your bill?" This caused the other person to interpret the first statement for me. If I tried to interpret first, I was always wrong, because I hadn't factored in the personal emotion or stress of the speaker. By asking the question instead, the other person would often respond with "I don't agree with the bill," or "Well, I can't pay it until I get my paycheck next week." Often "I can't" proved to mean "I won't" or "I will pay later."

This kind of listening demonstrates great respect for the speaker, which is especially important during conflict.

To summarize, to improve your listening, all you have to do is look at the other person with an attentive body posture and occasionally restate what you are hearing. Think about the people you know who are good listeners. Do you see all three of these tendencies in them?

Being heard is rare. The only way some people experience true listening is to buy it by the hour from a psychotherapist.

228

Before thinking these three steps are actually easy, however, try this. Ask a friend to discuss a problem with you. Promise yourself before you begin that you will not ask questions, give advice, preach or moralize. Simply summarize the meaning you are getting from what you hear. Listen for five minutes. Your only goal is to get your friend's perception of the problem. Caution: This will not be as easy as it sounds!

When the five minutes are up, discuss these questions with your friend: What was it like for you to really listen for five minutes? What problems got in your way? What was it like for the friend to be listened to? Did the friend feel you understood? Did he or she get a different understanding of the problem?

Unclear Communications Skills

When you're involved with other people, working with them on projects and tasks, the clarity of your own words makes a difference. Because you often don't have a very good idea of what your plan really is, it's often difficult to communicate it to someone else. Even if you do know, the words don't always come out the same way the knowledge is in your head. As a result, a lot of people (even those who really try to listen) begin work on a job without really knowing what it is they're doing, and why. Is it any wonder people don't like to delegate? "I told someone else how to do it, but it wasn't done right. It would have been easier to do it myself." Perhaps true, but how much of the fault was ours for failing express our wants and needs in a way that another could understand and act on them?

Most of us, too, are guilty of the same thing others often do to us. If someone asks, "Do you understand?", what's our first impulse? To say "yes"? Probably—even if we don't completely understand.

There are also different levels of understanding: If you understand 90 percent of something, are you inclined to tell the speaker you do understand? How about 80 percent? 70 percent? Now, which part is going to get you into trouble? Chances are, it's the 10-20-30 percent you didn't quite get.

It appears much of the fault could be laid at the feet of the speaker for ineffective communication. So, if you're the speaker, what can you do?

> *There are 7 emotions that are signaled on the face —anger, fear, sadness, disgust, surprise, enjoyment and contempt. These signals are the same for all people, regardless of race, culture, or sex.*

• **Be concise:** Use as few words as necessary. Prepare key one-liners to condense your thoughts on major issues and new proposals. Formulate your position and phrase it in one clear sentence.

Television-commercial writers know they have only 15 or 30 seconds to get their messages across, so they pack that time with clear, concise images to make their statements simply and powerfully, using words to create the mind pictures that are "worth a thousand words."

Writing-effectiveness studies consistently prove the best writing is concise. In fact, if the letter or memo runs more than one page in length, its effectiveness drops drastically. The same is true in speech. Keep to the point—don't wander. Know what you are going to say before you start. The fewer words you use, the better your communication will be.

ENOUGH IS ENOUGH!

• **Be simple:** Watch your word choice very closely. Just as there are no writing prizes for wordiness, there is certainly no award for being too complex when you speak: Don't use bigger words than are necessary. Be yourself. Use words the listener knows and understands. Unless you are certain of your listener's expertise on the subject, choose familiar, nontechnical words.

Think about your listener and the situation. Avoid the use of jargon. How much does your listener know about the project? Remember, that person certainly doesn't have the benefit of the time and thought you've put into planning something you already knew more about to begin with.

• **Be direct:** This is the old statement of "Say what you mean, and ask for what you want." Use specific language. Avoid generalities and assumptions. It's important to use the names of things (not "stuff"), names of people (not he, she, they) and numbers (not "some" or "more") whenever possible. Wishy-washy language comes from a lack of assertiveness—an unwillingness to

Forceful speakers use short active words, like "come," "cut" and "go."

take responsibility for what has been said, or not wanting the listener to get a wrong impression about us. In reality, we leave great voids in the picture that the listener has to somehow color in.

Here are a couple of examples on how to be direct:

GENERAL: We have to get on the ball around here.

DIRECT: Each person working on this project must increase personal production by five percent.

GENERAL: I hate to bother you, but we sort of need to go over some things.

DIRECT: I know you are working on the Smith report. Right now, it's important that I give you this information.

Sadly, directness is uncommon in many fields. We expect people to just "catch on," but sometimes we hope they don't. William Lutz' classic book, *Doublespeak*, addresses the problem clearly and humorously. Here are a few of the examples Mr. Lutz cites:

- In its 1981 annual report, Sambo's Restaurants boasted that the company had "achieved national prominence and publicity." They sure did; that was the year the company had filed under Chapter 11 of the Federal Bankruptcy Act.

- Standard Oil Company (Ohio)'s report in 1982 contained the following sentence: "The realities of 1982, as well as the ordinary changes that inevitably result in ongoing planning processes, have caused some modifications of refinements—which is probably a more accurate description—dealing with timing and degree that do not constitute any significant deviation from past thinking." What?

- They weren't all bad examples. Marshall & Illsley, a bank holding company in Milwaukee, included a letter to the stockholders with its annual report which said only: "Your company had a very good year. Some of it was due to luck; some of it was due to good planning and management. We hope you enjoy the numbers and the pictures." What a breath of fresh air!

The point here: You can't go far wrong if, when you talk, you

**SAY WHAT YOU MEAN,
AND ASK FOR WHAT YOU WANT!**

Lack Of Assertiveness

Effective communication literally dies because people would rather die, it seems, than to express themselves assertively. "Communication" comes from a Latin word "to make common." The word "assertiveness" also comes from Latin, "to join to oneself." Put the two together, and what you are doing is "making common (known) what belongs to you." For example: "You're standing on my foot!"

If you take these origins into account, assertiveness has gotten a bad rap. Being assertive is a basic survival tool for human relations, and certainly for protecting every priority list. To be assertive means you adhere to the following practice:

I SAY WHAT I MEAN AND ASK FOR WHAT I WANT.

Assertiveness is not, and should not be confused with, the two extremes, aggressiveness and passivity.

Assertiveness is not **aggressiveness,** which is often when you end up saying something you regret. Aggressiveness shows no consideration for the other person. An aggressive person walks in and totally takes over a situation, mashing beneath itself anything that dares get in its way. It's knowing you're standing on someone else's foot, and not moving!

Assertiveness is also not **passivity**. Passive people never finish their priority lists, because they are always changing the lists or adding to them. But because passive people never speak up, there is the tacit acceptance or approval of the new project, no matter how trivial or unrelated to the mission statement it might be. It's allowing someone to continue to stand on your foot. The passive person simply never speaks up. Instead, the emotion and energy (and pain?) are all kept inside. People who do this long enough end up killing themselves by the stress and pressure they create within. (Incidentally, the Latin origin of this word is "passivius" — capable of suffering.)

What is assertiveness? Assertiveness is saying, "I have a problem. (And you are the problem?) This is what's happening. This is what it's doing to me. And this is what needs to be done. This is what I want."

"You're standing on my foot. It hurts. Please step back."

With a good priority list (the "good offense"), it's possible to do this. With a well-thought *Daily Action Plan*, you can say: "I understand what you're asking me to do. Where would you fit this in the priority ranking I have here? Are you saying this new project is more important than what I'm already doing? If I take this project on at this time, what responsibility can you relieve me of? What deadline can be pushed back?"

Or, while you probably won't want to actually make the following statement, keeping it fresh in your mind is sure to help you maintain a healthy perspective toward the intrusion:

A LACK OF PLANNING ON YOUR PART DOES NOT CONSTITUTE AN EMERGENCY ON MY PART!

You might even want to post this statement somewhere around your desk in plain view—to be read by one and all, of course.

With practice, you can become great at assertiveness, so please, don't throw assertiveness out the window just because it doesn't work for you every single time. Assertive thinking and an assertive response will always be better for your own mental well-being. Remember—assertiveness is not aggressiveness—assertive statements can be made in direct, but nonconfrontational, ways. If you've already taken the time to plan and prioritize, assertiveness is the communication key that makes them happen.

Do Your Priorities Match Your Boss's?

Now for the sticky part. All this stuff about planning and setting priorities would be easy if (a) you functioned independently of anyone else, or (b) you had wide-open, regular communication with your superior(s) and (c) you always had complete agreement on what was important and in what order. Unfortunately, these statements apply to very few of us.

Nothing is more frustrating than having your plans and priorities change. It's hard enough to adjust to circumstances as they develop and situations change, but mix in an unorganized person, or one who loves the power and control from releasing information a little bit at a time, or someone who makes non-negotiable demands on your time, and you might be tempted to throw this manual out the window. But don't do it! You're too close to success now.

Get all your communications skills out, because this is when you're going to need them. Meeting different demands begins and ends with how effectively you communicate. Remember the good offense? It's time to get your own priorities planned and in order before making the first move. Know what's important to you. Commit the organization's and your personal mission statements to heart. Have the GANTT and PERT charts with you. Then, begin.

First, we must know the priorities of our superiors. If you work for someone who has clearly and effectively communicated this, go ahead to the next section. If you don't know your boss's priorities, there's only one way to find out.

ASK!

Possibly the best way to begin is to put your request in writing.

Do it like this. Draft a short note to your boss, and

- Communicate the new commitment you've made to organizing and managing your priorities.

- Pass along at least one or two new habits (from the many ideas in this manual) you've determined to work on.

- List in ranked order your three top priorities for the day, or for the week.

- Finish the note with a statement like: "If these are not in line with your priorities, please let me know."

This is assertion that generates feedback. It clarifies thinking, feelings, opinions and understandings. But most important, it creates a path of action. If your boss agrees, you know what to do. If the boss disagrees, you'll be told what is important.

What are the best-case and worst-case scenarios here? The best is that you'll find out that your priorities are exactly in line with your superior's, which is a green light to proceed! The worst-case scenario is that you'll find out your priorities aren't even close. But, you still have opened the communications channels in a very positive and constructive way, so the worst that can happen is that you improve your ability to communicate with your boss.

At the onset, you might consider doing this fairly regularly. Do it every day for a while to get the insight that comes from regular and ongoing awareness of your own needs and those of the other person.

How long it will take to establish a foothold for this type of communication depends on the relationship you have with your boss at the present moment, or the amount of authority your position holds:

- Lowest position—You wait for the boss to tell you what to do.

- Next lowest—You ask what to do (your boss still has to tell you).

- Not so bad—You make suggestions and recommendations (answers, not questions). You're taking solutions, not problems to your boss.

- Better yet—Your plans or priorities are pre-approved. Perhaps you give a weekly report, but you're pretty much on your own here.

Cooperation is spelled with two letters —WE.

- You made it!—You and your boss have reached the point where you don't have to bother him or her with anything. You're in complete control of your own destiny. If the building is burning down, you'd probably tell your boss, but that's about the extent of it.

Where do you stand along this continuum at this time? Where would you like to be? Are your ambitions for growth reflected anywhere in your mission statement? Have you told anybody about it?

Now, you may be thinking something like: "This would really work great, but you don't know my boss. My boss is the world's largest living bottleneck. He loves the control that can be obtained by waiting and procrastinating on everything. If I were to write a note like the one just described to my boss, I guarantee you, three weeks later it would still be lying on the desk, unanswered."

No doubt about it. There are people like that out there. And that's why a little bit of assertive wording can eliminate the agonizing, directionless waits some people suffer through. If you believe your boss would ignore a priorities-oriented memo, consider wording your last sentence like this: "If I don't hear back from you by (and put a deadline you are willing to live with here), I'm going to assume I have your OK on this."

That's assertiveness. This is not a threat—it is merely a factual option for the reader.

What does a sentence like that do? It eliminates forever the limbo of "no answer." Instead of no response meaning "wait until I get around to telling you, if I ever decide to," no response means "yes, go ahead!" There's an unbelievable world of difference between these two formulas. Grab your own priorities with both hands and take control !

As you build and develop this effective communication of priorities with your superiors, your contact can become less frequent in many cases, and you can keep the relationship fine-tuned by asking your boss for....

An open door is meaningless if the manager doesn't have an open mind.

The Eight-Minute Meeting

If you and your boss must work closely as a team, you may decide to establish a regular face-to-face meeting. If you work for a number of different people, you probably don't need to meet with each one every day, so the meetings can be less frequent as long as you maintain contact with all of them often enough to have a sense of priorities, control and planning. But, if your *Daily Action List* and priorities are going to constantly depend on what your boss is doing, ask for an eight-minute meeting.

Eight minutes? Why that number? Why not five, or ten? You can pick another number, but we feel this is just about the right amount of time to cover what needs to be done in this meeting. The problem with lengths like "five minutes" or "ten minutes" (or the famous question: "Do you have a minute?"—which is never just a minute) is that people tend to think of these time frames in very general terms. A length like eight minutes implies a specific amount of time. It commands respect, and gives you the "halo effect" of being a well-organized person.

In this meeting, you and your boss can:

- Go over both of your calendars, making sure everything is coordinated.

- Review your accomplishments. It can really show someone else just how much you are accomplishing.

- Consider the priority ranking of your *Daily Action List* for the next day.

- Ask questions like: "What is it you know is coming my way?" This is an example of assertion with empathy—for you, or is it for your boss?

The success of this meeting will depend on you. Whether it becomes a regular planning activity depends on how effective you make it. The value of regular planning with someone you work so closely with is immeasurable.

A couple of final tips on making sure your priorities match those of your superiors. First, if you have bad news, pass it along early. People don't like to be surprised. As soon as you know a deadline is going to be missed, let your boss know. Perhaps a solution can be reached. Maybe some help can be made available to you. Possibly, the deadline isn't as critical as you thought it was. Second, remember to clarify your own priorities first. Always. Never, never be caught with a "What should my priorities be?" attitude. Know them yourself, first—it's all part of having a good offense!

Dealing With The Interrupting Boss, Or Dealing With Multiple Interrupting Bosses

Sometimes people develop habits that are hard to break. Nothing is more irritating than having to work with a person who's never organized enough to allow us to maintain priorities or stick to our *Daily Action List*. But that doesn't mean you should give up on prioritizing. In fact, you may notice that, the more you practice organizing and managing your own priorities, the less some of these people will bother you with their unscheduled requests, and the more fun your work may become.

Having a good offense means that a strong wall of protection is built around you and your list. It's true! If these people have somebody else to go to with their projects and requests, the more organized you appear to be, the more likely they will go elsewhere and leave you alone.

Assertiveness is a powerful shield. The more your priorities are identified and ranked, the stronger the shield will be. So, here you are, hard at work on whatever you have decided is "The Best Use of My Time Right Now," and along comes Mr. or Ms. Unorganized with an urgent request. What do you do?

1. Ask for priority or impact. It's amazing to us how some people will automatically assume whenever a boss asks them to do something that the request is top priority. Is it? Have you asked? When working as a team member, someone else's rank may often establish the priority, but remember these words:

VERIFY AND CLARIFY

Ask! Be selective of the wording of your question, however. If you ask "Is this top priority?" this person will undoubtedly say, "Of course it is, stupid! Why would I be asking you to do it if it weren't?" People like this are good at transferring the guilt, blame and bad feelings to someone else. So choose a question that is open-ended: "What do you think? Is this a medium priority, or what?" Just make sure you ask a question regarding priority or impact in such a way that it allows for an answer other than "yes, it's important."

> **JONATHAN:** I had a boss who was constantly trying to catch up with yesterday. He dropped last-minute requests in my lap every day. First I assumed they were important, and did them. Then I asked if they were important and felt like an idiot for asking. One day, in desperation, I tried a different approach. I looked him straight in the eye and asked, "Is this medium priority, or what?" I couldn't believe what he said. He mumbled something about yes, it was medium priority, and wandered away.
>
> The minute he said it was medium priority, he gave me the right to choose to do this **any time I wanted**; to fit it into my *Daily Action List*. The question didn't always get the same answer, because sometimes he would say "No, this is top priority." But this way, I was causing him to tell me it was, rather than assuming myself that it was or asking him if it was.

Before going on, this is a great time to discuss **how** you ask—which is just as important, if not even more so, than just asking.

When your voice is firm, strong, relaxed and self-confident, you will have more appropriate communication with your boss or anyone else. The voice, as well as facial expression, influences others even more than rational, logical facts. This has been documented by many well-established communications studies such as those noted in Dr. Albert Mehrabian's *Silent Messages*.

Stating your questions with confidence—firm, strong and relaxed— eliminates the tone that tells your listener, "I'm judging or evaluating your request," which only puts the other person on the defensive. With assertiveness, your boss always knows where you're "at," for better or otherwise.

2. Ask for deadlines. The question, "When do you want this?" will inevitably be answered "yesterday" or "right away" or "by 4 p.m. today." Yes, this is a deadline. But what kind of deadline is it? We've all had this experience: Someone comes to us and asks us to do something very important, with a really tight deadline. We clear the desk, go to work, maybe work a little late or skip lunch, and somehow get the job completed by the deadline. Five days later the project is still sitting on that other person's desk, and nothing has been done with it.

Let's face it. People tend to give phony deadlines. They may do that because they don't trust you. If they need it Friday, they think they'd better tell you Wednesday, because surely you're going to be late.

If you ask the question the right way, and phrase it properly, you may be able to find out what the **real** deadline is. If we ask, "When is the latest I can get this to you?" It sets up a completely different answer than "When do you want it?" Now the other person may say, "Well, I really need it on Friday, because I'm going to use it in the meeting I have that afternoon." Now we know the real deadline.

By the way, a favor you can do for yourself and for the other person is to **beat the deadline by as much as you can**. This person has been honest with you about the time frame—now, honor that trust by showing you can be depended on. Don't violate it by making this person worry up until the last minute. You'll appreciate the peace of mind, and your boss will, too. But the best news is that the more you deliver on time, the more trusted and accurate the deadlines become.

You will also find out pretty quickly if the boss has been honest with you. Sometimes, because standards are not specified, there may really be two deadlines: Your deadline for getting something to the boss and his or her deadline for getting it to someone else. So, it could backfire when the boss gets out the red pencil and the project comes back: "Rewrite this...expand on this...tighten this up, etc." Now, your reward for turning this project in ahead of time is more work.

One key is consequences. Keep track of the possible consequences as you respond to these kinds of requests. In the future, it will help you to give you immediate knowledge of whether an item is important or urgent.

The above steps will work for you, whether you have one person interrupting you or several. If you are trying to satisfy many bosses instead of just one, there is one other plan of attack that can help you preserve your priorities and stay out of the stress and conflict that may be created by competing projects from bosses who may not even appreciate each other.

The valuable lesson to be demonstrated by this plan of action is:

PEOPLE WILL DO THINGS THAT LEAD TO POSITIVE CONSEQUENCES AND AVOID THINGS THAT LEAD TO NEGATIVE CONSEQUENCES

Begin by clarifying the importance and deadlines by asking questions. Let's suppose Boss A has already visited you and given you a high-priority project with a tight (not phony) deadline. You're hard at work and suddenly Boss B arrives on the scene with another high-priority, need-it-now assignment. Time for action on your part—here's what to do.

1. Communicate the conflict. Let the second person know that what you're being asked to do is creating a conflict because of the first person's project. "We've got a problem, because I'm already working on something Boss A has just given me with a really tight deadline."

2. Let the asker make the decision. "What do you think I should do?" Ask this question and shut up. Boss B has created the conflict, let him or her make the decision as to what should be done. Many times you'll get the OK to work on Boss A's project first if you ask that question.

Of course, sometimes the response will be: "I don't care what Boss A told you to do; this is more important!" If so, on to Step 3.

3. Get the asker to initiate. If, at this point, you try to decide what's best, it will backfire on you nearly every time. If you surrender and take on Boss B's project, who is guaranteed to walk up just as you're getting started? Boss A, naturally. So don't try to resolve the conflict. If these two people are the ones who have put you in this compromising position, they must resolve it. "I hear what you're saying, but Boss A considers this to be a very important job. I'll be happy to do your work too, but you and Boss A need to get together and decide which job I should do first, and which to do next."

All too frequently, if you work for more than one boss, you become a pawn in a manipulative chess game among bosses to get the upper hand on each other. Children should be treated like children, and you are an adult. Send both players to their rooms until they can resolve the problem themselves. And, in the meantime, work on something else!

Once again, remember the behavior principle here: People will do things that lead to positive consequences, and will avoid things that lead to negative consequences. If you don't encourage them to resolve their problem, it becomes your problem, which makes it possible for them to persist in poor communication. People will continue creating conflict if there is a positive consequence to their action. It shouldn't take too much to do a little teaching here if you keep sending both players away until they can decide, rather than rewarding them for acting inappropriately.

4. Offer alternatives. You can help out, of course, through your own initiative and creativity. Is there a way one job can be accomplished without you? Is there someone else to delegate something to? Could you go back to Boss A, show how much you've done already (since it may be enough for that person to work on for a while) and get permission to handle the other job for a while?

Remember, the best defense is a good offense. It's possible to assertively manage your own priorities and *Daily Action List*.

CASE STUDY

Jan Warburton, the supervisor of the data-processing operation at a mid-size educational institution, supervises a staff of four people, and her operation has run successfully for five years.

> *Confront minor issues as they occur. Dealing with small matters keeps people from building walls of resentment that make resolving big problems nearly impossible.*

Several months ago, Jan's department was placed under a different manager. Gloria Sherman, Jan's new manager, worked in a different building and communicated with Jan primarily over the telephone and through electronic mail.

Gloria normally began her work day at 4 a.m. (she told Jan it's her best time of the day when she is uninterrupted), and by the time Jan arrived at work at 8 a.m., her E-mail system contained as many as 25 separate messages from Gloria, most of them jobs and projects Gloria wanted her to handle. These assignments came with detailed instructions and, in Jan's view, represented "busywork" activities. Even though Jan had already planned her day, the new assignment load usually disrupted her plans.

In addition, Gloria developed the habit of contacting Jan late in the day, about 3 p.m., with other "emergency" assignments that she wanted done by "the first thing tomorrow." Jan often took this work home with her and, using her home terminal, worked late into the night—sometimes until 1 or 2 a.m.— getting the work finished so it was ready in the morning.

Even though Jan finished these assignments on time at great personal sacrifice, Gloria often criticized what Jan had done. If Jan submitted material to her already typed, Gloria always completely retyped it herself. If Jan gave her handwritten information, Gloria criticized her for not typing it.

The other workers in Jan's department were pretty insulated from Gloria's work and critical remarks (thanks to Jan), but on days when Jan was out of the office, they too felt the brunt of Gloria's comments and unreasonable work assignments. Jan worried that some of them would leave for other less stressful jobs.

Jan enjoyed her job but often found herself frustrated by the lack of balance in her life. She was also discouraged by her inability to complete her own work because of the numerous additional last-minute assignments from Gloria. Also, even though she knew she did a good job at her work, Jan began to wonder because of the frequent criticism from Gloria.

CASE STUDY

QUESTIONS:

1. What is Jan's biggest problem?

2. If you were Jan Warburton, what would you do?

What Actually Happened

Jan decided that, even though Gloria's problems included her inability to stay out of Jan's department and "micro-manage" things she knew nothing about, the biggest problem was her own lack of assertiveness and communication with Gloria. To overcome her problem, Jan concentrated on doing some things regularly.

Good followers help good leaders by speaking out when they disagree.

• Jan began planning her upcoming day the afternoon before, and before she left work (Gloria was long gone by then), Jan sent an electronic mail message to Gloria, summarizing her plans and top-three priorities for the upcoming day. The message included both personal and departmental priorities.

• When Gloria dropped an "urgent" project in her lap at 3 p.m., Jan responded, "Gloria, I estimate the job you've just given me will take eight hours to complete, perhaps even longer if I take time to type up all the information. Even if I abandon all my priorities right now and work on this project exclusively, the earliest I could get this to you would be 3 p.m. tomorrow. Before I begin working on this assignment, I need to know if this is more important than the priorities I'm already planning to do; and, if it is, if my anticipated time line is agreeable to you."

• Jan began attaching notes to the material she submitted to Gloria, particularly when the material was handwritten, reminding her that the work was not typed because she knew Gloria wanted the project quickly and usually retyped the material anyway.

• When Jan knew she would be out of the office for a period of time, she notified Gloria well in advance of her absence and asked Gloria to provide any input or assignments to her by a specific time, so that this work could be passed along to her people before she left. Then, before she left, Jan sent a summary of her people's priorities to Gloria's E-mail.

Analysis

Gloria liked to show her power by overloading her people. And, even though she didn't really understand a lot of what went on in Jan's department, she insisted on controlling every detail of the work done. Gloria wasted a lot of her own time creating busywork projects and redoing work already completed, usually to make sure her name was on top.

Jan couldn't control much of Gloria's action. But Jan could protect her own priority list by communicating her plans to Gloria, which she did. Further, Jan had every right to expect reasonable deadlines from Gloria, and to get the work done during normal working hours instead of working half the night at home. By telling Gloria as soon as an urgent project arrived about how long it would take to complete and the earliest she could expect to receive it, Jan could defend herself against unrealistic deadlines.

Only when she had a thorough knowledge of her own plans and priorities could Jan assert herself to Gloria.

When Jan began to do this, she discovered a truth about many demanding people in the workplace: These people will push others just as far as someone will let them. Throwing her own priorities aside and giving up her personal time was not beneficial to Jan; it merely subjected her to more unreasonable requests and expectations from Gloria.

Getting Others To Commit To Your Plan

At the beginning of this book, we exploded the fantasy that no one ever has enough time with the reality that everyone has the same 24 hours a day...no more and no less. This is true, but how much you accomplish in that time can be expanded. There is a way to add time to your day by getting a commitment of other people to your plans and projects. With their added time, your day can actually be much more than 24 hours, and productivity can be increased proportionately. In management circles, the process is called:

Delegation—Team Spirit. In employee-peer groups, the process is called: Job Descriptions—Rules of the Game. In family circles, the process is called: Family Love and Care.

However it is described, when you enlist the help of others, you come out ahead. By enlisting others' help, you gain their commitment as well. The process of obtaining the commitment involves delegation, negotiation and cooperation. It all happens by recognizing the questions every journalism student learns the first day of class. People want to know "the five Ws and the H:" Who? What? When? Where? Why? and How?

What To Know

Here's how you can gain commitment. Use the following nine steps:

1. Relate your plan to the overall mission. (Answers: "Why?") Get out the organizational or departmental Mission Statement and demonstrate the current project's connection to who we are, and what we are doing.

2. Pinpoint the responsibility. (Answers: "What?") This step involves performance specification: Have you made it clear what requires action? Do you have a PERT or GANTT chart for this project? This visually focuses attention on just what is needed and how it relates to the overall project.

3. Select the right person. (Answers: "Who?") Knowledge and skill is usually your starting point—who has the physical or mental resources to accomplish this task? Go back through steps 1 and 2 with the person you've selected, and communicate to that person why he or she is the "who" for this job.

4. Communicate clearly. (Answers: "How?") Review the earlier section of this chapter on Be Concise, Be Simple and Be Direct. During this step of getting the commitment, you want to both give and get feedback on the project. Ask lots of open-ended questions— the ones that really pull information and understanding into the situation. Questions beginning with words like "how," "what" and "why" foster good communication between both parties.

5. Agree on conditions. (Answers "When?" "Where?" and anything else not yet resolved.) Here's where you communicate, and get agreement on things like deadlines, progress reports, expectations, how you'll monitor results, where the work is to be done, and to whom it will be submitted.

This is the time when negotiating is your best tool. Negotiation is what produces cooperation, especially if you are dealing with a peer and have no authority to delegate. When you can't take no for an answer, it's going to cost you something!—but that's all right. What can you do in exchange, either now or later?

Negotiation will happen in several ways. Perhaps you can convince one of your superiors, someone with the necessary authority, to involve others in your project by delegating. Maybe there are people you work closely with—closely enough to have developed the informal alliances. These mutual relationships are designed to help each other out when possible. And, we'd bet, right now, somebody owes you something. Or, as in the previous paragraph— you will now owe them something because you can't take no for an answer.

6. Clarify the degree of authority and responsibility. One of your most vital steps is knowing who is responsible for what and how much authority each person involved has. We've all been frustrated by not knowing just how far we could go. We've all wished we had enough authority to effectively carry out our responsibility, but it was never given to us.

Only when you know just what you can do is it possible to do the job. Take the time to make this perfectly clear before work begins on the job. What might that other person want to know—Can I get other people to help? Can I spend any money? Are certain tools or equipment available for my use? What do I need approval to do?

How much authority you grant to another person will depend on how well you already know and trust his or her abilities and responsibility. If you have worked with this individual for years, and know exactly how well he or she knows a certain job, you would probably entrust that person with quite a bit of freedom to make decisions. On the other hand, if this person is relatively new or inexperienced, you may want to be kept posted, and have him or her check with you before making certain moves or taking the next step. Either way, the point is the same. The amount of authority and responsibility must be clarified and understood by all parties at the onset.

7. Provide support and backup. This individual is now helping you out on a tough job. What can you do in return? Are there any wrinkles you can iron out of the situation? Any other projects or

How to Delegate

- *Spread out information.*

- *Let others think for themselves.*

- *Give assignments and needed tools.*

- *Share the glory.*

deadlines that can be delayed? Any of his/her work you could do yourself, or assign to a third party? Any interruptions, either human or telephone, you could divert your way?

8. Check on progress. The worst thing you can do here is simply walk away and expect to get exactly what you asked for just when you wanted it. After all, if the ultimate responsibility for the success of the task is in your hands, you want and need the control of knowing what's going on at all times. You can mark certain dates on your calendar, or write notes to your Tickler File, reminding you to check at various times. Getting feedback at this point is critical.

How you get that feedback is your decision. Some people like to have a formal, scheduled meeting so the project is discussed in detail. We like to do this more informally, and would usually do it as we walked around the office. Often an informal method is more effective because it's much less intimidating and usually elicits more honest answers. An informal briefing might begin by your asking, "As long as I'm here, update me on how the project is going."

9. Evaluate the completed assignment and give feedback. We believe you can get anybody to help you. One time. Whether you ever get help again is determined by how well you can give evaluation and feedback once the job is done. Most people's attitude is: "Let me know how I did!" Each person is entitled to an evaluation, if you want help again.

Look at it this way: There are really five questions related to the job that any person wants answers to. The five questions are often merely thoughts asked in the same order, because the next question never comes unless the person gets the right answer to the previous question. If you want a team of productive, enthusiastic players, you need to give the right answers. (As an employee, these are thoughts you ponder, as well.)

1. What's my job? The first thing someone wants to know. What am I here for? What's expected of me? When a person knows the answer to this, the next question is:

2. **How am I doing?** The need for evaluation and feedback is so strong it's part of the second question. The answer needs to be clear and specific, with useful information.

For example, there once was a boss who did not communicate well. One day, wanting some helpful feedback, an employee asked the boss, "How am I doing?" The boss's response was, "We pay you, don't we?"

Obviously, employees want quite a bit more than that! And, if they get the right answer, their next question is...

3. **Does anybody care?** "OK. I know what my job is, and how I'm doing. But what I'd really like to know now is, who cares? How much? How are you telling me? Does it seem sincere? Do I feel like anything more than the social security number on my paycheck, or my employee ID number?"

These are tough questions to answer, and should tell us we'd better be as open and responsive as we can with thanks, recognition and appreciation for work well done. Because if we don't give it, the next question never comes!

4. **How are we doing?** Now, that's a good-sounding question that everybody wants to hear! This question tells us that employees' individual needs are being met, they feel good about what they're doing, and they feel a part of a team. And, if they get good answers to this question, here comes the best one...

5. **How can I help?** I know what my job is. I'm doing well, and someone is telling me that. I feel good about by contribution, because I know people appreciate my efforts. I belong to a team, and it's helpful to know what the score is. Therefore, what can I contribute to help us become even more successful?

Make sense? If you want continued help and willing participation, the better you can anticipate and answer these questions, the more help you're going to get. It's truly a situation where everyone wins and no one loses!

These nine steps guarantee you'll be able to multiply your own time and efforts because you've gained the commitment of others to your projects. Review the list again, and note the ones most important in

> *"Thanks" is a neglected form of compensation.*

achieving the desired results. In our opinion, #4, #6 and #9 are the most important. If you can communicate with power and clarity, provide specific directions regarding authority and responsibility, and give prompt and useful feedback and evaluation, you're nearly there! Practice, practice. When these steps become second nature to you, you will hold a set of priceless keys in your hands!

One Tool And One Idea To Ensure Success

If you do a lot of delegating, negotiating and asking for cooperation, it's a very good idea to keep some sort of log to help you to stay on top of all the assignments and not let anything slip through the cracks. The Project Planning Chart will do just that.

PROJECT	PERSON RESPONSIBLE	FIRST PROGRESS REPORT	SECOND PROGRESS REPORT	THIRD PROGRESS REPORT	DUE DATE	COMMENTS

This chart may be used in lots of ways, but here's how to use it for logging your communications. List the project and person to whom it was delegated in the first two columns. If you already know a due date, go over to that column and enter the information. Then, determine how many times, and when, you want to check progress between assignment and completion.

As a part of your 15 Minutes of Planning, review your Delegation Log. Do you need to check on anyone? How will you do it? You can do it formally (in a meeting) or informally, as part of conversation during the day. When you've gotten your progress information, cross off the date on the log.

That's the tool. Now, the idea. To increase your awareness, and ability, of delegating work to people, here's a recommendation for your *Daily Action List* for the next 30 days (enough time to develop into a habit, right?): Next to every item on your *Daily Action List*, every day, write this question next to the task:

WHY ME?

Remember, much of successfully organizing and managing your priorities comes from making sure the task is appropriate, that it's the right time to do it, and that you are the one who should be doing it. Asking the "why me?" question forces you to evaluate what you're spending your time doing. How important is it? What is the best use of MY time right now?

Assertive communication skills literally grant us unlimited power to live out our destinies! Wayne Dyer, in his book *Pulling Your Own Strings*, advises us:

"MAKE ALL YOUR ENCOUNTERS FUN AND CHALLENGING EXPERIENCES, RATHER THAN BATTLEGROUNDS IN WHICH YOU PLACE YOUR HUMANITY ON THE LINE. HAVE FUN SEEING HOW EFFECTIVE YOU CAN BE. RELAX AND ENJOY THE CHALLENGE."

Making It Work

CONCERN	REASON	STRATEGY
people change your list regularly	you don't have priorities	establish your priorities to prevent list violations
difficulty understanding others when they talk	listening skills poorly developed	practice the three easy listening ideas
people don't listen to you	inability to speak with clarity and directness	speak concisely, simply and directly
people often seem to take advantage of you	you let them do it	say what you mean and ask for what you want
you and your boss disagree on what's important	priorities not known or clarified	ask! ask! ask! meet regularly with boss
interruptions by boss(es)	your vulnerability is well known	know your own priorities; be "organized" by reputation
can't get the job done	trying to do it all yourself	get others committed to your plan
feel like all the weight's on your shoulders	no delegation/ negotiation	write "why me?" next to every item on your list

Putting It to Work

- Remember that when it comes to protecting your priorities, the best defense is a good offense.

- Always have your own priorities in order; become known as a person who is always totally organized and planned.

- To listen better, make eye contact, keep good posture and give verbal feedback to the speaker to ensure you understand.

- Good communication is a two-way street. The more concisely, simply and directly you speak, the more effective you will be.

- Learn to assert yourself by saying what you mean and asking for what you want.

- Ask your boss to find out if your priorities are the same as his/hers.

- Meet regularly with each of your bosses to communicate priorities and plans and to ensure yours are coordinated with theirs.

- If you get conflicting requests from multiple bosses, pass the responsibility of resolution back to them, rather than doing it yourself.

- Others will commit themselves to your plan if you answer the questions: Who? What? When? Where? Why? and How?

- Give plenty of feedback to people who help you to guarantee their cooperation on future projects.

- Keep a list of tasks you delegate, with progress report dates, to keep jobs from being overlooked or slipping up on you.

- Asking the question "Why me?" of every item on your *Daily Action List* will keep you from doing things you should delegate to others.

Check Your
Working Knowledge Of Communication

1. What is the best way to protect your priority list?

2. Name the three easy steps to better listening. Which one(s) do you need to work on?

3. Why do we fail to tell other people what we want them to do?

4. What is the definition of *assertion*?

5. Why is assertion critical to effective communication?

6. Do your priorities match the boss's? How do you know?

7. What is the importance of meeting regularly with your boss(es)?

8. If you're the boss, do your people know your priorities?

9. What's the best way to handle two bosses who assign you conflicting priorities?

10. How can you identify the "real" deadline for a project?

11. What should you do if you know what the real deadline is?

12. What are the three most important steps to get others to commit themselves to your plans?

13. What are the five job-related questions everyone wants the right answers to?

14. What two-word question can keep you from trying to do it all yourself?

MY SLIGHT-EDGE IDEAS FROM CHAPTER 10:

_____

_____

_____

_____

_____

_____

_____

_____

_____

*C*HAPTER 11

Working Timelines/
Deadlines/Lifelines

- **It's a matter of life and death**
- **Timelines that work**
- **Getting someone else to accept your timeline**
- **Nine ways to get a bogged-down project running again**
- **The value of substitution**
- **What a specific timeline creates**

The ultimate goal of any project is **completion.**

How do you feel about deadlines? Do they cause a lot of grief in your life? Are they stress producers with little benefit to you? Or, do deadlines give you a target to shoot for? Do they tell you where you stand? Do they give you direction? Do they give you the motivation and determination to achieve? Are they helping you plan your project for success?

Chances are, deadlines have caused some stress in your life, but when you really think about them, you'd probably agree that they are useful. Perhaps "deadline" isn't even the proper word for this concept: Maybe "timeline" is better, because that's truly what it is—an indication of a future time at which an activity must be completed and of the intermediate steps that occur as time passes and moves ahead to the scheduled completion date.

A TIMELINE, therefore, can develop one of two ways. If it doesn't work, we'll use that old term DEADLINE, because dead is what we may be, figuratively, if we don't make it. On the other hand, a timeline that works becomes our LIFELINE assuring success and achievement.

The timelines in your projects provide a motivation for action. They enable you to develop meaningful plans, with mileposts along the way to chart your progress relative to a predetermined completion date. In short, the difference between success and failure in your projects will depend on timelines that work. An old English proverb states:

THAT WHICH CAN BE DONE ANYTIME
IS NEVER DONE AT ALL

But, when a timeline is set, others come through for us! It gives them the frame of reference they need, too!

Self-Quiz: Can You Set Workable Timelines?

Directions:

What do you already know about timelines? Indicate your agreement to these statements as follows: (3) I agree; (2) maybe; (1) no!

1. I nearly always complete my projects on time.	3	2	1
2. Others willingly abide by timelines I set for them.	3	2	1
3. I know what makes a timeline work, and why it doesn't.	3	2	1
4. If a project gets off track, I can always get it going again.	3	2	1
5. I know when to use incentives or compliance to get results.	3	2	1

Add your score:

12 or more:	Old reliable, that's you!
11-8:	People hesitate before asking you
7 or less:	You're usually a day late and a dollar short

Make It Specific!

For a timeline to be useful, it must be specific as to date and/or time. Totally ineffective phrases that don't work include:

- "Please advise"
- "As soon as possible"
- "At your earliest convenience"
- "When I get around to it"

All of these phrases provide built-in automatic excuses for not performing: It wasn't convenient. I couldn't get around to it.

A specific timeline should not only spur people to action, it should do so in a positive way. It's unhealthy when a timeline pushes you or others against such tight constraints that it's virtually impossible to achieve. Therefore, whether you are establishing your own timelines, working with somebody else's or setting a timeline for others, you need to recognize the three types of timelines that actually work:

1. A reasonable timeline. How much work is required? How much time is available? What else needs to be done at the same time? Is this realistic and reasonable?

If you (or someone else) believes the date or time of a timeline is indeed reasonable, there is every reason to expect the timeline will be met. It's a conscious decision, but the subconscious operates strongly in these situations as well. When there's a deep-down-inside feeling that "I can't make it," achieving the timeline becomes unlikely.

Remember, it's always more acceptable to negotiate a reasonable timeline at the beginning of a project than at the end. This helps you establish your planning effectiveness rather than emphasizing your inefficiency.

2. An equitable timeline. Is this timeline fair to me, if I accept? Am I already overburdened with responsibilities and tight time frames? Am I being penalized for my productivity? (How often this is the reward for people who get the job done—to throw that much more at them!)

If it is not equitable, establish some facts here. A GANTT chart is an excellent tool to visually verify all that is being required from one person or department. This is the time to focus on facts, not personal opinions.

If people believe they're being dealt with fairly with regard to the work required and the timeline, they can and usually will work within it.

3. A self-imposed timeline. No timeline will work for you until you personally buy into it. Of course, many times you set your own timelines, and there's certainly no reason to think you won't achieve them, because you chose them yourself. Presumably the time frame you have chosen is also realistic (reasonable) and equitable (fair).

Do a self-assessment here—are you buying into all three aspects of a timeline at this point? If you are, this will ensure a proactive position toward achievement instead of later assuming and reinforcing a passive "victim" position, which is never healthy.

What about the times when someone else sets a timeline for you? The timeline will be achieved IF you buy into it and essentially accept it as your own timeline. At that point, it is not somebody else's timeline: It belongs to you. It has become self-imposed. It is yours.

How can you get someone else to accept the timeline you set? The same process must take place. The timeline must be reasonable and it must be fair for the other person to decide to make the timeline his/her own. It is now self-imposed, and should be achieved.

To get the other person to that point, here are a few key questions you can ask to help establish your position:

- "Does this time frame seem realistic to you?"
- "What obstacles do you see that might prevent you from achieving this deadline?"
- "What are some reasonable intermediate goals we could set here?"
- "Is it fair for me to assume you're going to be able to do this?"
- "Can I count on you to have this back to me by (timeline)?"

A key point to remember here:

> **A PROJECT DOESN'T GET SIX MONTHS BEHIND**

Think about fair, reasonable, self-imposed timelines. Ask questions. Chart progress. Get agreement.

OK, But I Just Got Bogged Down...

The most realistic, fair, self-imposed timeline can still encounter unexpected difficulties as events develop. Because other priorities arise, suddenly a project that was going so well can be placed on the back burner. A once-realistic timeline is now a huge, negative, de-motivating factor. Somehow, someway, you're suddenly way off the track, and you're not even sure how you got there.

The best news, of course, is that you aren't faced with an empty bag when you encounter a side-tracked project. In fact, there are nine steps you can take to get out of the mud and back on the main track. It's not necessary to try all nine steps—this is not a sequence. It's a listing of nine different options that are available. It's more a matter of finding or choosing the one that works to get back on your feet again. The steps are:

1. Re-negotiate the timeline. Perhaps all you need to recover momentum is to get some relief from the timeline. It may be possible for you to go back to the person to whom you committed yourself and get a change or extension, particularly if the circumstances make this reasonable. Perhaps now you will find out if the first timeline you committed to is the real timeline or simply someone else's "wish list." With a timeline change, you're no longer behind the program, and you're rolling again.

2. Re-examine the timelines within the project. If you're seriously behind schedule, look at your flow charts. Were you able to build a PERT or GANTT chart with a cushion or two in the schedule? Or, if you have used up the cushion already, what individual step can be shortened or sped up? Maybe there's a step that involves the mailing of a draft of a report to someone else. This might be a great time to send it by overnight delivery...or put it on the fax machine.

3. Eliminate the nonessential. Are some steps in your plan ones you thought would be nice to have, but aren't really critical to the success of your project? This could be the time to eliminate them. Does it have to be this big? Maybe it's time to downsize a little. Perhaps the final result won't be quite as elaborate, but cutting out a few frills may be just the thing to get your project going again.

This could be a way to provide help for the perfectionist. Some people, when given more than enough time to complete a project, fill all the time by adding nonessential elements, which is actually a form of procrastination. By consciously eliminating nonessential items before starting, you may be able to set a timeline that is tight enough to force the perfectionist (you?) to stick to the project. The project never gets off track in the first place.

4. Resources—develop more! What resources do you have? Is it possible to get any more? More people, more help, more money? What would make a difference here? There's almost always a point in any project when so much time and money has already been invested that spending a little more is worth it. For example, construction companies often get this kind of motivation through the agreement (in the beginning) to substantial daily penalties for each day a project runs past its agreed deadline.

(Incidentally, the incentive can also work the other way. The city of Seattle has promised a company $18,000 per day for every day it can beat the deadline for completing a storm-damaged bridge over Lake Washington. That's the amount the city figures it costs every day not to have the bridge operational.)

5. Substitute something else. Is there a certain item you need for your project that you just can't seem to obtain? Would something else, which is already available, work just about as well? Would the substitution make any qualitative difference in the finished project? If you can answer "no," go ahead and make it.

Many products have come about because of substitution. This could be an asset defined by a liability. The story behind the "Post-It" note paper is a classic illustration. Ask 3-M if it was worth the millions of dollars that have been earned because someone found a substitute use for a glue that didn't stick!

6. Alternative sources. Where (or how) else could you obtain what's holding you up? Is there another source or way you could do it? A supplier who's been asking for a chance to do business with you? When can your supplier get the materials to you? Is it already in their warehouse? What if you got it yourself instead of waiting for a delivery?

This philosophy is well explained by Roger Von Oech, author of *A Kick in the Seat of the Pants*, who suggests looking for another right source or solution. If you ever found the best way to do a job, how would you know you had found it? We call this the "Two Good Ways" rule! Another way of looking at this idea is this: That's one right way. Now, what's another right way?

7. Accept partial delivery or shipment. Suppose your entire mailing is being held up because the 10,000 envelopes aren't available. Call the supplier. Are any of the envelopes printed yet? 2,000 of them? Great! You'll accept that much right away, a partial delivery, because that will give you something to work with. That will give your supplier time to finish the order.

8. Incentives. Here's where the human-relations side of getting your projects back on track enters into play. What kinds of rewards, either for yourself or for others, might spur renewed commitment to the project? The "carrots" of life are sometimes strong enough to do a job nothing else can do.

9. Compliance. Likewise, the compliance factors—the "stick," if you would—can be effective, too. Sometimes the avoidance of bad consequences is an even stronger force than the pursuit of good consequences.

In working with people, consider both the incentive and compliance options. April 15 is a good example of this. Think about the lines of people at the post office at midnight turning in their tax returns! Yet, many tax preparers offer the early-return incentive of "get your refund sooner." The same date provides incentive for some people, and compliance for others.

We can regain our momentum on bogged-down tasks by remembering:

> **IF I SET THE RIGHT KIND OF TIMELINES TO BEGIN WITH, THERE ARE MANY WAYS I CAN GET MY PROJECT BACK ON TRACK!**

And, only one step that works is all you need!

Here is an exercise to help determine that one step. Asking these questions can not only keep your project on target to begin with, they can also help you know the best way to regain your lost momentum when that happens.

WORKSHEET—Project Timelines

Directions: Select a project you're currently working on (or one you've completed, but which didn't go as well as you'd hoped) and answer the following questions about it.

1. How can I minimize this project? What could I subtract or shorten?

2. What could I change about my plan? By adding or duplicating or extending a timeline, what might happen?

3. Can I rearrange anything here? Are the sequences, the people involved, or the steps inflexible, or is there some flexibility?

4. What substitutions would make this project work even better? Take even less time?

5. What other ways can I use the time, materials, ideas and energy going into this project?

6. How many different ways could this project be accomplished?

> "GENIUS MEANS LITTLE MORE THAN THE FACULTY OF
> PERCEIVING IN AN UNHABITUAL WAY."
> —William James

Making It Work

CONCERN	REASON	STRATEGY
people don't respect the timeline	haven't "bought in" yet	make reasonable, equitable suggestions and ask questions for agreement
timeline doesn't work	something is missing	better planning use flow chart
project gets bogged down	something else took top priority on the list	make it top priority again take one of the nine steps
job is held up	lack of materials	accept a partial delivery

Putting It To Work

- Make your timelines specific as to date and time.

- That which can be done anytime is never done at all.

- Timelines will work if they are reasonable, equitable and self-imposed.

- Remember, there is normally more than one "right way" to do something. Don't let your preconceptions get in the way of your creativity.

- By using flow charts, you will be able to see your options for getting the project back on track.

265

Check Your Working Knowledge: Timelines

1. What are the three types of timelines that work?

2. What questions can you ask to get someone else to buy into your timeline?

3. Why is it good to eliminate some nonessential items before starting your project?

4. How many right ways are there to do most things?

5. What are some of the benefits of timelines?

MY SLIGHT-EDGE IDEAS FROM CHAPTER 11:

_____

_____

_____

_____

_____

_____

_____

_____

Crisis And Conflict—
Things Just Might Go Wrong

- **Anticipating Murphy's Laws**
- **Where crisis is most likely to occur**
- **Preparation begins with a plan**
- **Be ready for anything!**
- **Crisis survival tactics**
- **"This, too, shall pass"**
- **The $10 million education**
- **Spotting opportunity in crisis**
- **Conflict: the human factor**
- **Be glad you don't have a hobby!**
- **Disagreement is not the same as conflict**
- **Don't worry, let yourself relax!**

There's not a single idea in this entire manual that is guaranteed to work 100 percent of the time! Crises happen—they're a fact of life. Remember Murphy's Laws:

> **IF ANYTHING CAN GO WRONG, IT WILL.**
> **Murphy**

> **NOTHING IS AS EASY AS IT LOOKS.**
> **Murphy**

> **EVERYTHING TAKES LONGER THAN YOU THINK.**
> **Murphy**

> **LEFT TO THEMSELVES,**
> **THINGS TEND TO GO FROM BAD TO WORSE.**
> **Murphy**

> **IF THERE IS A POSSIBILITY OF SEVERAL THINGS**
> **GOING WRONG, THE ONE THAT WILL CAUSE THE**
> **MOST DAMAGE WILL BE THE ONE THAT GOES WRONG.**
> **Murphy**

> **MURPHY IS AN OPTIMIST.**
> **O'Malley**

We enjoy these whimsical statements. They make us laugh. Why?
Probably because every one of them contains a substantial element
of truth. Sure, they are exaggerated, but we've all experienced
things similar enough to the situations they portray to find a great
amount of personal identification with each "law."

The fact is, everything won't go according to plan. Sometimes the most unexpected event works its way into the project. And the best crisis-prevention technique you have is to keep the wary eye out for one of Murphy's Laws to appear, and to knowingly smile when it does, because you're prepared for it.

You learn a lot more of what's really inside you when you look at how you respond when the wheels falls off and everything goes wrong. How you deal with it is often much more important than what actually happens to you.

It's neither good nor bad. It's inevitable when organizing and managing multiple priorities. Conflict and crisis are often necessary to keep things on track, encourage integrative solutions and recognize potential problems. It is the consequences of how you manage the process that determine how effectively you use the energy stemming from crisis.

You need to be ready, and you must have the right attitude. When do crises occur? Collected research from priority management indicates that crisis and conflict happen most frequently in these areas, in this order:

- Schedules

- Project priorities

- Human resources

- Technical options and performance trade-offs

- Administrative procedures

- Personality and behavior

- Cost (surprised this is last?)

What can you do when crisis occurs? Obviously, you must do something, because effective crisis management is essential for project success. Neglect, avoidance and denial only doom your efforts to ultimate failure.

Self-Quiz: Are You Ready for Crisis?

Directions:

Time to see where you stand on preparedness! Read the following statements and circle the number that best indicates whether you (3) agree; (2) are not sure; (1) disagree.

1. I know my department's most vulnerable areas.	3	2	1
2. If I got into a real bind, several people would help me out.	3	2	1
3. I have a written contingency plan for my worst nightmare.	3	2	1
4. I already use flow charts to track my projects.	3	2	1
5. I learned a valuable lesson from my last mistake.	3	2	1
6. I tend to avoid others if the potential for conflict exists.	3	2	1
7. I welcome conflicts and crises on my job.	3	2	1
8. When things go wrong, I can always keep control.	3	2	1
9. I can be very flexible when change needs to occur.	3	2	1

What it means:

22 or more: Emergency? You're prepared!

21-14: You're holding back water, but the dike is leaking

less than 14: Did you know your building is on fire?

Contingency Planning

Preparation for crisis begins simply with a plan for what you are going to do if and when something unexpected does occur. Remember the story about Johnson & Johnson and that company's quick and effective response to the Tylenol scare? That's an excellent example of a company being prepared and having a plan to implement immediately.

An example of not being prepared was the Exxon tanker at Valdez, Alaska, which ran aground, resulting in one of the largest oil spills in history. Not only was the company not ready, neither the city nor the state governments of the area had much to brag about as far as preparedness was concerned. The tragedy of the Exxon oil spill is that there once *was* a contingency plan. The equipment was there, and the people were trained and ready. But it was decided that a spill of this enormity really couldn't happen, so the workers and equipment so vital to preventing disaster were sent elsewhere.

There's a lesson for all of us here:

BE READY FOR ANYTHING!

Your preparedness will be further refined if you ask some specific questions, such as:

1. What is likely to go wrong? To be ready for disaster, you must identify where you might be the most vulnerable. Imagine a worst-case scenario, and ask: Can I live with this? What is the likelihood of this happening? Your *challenge* is to establish techniques for discovering problems before they become crises.

To meet this challenge, remember the feedback system from Chapter 4—the FAR way: Feedback, Appraisal and Revision. Being aware of and open to this process creates an atmosphere of openness, honesty and fairness among your project team. With an effective team-member feedback system in place, you will have the information necessary for anticipating problems.

2. When will I know about it? Obviously, the sooner the better. This is the real plus of flow charts like PERT and GANTT. These tools are capable of giving you the early warning critical to surviving the crises. Your **challenge** is to have systems in place that properly communicate project status.

To meet this challenge, establish guidelines for proper reporting so the first signs of a problem are quickly visible. Here are some suggested guidelines for establishing such a reporting system:

- Schedule weekly or regular team meetings. Circulate the agenda before the meeting.

- Use charts whenever possible, and make them visually available to the people working with you.

- Put goals, procedures and expectations in writing.

> *Have written plans describing steps to take in case of a fire, flood or similar event for all employees. A disaster can happen during off-hours when no managers are around.*

- Make this a positive information reporting system—not a cause for discipline or reprimanding. Don't shoot the messenger.

- Determine when a trend has developed.

3. What will I do? You must have a plan and be prepared to move into that plan as soon as the trouble arises. Your challenge is to be able to make immediate decisions.

To meet this challenge, here are some possible solutions:

- Have backups already in mind. Think and prepare your basic resources of money, machines, materials and human resources.

- At the earliest point of detection, immediately re-schedule those tasks likely to be involved in the crisis.

- Be sure your decisions can be justified.

- Know the objective—the driving factor of the project.

- Gather facts from the people most directly affected by the situation.

Steps To Crisis Survival

For those times that we hope never happen, here is an eight-step survival plan that affords you the necessary persistence, openness, wisdom, energy and responsive action:

1. Step back, and collect your thoughts. It's imperative you see the big picture, and see it as quickly as possible. Try to assume the role of an outside consultant—someone brought in to solve the problem. If you can see what's really going on in a detached, objective way, the necessary action will become more clear.

Our friend Steve once worked for the Federal Emergency Management Agency (FEMA). His job was to go to disaster areas (following floods, tornados, air crashes, etc.) and begin the initial steps to return life to normal in the affected area. The objectivity of a consultant when we encounter our own crises is vital to survival.

2. Clear a space on your desk. In order for something to happen, there has to be a place for it to happen! Take the minutes necessary to create a workable, productive environment for taking action.

3. Control (or reduce) interruptions. What can you do to avoid as many distractions as possible? Is there a secluded spot in your office (or somewhere else) where you can retreat? Can you divert your calls or your visitors to somebody else?

4. Clarify priorities and deadlines. Right away, determine if the deadline creating the crisis is a true deadline or simply one that "would be nice." Maybe you don't have a crisis after all. If you do, it's time to redouble your efforts. What else is important? Does something else need to be assigned someplace else while you work on putting out the fire?

5. Stay focused—work on one thing at a time. Remember that "you can't catch one hog by chasing nine"? Since you can only do one thing at a time, concentrate your energy on finishing something. Stick with it until it's completed. Then you can focus your attention on another task.

6. Ask for help! This is not the time to be the Lone Ranger of priorities. Remember that "connectedness" is vital to reaching your goals. Ask for any assistance you can get, and use it!

7. "This, too, shall pass." This is a handy phrase to keep in the forefront of your mind during a crisis. No matter how bad it may be, eventually you will get through it. You have before, and you will again.

8. Learn from it! In the charred ruins of the worst disaster can be found seeds of future success. What kind of learning experience has this disaster given you? Did you learn something you need to do next time to keep it from happening again? Was there something you did that you shouldn't have? What new insight will make you better able to cope with the next experience? History can be an excellent teacher—if you remember to use it.

In the early growth days of IBM, when Tom Watson, Sr., was still head of his little business machine company that was on its way to becoming a corporate giant, one of Watson's most trusted associates, a vice president, made a judgment error that was so bad it cost the company ten million dollars.

Can you imagine making a ten million dollar mistake? How could you live with it? What would you do? Many of us would do just like this humiliated vice president did. He went into Watson's

Solve problems quickly —right or wrong. Lying dead in the water and doing nothing is comfortable, but it is a bad way to manage a business.

273

office, closed the door and said: "I think I had better resign before you fire me."

Watson stared at his associate in disbelief. "Resign?" he thundered. "Fire you? We can't afford to do that. We have just invested TEN MILLION DOLLARS in your education!"

What a great attitude toward disaster! The past is past. You can't go back and change it. You can only learn from it, and, you had sure better hope you learned something!

The Chinese symbol for "crisis" is actually two symbols together: The symbol for "danger" and the symbol for "opportunity." How often does our vision get so nearsighted when crisis closes in around us that we only see the bad, the danger, in the situation? Actually, lurking right behind the fence is a fantastic opportunity, if we can only recognize it and seize it.

Two examples: When Johnson & Johnson was dealing with the Tylenol scare, a large toll-free telephone network was quickly established as a crisis hotline for people with concerns, questions and information. The crisis passed but the system remained.

In the years that have followed, that system has been used many other times when quick and far-reaching communications capability was required. When Hurricane Hugo's devastating winds pounded the Atlantic seaboard in 1990, Johnson & Johnson opened up that toll-free system as a public service to enable emergency communication to take place.

Individual lives and careers are often positively affected by crisis, as well. That no more deaths occurred during the October, 1989 earthquake in Northern California than did occur is a tribute to fantastic contingency planning by the many municipalities in that area. We were in the Bay Area exactly thirty days later, the day the Bay Bridge was re-opened. The newscasts all contained much reflecting on the events of the month, and it was amazing to see how some people's lives and careers had reached new levels of achievement due to the opportunity the earthquake provided. An ability to perform often springs forth in crisis situations.

Where's the "seed of benefit" in the crisis you're enduring? Keep looking, it's there. And the opportunity and lesson may even make it worth the pain of the crisis.

> *Anyone can steer the ship when the sea is calm.*

Dealing With Conflict

One difference between crisis and conflict is this: Crisis involves activities. Conflict involves people. All of us have conflicts with ourselves, with other people, and with the organizations we work with. Conflict, like crisis, can throw our best planned projects onto the scrap heap.

The emotional and stress level of conflict is likely to be much higher because the situation is usually personalized. Once again, how you meet conflict is more important than what happens to you. Psychologists say that people cope with conflict in six basic ways:

1. They back off.

2. They become indifferent to the situation.

3. They make concessions.

4. They use a third party for counsel.

5. They establish the "enemy" position.

6. They problem-solve.

You can look at this list and quickly see methods that are productive. Also, you can see how a combination of methods might be useful. You can't always control what happens to you, but you can control how you deal with conflict. Make a plan involving what you can control and leaving out what you can't control. In your survival plan, consider the following:

1. Assess the situation. Ask yourself, "What is the real problem here?" Frequently what appears to be the problem in a conflict is only a symptom of something else underlying the reactions. Analyze. Look deeply. Ask someone else (the person you're having the conflict with?).

Begin by determining what areas you might have in common. Most people focus instead on areas of disagreement or difference. Then, they tend to accentuate those differences and polarize against each other and their work. Creating a common ground and enlarging your areas of agreement lead to win/win conflict resolution.

Conflict in work relationships is the biggest cause of stress in workers' lives. People who have the most contact with individuals with whom they have no personal relationship—such as sales reps—are most prone to serious psychological stress.

275

Once you have identified the areas of agreement or discovered the real problem, ask "Can I change this?" If you can, then change it. If not...

2. Accept the situation. Accept conflict as something that can't be eliminated, and as it probably is: A necessary part of your job. Malcolm Forbes, the late publisher of *Forbes* magazine used to say:

> **"A JOB WITHOUT A CONFLICT IS ONLY A HOBBY."**

Interesting thought, isn't it? Do you know anyone with a job involving work with other people who has no conflict at all? Hardly. The more responsibility you assume, the more your chances for conflict increase.

> **CONFLICT IS NORMAL AND SHOULD BE EXPECTED.**

To maintain perspective, separate what is merely annoying and frustrating from what is serious—just like distinguishing the important from the urgent. Is it consequential? Are you looking at personality traits here, or it is a matter of production skills? You can take comfort in this thought:

> **I AM THANKFUL FOR THE CONFLICTS ON MY JOB!**
> **WITHOUT THEM, SOMEBODY ELSE COULD DO MY JOB**
> **FOR HALF THE MONEY I'M PAID!!**

Isn't it true? Your value to your organization (and to yourself) increases in direct proportion to how effectively you can manage the conflict of your job and life.

3. Distance yourself emotionally. And, if necessary, distance yourself physically. Tough, but necessary! Once again, the more you can detach yourself from the emotional stress of conflict, like a consultant could do, the more effectively you can deal with it. When you can really see yourself outside the situation, looking in, then follow the steps below:

- **Acknowledge responsibility.** There's no sense passing the buck. Because of what you did, or who you are, the responsibility for resolving this conflict is lying at your feet.

- **Accept the challenge!** There's going to be a wonderful growing and learning opportunity here, should you choose to take it on.

- **Brainstorm for ideas.** How many different ways could you possibly try to resolve this situation? Come up with as many as you can—consider even those that seem a little far-fetched.

- **Choose the best idea.** As well as you can, identify which idea has the greatest chance for success. Don't be caught up with indecision here. If several ideas fall into the "pretty good" category, pick one and run with it.

- **Remember, disagreement is not the same as conflict.** Some people even consider this idea in decision-making: Don't make a decision unless there is some disagreement. It's healthy for stimulating thoughts and options.

- **Formulate a plan.** Based on the idea you've chosen, what steps could you take to put it into action? Try to visualize the situation as it may work out and project what might be done.

- **Implement, monitor and modify.** Put your plan into action, and watch it. Look for results or effects of the idea as it evolves. If you're not getting the hoped-for outcome, don't be afraid to alter the idea a little and come at the problem from a different direction.

Even if the person with whom you are dealing is acting emotionally, keep your emotions and reason in balance.

"I Give Myself Permission To Relax, Not Worry"

When everything goes wrong, can you give yourself permission to take a deep breath and quiet your mind? If you can't, who (or what) is controlling you? You don't have to surrender leadership of your life, your attitudes or your priorities to your circumstances!

When you find yourself in a situation you can't control, ask yourself: "Will this matter be in my life five years from now?" You'll realize most short-term problems aren't worth worrying about.

JONATHAN: When I travel, I'm frequently hurrying to catch a flight, rent a car or check into a hotel. There are many circumstances surrounding travel that simply can't be controlled: the weather, traffic, flight delays, uncomfortable situations.

Delayed flights used to particularly irritate me, especially if I was worrying about a connecting flight or my evening plans getting botched up. I'm not proud to tell you, but I frequently became some sort of terror when things went bad at the airport. My blood pressure would rise. I would yell at people who had no control over the situation, either. At that point, if you worked for the airline causing the delay, you were my enemy.

Once, in Huntsville, Alabama, when I arrived for a flight, I found the flight was overbooked. I became so angry at the gate agent he called a security guard down to make sure I didn't do anything violent. (I'm certainly not proud of that!)

You know, for as much as I got upset, and as loudly as I ranted and raved, I never had any effect on getting the flight off the ground one minute sooner?

Then one day, the futility of being upset hit me. I realized I was the one who controlled my own emotions, and I was choosing to let them control me. I began to tell myself: "I give myself permission to relax." It really worked! Once I allowed that to happen, I discovered there were some wonderful things you could do when a flight was delayed ("In Between" Time). I started making phone calls—in fact, I often reward myself by phoning favorite friends rather than concentrating only on business matters. I do paperwork (there's always more room in the terminal than on a plane in a coach seat). I treat myself to real dinners in a real restaurant, and enjoy after-dinner coffee on the plane, instead of complaining about the airplane food. Sometimes I just sit back and people-watch, a fascinating activity at an airport.

I won't say I look forward to the delays, but I have certainly learned there are a lot more productive uses of my energy than choosing to be upset over something I can't control.

I GIVE MYSELF PERMISSION TO RELAX, NOT WORRY

Crisis? Conflict? Sure, it's going to come, no matter how well you plan or how hard you work. But it doesn't have to mean throwing in the towel, and it might even give you a chance to grow in ways you hadn't expected.

Making It Work

CONCERN	REASON	STRATEGY
not knowing what might happen	haven't thought about it	develop a worst-case scenario
lack of cooperation	team concept not implemented	have regular meeting with positive orientation
problem sneaking up on me	visual aids not available or not working	develop flow charts and up-date frequently
being too subjective	too close to situation	become a "consultant"
losing focus during crisis	doing too many things at once	pick one activity, work on it until completed
mentally or emotionally overwhelmed	taking problem too seriously	"This too, shall pass" — recall past experiences
tend to ignore crisis	see as negative situation	look for learning benefit
many conflicts with others	dealing with symptoms focusing on differences	look for real problem identify areas of agreement
avoidance of conflicts	dislike negative emotions take conflicts personally	expect conflict as natural distance self emotionally
loss of control, loss of temper	try to control everything, actually believe I can	identify what you can/can't do, use to your benefit

Putting It To Work

- How you deal with conflicts and crises is more important than what happens to you.

- Recognizing the truth of Murphy's Laws gives you a healthy mindset toward crisis.

- With a good contingency plan, you can be ready for anything!

- Flow charts and regular reporting will establish early warning of potential problem areas.

- Put yourself in a consultant's role as you objectively observe conflicts and crisis to determine what is happening and why.

- Work on one thing until you have completed it. Then tackle another.

- Don't be too proud to ask for help when things go wrong.

- Look for the seeds of benefit and the lesson to be learned in every crisis.

- Acknowledge conflict as a necessary part of your job: It's what you're being paid for.

- Welcome disagreement as a chance to exchange ideas and look at a situation from another's perspective.

- Give yourself permission to relax. Nobody can control every aspect of his or her life!

- Ask yourself: "If I can't control this, what can I do instead?"

Check Your Working Knowledge Of Crisis And Conflict

1. What is the #1 cause for crisis and conflict?

2. What is your organization's Mission Statement? Can you relate

this to a specific approach you can take if a crisis occurs?

3. Where is your current top-priority project most vulnerable?

   How likely is it that a crisis will happen (express in percentage)?

   Could you live with the situation if it did occur?

4. How can you make other members of your team more cooperative and helpful when things go wrong?

5. What is the best early-warning system you have for spotting problems?

6. Is there room on your desk right now to deal with the next crisis?

7. How many things should you work on at once during a crisis?

8. Describe a recent setback you experienced on the job. What did you learn that can be applied to future situations?

9. How do you tend to react when you experience conflict with someone?

10. Before determining what the problem is when you have conflict, what should you identify first?

11. Why is disagreement healthy?

_____

_____

_____

_____

_____

_____

_____

Balancing Priorities: Life Itself

- **Randy's story**
- **Your balance wheel**
- **How do you see yourself?**
- **The balance checklist**
- **Reducing stress on the job**
- **The power of assertion**
- **Seven approaches for building energy and balance**
- **Jonathan and Susan's three philosophies of life**

Recently, flying from Oakland to Seattle, we sat next to a young businessman named Randy. He was going to be 39 years old the next month, and two weeks before had suffered his second heart attack. His first was at age 34.

This man took over a business his father started and built its sales from $3 million to over $60 million annually. Someone had recently offered to buy the company at a price that would have left him with $10 million in his pocket—after taxes.

That's enough money that, even if you left it in a checking account, you would earn over a half-million dollars a year. Most people could live pretty well on that. Randy hadn't decided yet if he would accept the offer, but thought he was going to turn it down.

"I love to work!" he exclaimed to us. He said he averaged working 16 hours per day, six days a week. Sundays he only worked a half day. Last year, he never took his 40-foot yacht out of the marina. Not enough time.

Randy and a friend owned a large tract of waterfront property on an island north of Seattle. "It would sure be nice to live up there, but I don't know what I'd do with myself. I'd probably go crazy with boredom."

Before getting on the plane, he talked with his girlfriend. She was going to pick up his daughters from their mother's for the weekend, and meet him at the airport. He wasn't pleased with the attitudes the girls were developing. Too much influence from his ex-wife, he thought.

He was at least 50 pounds overweight. He eagerly dug into his filet mignon and ordered another scotch on the rocks. As the plane pulled up to the gate and Randy straightened his tie and picked up his briefcase, he said, "I guess I really should pay attention to some of the other areas in my life."

Why is it so hard to keep a sense of perspective in life? What good does it do to achieve great financial success or notoriety if the other areas of life are nonexistent?

At the beginning of this manual, we encouraged you to maintain a little perspective on the subjects we were going to cover...not to become so fanatical about productivity and effectiveness that you merely replaced the tyrant of disorganization with that of absolute time control. Have you been able to find your own personal truths and usefulness from the ideas and solutions in this manual? How's your balance?

Maintaining A Perspective

One of the goals charts we looked at in Chapter 4 showed eight different areas in which you could set goals to maintain a well-rounded approach to matters of life and business.

The balance wheel on this page represents four areas, shown in a shape resembling an old airplane propeller. Take a moment, and take stock. Rate yourself, your satisfaction and success in these four areas. The numbers 1 through 10 on the propeller blades serve as a rating system used in so many areas—10 is best, 1 is worst.

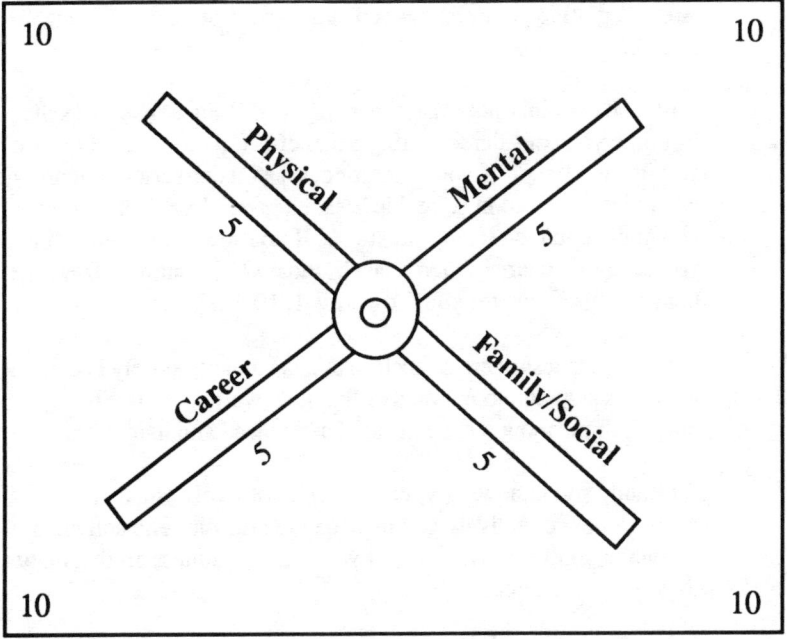

Let's start on the *career* blade. How would you rate yourself in your career, on that scale? Are you satisfied with who you are, what you've achieved, your professional respect, your income (if your field measures success in that way), your responsibilities? Do you enjoy your work? Are you pretty good at it? Put a dot somewhere on the propeller between 1 (the center) and 10.

Next the *mental* scale. This doesn't mean "mental health," but from a standpoint of mental growth and development...are you still learning? Seeking new ideas? Developing new interests? Challenging your mind and thought processes in ways different from the old ones? Had a class recently? Read any good books lately? Put a dot on that propeller from 1 to 10.

What about the *physical* side of life? So many elements can come into play here. Are you taking care of the only physical body you're ever going to have? Exercising it intelligently? Have you seen a doctor for a physical check-up lately? What have you been putting into your body recently? Consider the quality of food, the quantity. Caffeine? Alcohol? Nicotine? Narcotics? Prescription drugs? Are you getting your body to bed at a reasonable hour? Rate it, 1 to 10.

Last, and certainly not least, the *family/social* side. When was the last time you considered putting a real effort in this area? Or were you just too busy? If you're married, are you delivering in marriage what you promised in courtship? Got a good close friend or two you could count on in any situation? If you're a parent, how did you celebrate your children's last birthdays? Valentine's Day? Be honest. This is just for you. Lowest is 1, 10 is tops.

A self-awareness exercise such as this is valuable simply because it makes us stop and look. Most of the time, we're too busy being busy to think about the elements of a balanced and happy life.

As Randy so unknowingly reminded us last week, you can't measure how effectively you manage the priorities and activities of life when you're looking only at your career...unless all that matters to you is that career.

What can you learn from the dots on your balance wheel? First, connect those dots with a rounded line as if you were drawing a circle. Warning: It may not look like a circle!

Well, what does it look like? This is a wheel, or a propeller, designed to take you smoothly toward your destination. If it's a wheel, what does it look like? Do you have a flat tire? Are you in for a very bumpy ride? If it's a propeller, does it look like something that will fly you in a straight line, or one that may well run directly into the ground and crash?

"In a narrow circle the mind contracts. Man grows with his expanded needs."
— Schiller

286

Are some things out of balance here? Do you see some areas that maybe you should devote a little more time and energy to? Is one aspect so high it throws the rest out of balance?

We can't tell you what to do, because we don't see your balance wheel, but it shouldn't be too hard to figure out what needs to be done, and in what areas. What are you willing to do? Is this important enough to consciously try to develop some more new habits? That's your decision. But if you choose to do nothing, you need to know that you've chosen to accept your life as it is—you can't expect anything to change unless you're willing to put some effort into making the change happen.

The real limitations that rob us of our freedom to make the best of what we have, and what we are, relate to the way we see ourselves and the world around us. Did you know that:

- Colonel Sanders was "too old" to start a business?
- Fred Astaire's first screen test stated: "Can't act! Slightly bald! Can dance a little."?
- Florence Chadwick knew that other people had died trying to swim across the English Channel?

Had these people given up because someone else had said their efforts were doomed to failure, they'd never have succeeded. But each believed in himself or herself. So must you believe in yourself, because you're the only one that can effect real change in your life.

You have the freedom to choose how you will respond to the circumstances that have created where you are on this balance wheel.

Check Your Balance

Just as you balance a checkbook, make a regular practice of balancing your life account. You can't (or at least, you shouldn't) write a check without knowing the balance, i.e., what you have and how much you are spending. If you find some person or some activity is making unauthorized withdrawals from your life account, put a "stop payment" on it immediately!

Like so many areas of life, balance is an attitude, a set of specific actions. Take a look at the checklist below, and return to it from time to time. Compare your achievements and accomplishments with the goals you set for yourself. There is no need to compare yourself with the achievements of others, because you're not leading their lives, you're leading your own. Look at the list, review it monthly to keep fine-tuned, and check off the boxes you're taking care of:

Self-Assessment: Check Your Balance

Directions:
Review this list monthly. When you answer "no" to any of these questions, review why you answered negatively and think of ways you can make your answer positive.

YES   NO

☐   ☐   I have a sense of priority. I am able to look at options and make decisions about the relative importance of my choices.

☐   ☐   I have a variety of activities built into my life. They are not all work-related. I have friends who don't work at the same place, or in the same field, as I do.

☐   ☐   I plan my time. I have a pretty good idea how long things will take, and know what I have time for. I focus my energy into Prime Time periods of the day, and I schedule in a little breathing time, as well.

☐   ☐   I have a clear definition of what I want (a Personal Mission Statement). It helps me make intelligent choices of activities that will get me where I want to go.

☐   ☐   I don't let stress continue to build up inside me but I physically release it through a sensible exercise program based on my abilities and physical condition.

☐   ☐   I am happy at home and in my career.

How do you think you'll do when you check this list next month? Can you say yes to each of the statements? What new habits can you work on, starting today, to increase your chances of saying "yes" to these items in 30 days? Is it worth it to make the effort? Who will check on you?

When you were a child, your parents would probably leave a light on until you went to sleep. Later on, your teacher decided when you could put your head down on your desk or when you could go to the bathroom. Then, your peers gradually started to dictate and control the way you would talk, what you did and where it was "cool" to be seen. As a young adult, you took a job and let the boss decide what you would do. Now that you are "all grown up," you are, and always will be, a product of your own choices. You check on you!

Reducing Stress On The Job

For most of us, our work environment produces at least some stress and pressure. Of course, a certain amount is a good thing, because it can be a stimulant and motivator to create action. Unfortunately, far too often the stress becomes too much. Sometimes we don't even know where it's coming from, much less how to stop or change it.

One of the major causes, which this manual should certainly help you alleviate, is this:

TOO MUCH TO DO, NOT ENOUGH TIME TO DO IT!

Sound familiar? It's a tune we've been talking about throughout this manual. It has to do with deciding what's important and how you use the time you have available. It relates to how you communicate with others, and the tools you can use to control and track your priorities.

In other words, this entire manual has been solution-oriented. We know if you'll work and apply the ideas we've presented, the results will make a big difference in the problem of time vs. demands, and reduce your level of stress accordingly.

How do you stay on top of those situations? Remember three
questions to ask before you get started on anything:

IS IT NECESSARY?

(Will it benefit my organization or department?)

IS IT APPROPRIATE?

(Is it the right time to be doing this?)

IS IT EFFICIENT?

(Why me? Should I be the one to do it?)

Learn and memorize these questions. Practice asking them
frequently, every day. Pretty soon you'll have developed a great
new habit—that of automatically considering the answers to these
questions before you ever begin an activity. When you come up
with a "no," take the appropriate action. Reduce your stress, and
increase your value to your organization!

There will be days when you have less-than-successful results and
tend to replace the three questions with these three statements:

- Necessary—How could I have been so stupid?
- Appropriate—Why does this always happen to me?
- Efficient—What if my boss finds out?

Even when it all goes wrong, you need to take an assertive, self-
confident approach. Ask the questions one more time, but this time
in this way:

- Necessary—What did I learn?

- Appropriate—What can I do next time?

- Efficient—What can I do tomorrow to step back onto the right track?

Instead of punishing you, these questions take a more productive and professional approach to your situations.

The best coping tool for dealing with stress is still: ASSERTION.

If you want something, ask for it. If something bothers you, tell somebody. If you're having a problem, discuss it. If someone is taking advantage of you, acknowledge it, document it, and talk about it.

**ASSERTION: SAYING WHAT YOU MEAN AND
ASKING FOR WHAT YOU WANT**

All of us, as humans living in a free society, have the right to express ourselves and state our desires. Bottle up this right of expression, and you will invite stress and all its relatives back into the middle of your life. Even if assertion doesn't accomplish what you want every single time, the feeling of release that comes from having expressed your thoughts and feelings is one of the healthiest habits you can develop. Assert yourself!

Approaches For Building Energy And Balance

Here are seven ideas that will help you maintain and build energy and balance all day long, and they can work for you, too!

1. Develop a "support network." Like the Canadian geese, we truly do need each other. Are there people in your life who believe in you and support you? You need people who encourage you and with whom you can bounce ideas back and forth.

One man with just such a support network was Nathaniel Hawthorne. One day he came home broken-hearted to tell his wife Sophia that he had been fired from his job in a customs house and to admit he was a failure. Sophia returned his sorrow with joy. "Now you can write your book!" "Sure," said Hawthorne. "And what shall we live on while I write it?"

To Nathaniel Hawthorne's amazement, Sophia opened a drawer and pulled out money. "Where did you get that?" he asked.

"I always knew you were a man of genius. I knew someday you would write a masterpiece. So I've saved money every week from my housekeeping funds, and here's enough to last us for one whole year!"

With the money, support and confidence of Sophia, Nathaniel Hawthorne went to work and wrote *The Scarlet Letter*!

Do you have a support network, some kind of advisory group that can give you encouragement and energy? If not, why not put such a group together? It could be some of your friends or associates who might also benefit from the mutual sharing of ideas and support. Why not ask someone today?

2. Control your environment. Whatever control you do have over your environment, exercise that control. What can you do to make your workplace, your home, your relaxation spot, more positive? What kind of negative aspects can you change or remove? For some, it may be nothing more than replacing a picture on a wall that stirs up mixed emotions with something truly restful or motivating to look at. For others, perhaps a little remodeling is in order. In this complex world, consider how you could simplify your environment. Perhaps nothing more than a better organized environment (using some of the many tools in this book) is your key to a more positive outlook and more energy and balance as a result.

3. Assertion—taking control. This is truly a quality of life that creates energy and balance.

4. Nutrition. You are what you eat. We all know plenty about this already, and we won't attempt to superficially cover what you could find in an in-depth book on the subject. No doubt about it, though: Energy and balance (or a lack of it) result from the fuel you use to run your engine. What are you doing to help yourself here?

5. Exercise. Maybe you really don't have time to develop a disciplined program of body maintenance, but world-renowned speaker and health expert Dr. Kenneth Cooper says you don't have time not to. Even at a desk or on an airplane, there are small things you can do during the day that can make a difference. A good isometric exercise, just pitting one muscle against another, can relieve stress and build your physical plant.

6. Do the worst thing first. It also does wonders for energy and balance. How much negative energy is created, draining off the positive, by the dread of anticipating something you know you're going to have to do, anyway? Get up, go in to work, and hit the door at top speed, tackling that tough project right away. Having the biggest job of the day already behind you will boost your energy all day!

7. Gain more closure—finish things. We've said this separately, but here it is in a box to help you remember. The two greatest habits of self-management (directly related to managing your priorities) you can develop, are:

---

1. **HANDLE A THING ONLY ONE TIME**

2. **FINISH THE THINGS YOU START**

This may first mean deciding what you can't do. Don't start what you can't finish. That's what gaining closure means—simply finishing things. Work on one thing at a time. Stay focused until you complete it. Finish your *Daily Action List*. Complete that project. If you can't finish it, organize by putting the project back onto the Master List. Manage the problem by making a decision to work toward resolution. Completion is a great surge protector for energy and balance. And don't forget to reward your long hours of labor!

Conclusion:
Jonathan And Susan's Philosophy

We'd like to end this manual with a few thoughts from our own philosophy that have helped us build what we believe is a successful life with harmony and balance.

There are three sayings we constantly keep in our minds as we go through life. They are our own sayings—we didn't borrow them from anyone, or read them anywhere. We developed these as we thought about what we are achieving, how we're getting there, and what we believe.

---

1. TAKE A WALK

> *Live today, for tomorrow is but an extension of today.*

We have discovered that, no matter how stressful our lives may have become, no matter how much tension or pressure we might be experiencing (and life is never free from elements that create pressures), it doesn't seem to matter when we're out on a walk. We immerse ourselves in our surroundings, and cares seem to disappear.

The most creative ideas we get come to us when we're out on a walk. Any project that becomes challenging, any problem needing resolution, any major job that needs lots of creativity gets its best input from the creative power of two that comes as we walk and talk. We never have a specific agenda for our walk; we just go and let it happen. Sometimes we simply have a good time, and never talk about anything of consequence. (But we always bring a small notebook and a pen, just in case.)

You, too, can "take a walk!" No, it doesn't literally have to be a walk. Find your own way: Maybe it's unplanned, quiet time in a pleasant environment. It could even be created in your mind.

Psychologists tell us that the subconscious mind is unable to tell the difference between a real experience and one that is vividly imagined. Think of the nicest, prettiest, quietest, most relaxed place you've ever been. Now, do more than think about it. Imagine it. Call back from your memory as clear a picture as you can get. The sounds. The sights. The smells. The feel of the sun or the breezes. Take a walk. It'll do marvelous things for your energy, creativity and mental well-being.

---

2. TURN OVER A ROCK

Have you ever noticed that all kids seem to have a lot of curiosity? Nearly everything is of interest to them. How about when you were a kid? Did you ever go out into a field during the summer, see a rock on the ground that looked like it had been there for a while, and picked it up to see what was under it?

The things you saw! Yes, most of them were bugs and stuff. Sometimes it didn't look very nice and you put it back. Other times, the bottom of the rock revealed beauty and you took it home and kept it.

One day, we all stop being kids. We grow calloused to the novelty of life and its unexpected pleasures when everything was a wonderment—something to be examined and learned. And we stop picking up rocks, which is tragic, because as we walk down the road of life, there are many rocks along the way. In the road, on the road, along the side of the road. We consider the rocks a nuisance. We trip over one every once in a while, and angrily kick it aside.

But some of the rocks of life are opportunities. Are you so set in who you are, where you're going and what you know that you're no longer willing to pick them up and look at them?

Every time a minute passes, you have a new opportunity.

Personally, we don't choose that approach. We are interested in the rocks, and we stop, pick them up and look at them. Just like when we were younger. We don't always like what we see, so we put the rocks back down. But, some of the rocks we've picked up are fabulous! Not only have we kept them, we've used them, and we've shown them to others.

Your world is full of interesting things, just waiting for you to learn about, and wonderful opportunities to grow and develop, if you are willing to give them a try. New interests and new opportunties are what make life a continuous adventure, full of excitement and anticipation.

If you want energy and balance in your life, decide today to pick up the rocks of interest and opportunity you encounter along your way and look at them. Who knows? Once in a while, you might find a "keeper"!

---

3. LIFE MAY BE SHORT, BUT IT'S TOO LONG
TO BE LIVED ALL AT ONCE

We are bombarded by commercials and people who tell us "you only go around once in life, so get all you can while you can." True, we only get one time, but when viewed in perspective, for most of us life is really pretty long. Long enough that to try to live it all at once is not only unrewarding, it can be tragic.

Most of the really worthwhile things in life are not of the instant-gratification variety. They come as a result of time, learning and experience. The more we have to learn, the greater we value the experience.

Take your time. Stop along the way. Don't try to cram all the excitement of life into a few months or a few years. Learn to relax. To give of yourself. This is the true secret of happiness. The satisfaction of self-awareness and the joy of memory. The positive lessons from life's most negative moments. Slow down and let these lessons catch up to you.

Life may be short, but it's too long to be lived all at once.

Making It Work

CONCERN	REASON	STRATEGY
part of life out of balance	too much time spent here	reduce time in this area, develop more in others
part of life out of balance	too little time spent here	put more time, effort into this area to balance
high stress level on job	too much to do, not enough time to do it	develop assertive skills to ask for what you want
too little energy on job or in life	no human support network	put support network in place; ask friends to join you
too little energy on job or in life	negative environment	put positive elements in your environment
too little energy on job or in life	poor physical condition	regular exercise; you don't have time not to!
too little energy on job or in life	certain job anticipated with fear or dread	do it first—get it over with

Putting It To Work

- Balance in life comes from putting emphasis in different areas of interest and responsibility.

- Physical wellness is just as important as mental sharpness.

- Your real limitation is the way you see yourself.

- Check yourself regularly to keep imbalance from affecting your life.

- Use the ideas and techniques in this manual to keep you from having "too much to do, and not enough time to do it."

- The best coping tool for dealing with stress is assertion: Saying what you mean and asking for what you want.

- Build a support network of people who believe in you and encourage you.

- Remove as many negative elements from your environment as you can, and replace them with positive ones.

- To get your day off to a start that will keep you flying all day, do the worst thing on your list first and get it over with.

- Take a walk.

- Turn over a rock.

Check Your Working Knowledge Of Balance

1. What area of your life needs to be reduced for more balance?

2. What area of your life needs to be increased for more balance?

3. What is the major cause of stress on the job?

4. What three questions can help keep you on top of the demands of your job?

5. What is the best tool for coping with stress? What does it mean?

6. Which of the seven approaches to building energy and balance are you already doing best? Why?

7. Which of the seven approaches to building energy and balance are you willing to develop in your life? How will you go about it?

MY SLIGHT-EDGE IDEAS FROM CHAPTER 13:

_____

_____

_____

_____

_____

_____

_____

_____

INDEX